Devils & Blue Dresses

MITCH RYDER

CooL titles

Published by
Cool Titles
439 N. Canon Dr., Suite 200
Beverly Hills, CA 90210
www.cooltitles.com

The Library of Congress Cataloging-in-Publication Data Applied For

William Levise (Mitch Ryder)—
Devils & Blue Dresses: My Wild Ride as a Rock and Roll Legend

p.   cm
ISBN-13: 978-1-935270-14-0
1. Autobiography   2. Music-Rock   3. Pop Culture I. Title
2011

Printed in the United States of America

1 3 5 7 9 10 8 6 4 2

Book editing and design by White Horse Enterprises, Inc.

For interviews or information regarding special discounts for bulk purchases, please contact:
cindy@cooltitles.com

Distribution to the Trade: Pathway Book Service, www.pathwaybook.com,
pbs@pathwaybook.com, 1-800-345-6665

Also available through Ingram and Baker & Taylor

Dedication

To the memory of my mother and father;
and to my beloved sister Nina, much too late.

To Neil Wach, for being a good friend to Megan and myself.

To Megan Ryder, for all of the different meanings of love.

Acknowledgements

There will be people upset because they were not included in this book. I am sorry if you feel that way but take comfort in the fact that we talk privately, either with you or about you in the same color or manner with which you speak of me and mine. Good or bad, you have chosen the tone. Without the support of the following people I could not have accomplished this attempt to tell my story, so special thanks go out to Neville Johnson, Cindy Johnson, Lisa Wysocky, Geoffrey Fieger, Thomas Kenny, John C. Ray, Mark Sutton, Gert Leiser, Randy Erwin; and Dawn, Joel, Tom, Ian, and Megan.

Author's Note

THIS BOOK IS ABOUT TWO THINGS I share with most other adult humans on this planet. The first is my struggle to make a living in a job that will provide for myself and my family while I attempt to rise to the top of my profession. The second is my struggle to recognize who I am and, where necessary, change that person for the better.

We all play out these tasks within the environment we find ourselves. Some of us settle for less. Some of us demand more. Our choice is the result of the mental, physical, spiritual, financial, and political condition of the adults we are exposed to as children.

In these two struggles my life is no different from most of my fellow humans. We sometimes succeed. We sometimes fail. In our democratic system in America the odds of success are against most of us—unless we mysteriously overcome class separation and, in addition, fight a system of law that demands that justice go to the highest bidder. The end result is that corporate business is protected from real accountability.

The lower- and middle-classes barely resemble what many of us would have hoped for as a family. The parents, the parent, or in many cases, the caregivers to our children, struggle to finance an ideal that is no longer a reality. We leave the education, fate, and needs of our children in the hands of day-care keepers, the street, teachers, and whatever little time we can give the children after a hard day of labor. When you bring into the mix dysfunctional caregivers and parents, absent relatives, then add television, you begin to get a picture of the future for children exposed to these different formulas.

Stress plays itself out in so many ways because there are so many different levels of consciousness within the above-mentioned groups. The undeniable fact, however, is that stress has a negative impact on everyone who is connected to the family.

My favorite observation about free enterprise and its effects on our children is about health care. We are the only civilized nation in the world that does not supply health care to all of its citizens, big or small. There is no corporate health care hospital system, pharmaceutical company, or corporate health insurance company that can justify such a shameful state of being.

Greed. You want the easy answer? There it is.

The only thing that makes me different from you is a bizarre twist of fate. I found fame in America. Fame is a twisted concept that garners such odd reaction from the public that it borders on insanity. Did fame make me a better person than you? You read this book and tell me. Did fame solve any of my problems or make my life easier? Hell no. Fame only did one important thing for me. It gave me a goal to overcome, or die trying.

There is comfort in pain. I discovered this while learning why my life was different from many of the happier faces I've looked at (in bewildered fashion) as they floated past my aging, weary eyes. One of the biggest reasons we have such an enormous addiction to drugs, legal and otherwise, is the need to escape the reality of our situation. People, myself included, will try anything in excess—with the exception of money, which is the province of the wealthy. Still, the pain will not go away. We are smart enough to understand the problem, but powerless to effect any meaningful change. People lie to us and we lie to people. It is endless. I used to believe that only junkies lied to get what they want, but now I see it's a cultural phenomenon.

What a grand future we have given to our children. They believe money and "stuff" will save them from ill will. I think a society that prioritizes material gain as identification to your personal worth is a crime.

As for me, fame has allowed me to pass, if you will, because it is an exclusive achievement. But my God, look at what it has cost me. My fame cannot be taken away. The accomplishments are well documented, but so are the prices. At the end of the day all I have left has nothing to do with fame, and everything to do with how I conducted my life as a fellow human being. In this way my autobiography, while honestly discussing my life in music, also reaches out to you for understanding and compassion from one human to another. Bob Dylan once said, "Even the president must sometimes stand naked."

In the beginning of my career I was too young to comprehend and include in my search of meaning those things necessary to the achievement of a healthy lifestyle. And, being not too terribly intelligent, I settled for something temporary and pleasurable. Like many from my class of people, I looked for the easy way. When fame hit I began spending the rest of my life enjoying it, destroying it, retrieving it and finally trying to prove myself deserving. Today I consider myself an artist of accomplishment. Because I took my street sensibilities to my masters and defied them in a very offensive manner, they punished me. They punished me by minimizing my accomplishments and thwarting my growth by trying to write me out of their elitist, subjective opinion on who deserved their praise.

I applaud my peers—my fellow rock and roll artists—if they have found happiness in the membership of a musical genre that was never supposed to be defined. If anyone ever took the time to closely explore the lives, humiliations, pain and sacrifice made by the people who have given you so much pleasure, and who try to understand the true nature of the music business. . . .

Now that my book is finished and I continue to move forward with my other creative projects, try to believe that my fellow artists and I love you all. We don't have a lot, at least most of us don't, and we don't really expect a lot, but it would be nice to know that you understand we are no different than you. That would be a kind gift. I will continue to bring pleasant memories and pleasant performances to you as long as I can.

I will end this with something for you all to ponder: More than half of my Christmas cards in the last decade have come from law firms and accounting firms.

May God be with you, if that is what you need.

Mitch Ryder
September 2011

Foreword

WHERE TO BEGIN?

Understanding something with your head is one thing. All it takes is a little brain power, some thought, and an armchair psychology degree. Making sense to your heart is something entirely different, and I love Billy (whom most of you know as Mitch) with all my heart.

About two weeks ago Billy and I were discussing "us" while driving home from a gig. Billy looked at me and asked, "Have you always loved me, all the time?" I answered, "To my shame and horror, yes." To understand that statement you have to get into my head, and more important, into my heart.

My reality is that for Billy to have become a performer he had to develop a huge ego. When you describe someone as having an ego, many people imagine a person who thinks too highly of him- or herself. That is so far from the truth. Billy's ego is very simply (but with oh so much complication) a defense mechanism for a wounded little boy with low self worth. Each time Billy steps into the spotlight, his very existence is on the line. It is like this big secret that everyone who has spent any amount of time with him knows. Mitch is little Billy's alter ego, the persona he developed to survive the trauma of his youth.

Having heard his stories about his early life it is really no mystery to me why he is the way he is. The puzzle that I have spent the better part of twenty years trying to grasp is that it has largely remained a mystery to him—mostly because he chooses not to explore it.

Love has always been a confusing notion for Billy, because what he knew of it came with such a high price. When you don't earn love just by virtue of your existence you are forced to understand the ugly commodities market where your body and soul

XIV   Devils & Blue Dresses

are collateral. The younger the age at which you enter into this adult concept and the more traumatic the initiation, the more damage. Add to that the sexual identity issues that came from Billy's experiences and it is a pretty lethal cocktail to have to swallow. I am, quite frankly, surprised that he is only as emotionally crippled as he is.

Within this vacuum Billy was introduced to the narcotic of adoration. How could love ever compare to that? In his childish world, love was hurtful and elusive. Then, as an adult, love had the audacity to ask him to do the hard work of exploring his issues and becoming emotionally vulnerable? Not hardly.

When you look at it comparatively, love says, "I love you but I also love myself. Therefore I have boundaries and expect you to respect me and my needs," whereas adoration says, "I have no sense of myself and therefore no boundaries. So treat me as you will and I will still stand here and worship you." Really, that is so much easier. No accountability. No sacrifice. No stepping outside your comfort zone. No growing up.

So here I stand in my unenviable position as a wife rather than a fan, insisting that Billy not engage in behaviors that are contradictory to a healthy, mutually respectful relationship, playing pass interference between him and what he really wants. I am being pummeled.

This is where the shame and horror come in for me. Why do I stay for the whole game when it is painfully obvious to myself and everyone around me that my team has no chance at a Hail Mary in the fourth quarter on this one? The easy answer is that apparently my psychosis fits very neatly into the grooves of Billy's psychosis. But then we would only be talking head knowledge. And as I said earlier, to completely understand why, you have to ask my heart.

The ultimate answer lies in the fact that I love Billy. That flawed, vulnerable, playful, confused, funny, confusing, infuriating, hopeful, depressed, talented, happy, shallow, deep, subtle, forceful, sometimes kind, sometimes abusive, entertaining, never easy, all consuming human being that Mitch was never able to completely kill no matter how hard he tried. I love him. I do.

Megan Levise, wife of Mitch Ryder
September 2011

Introduction

I WAS GOING THROUGH MY THIRD divorce and living alone in an apartment with no furniture except a bed, dresser, kitchen table, chair, desk, telephone, and computer. A male friend called and suggested we get together at a bar not too far from me. We had quite a few drinks and the ashtray was filled with stinking butts, the juke box was too loud, and the smoke was choking me when he asks, "So, what are your plans?"

Plans? What plans, I think to myself. I've got no money, all of my bills are late, my soon to be ex-wife got an attorney who thinks I've got a fortune stashed away somewhere, the IRS is on my ass, and I'm pissed off because this is the third time I've been married and I don't know why I keep wanting to hurt myself this way.

I throw back the Sambuca and quickly grab for the Heineken to stop the burning in my throat. I look him in his eyes and say, "Plans? I don't have plans. I got dreams, but they're just dreams. However, I did manage, in my financial ruin to somehow save a hundred dollars for drinks. You ready for another one, Nick?"

Nick laughs. He loves watching me suffer. He especially likes it when I drink enough to become comically cynical. "Sure," he says. "You're buyin'." Then he becomes more serious. "Listen," he says." I know this is a tough time for you but you're not the first man to go through a divorce."

I immediately shoot back, "Three, Nicky. Three times a loser. How many guys do you know that can't get it right three times? What the hell is wrong with me? I can't afford this anymore."

He leans back in his chair, thinking about what to say, and moves his bottle around the table as if it was some kind of figure skating champion. Then he offers these hidden jewels of stunted knowledge, "You know, my old lady's got a really hot girlfriend an' she knows you're getting divorced an' she'd really like to meet you." Then he moves his eyebrows up and down and smiles. "What d'ya think? I mean she is really hot and she just got divorced an' she's horny as hell, at least that what my old lady says. She says she'd really like to meet you."

"I'll think about it," I say. I was a little horny myself, but sweet Jesus where would we go to have sex? If she saw my place she would wonder where my money was, given the lack of furniture. Where would we sit? On the bed? Or, I could let her sit at the table and stand there like an asshole, or we could sit on the bed and I could tell her all of my considerable fortune was tied up in escrow until the divorce was final.

Then Nick pulls her picture out of his wallet. She is beautiful. "Don't worry about the kids," he says. "They're real small. Besides, I hear her ex is trying to get custody because he claims she's an unfit mother."

"Why did they get divorced?" I ask.

Nick raises his shoulders and says, "I don't know. He claims she was cheating on him, she claims he was cheating on her. You know how it goes by now, right?'

"Who filed for divorce, Nicky?"

"I think he did. Yeah. I'm pretty sure he did. But don't worry about money. He's rich. He's some big auto executive an' she says she's gonna clean him out."

Right about then two women come over and ask if they can join us. Before I can open my mouth Nicky says, "Sure, beautiful women are always welcome at our table." I don't even see them. I just stare at Nick and think, this is *my* money motherfucker. What the hell is wrong with you?

Who knows, I probably would have lost it in the poker machine anyway. Oh well.

Nicky orders drinks for them and I am lost in my thoughts when the woman next to me says, "So, what do you do for a living?" Just as I'm ready to say "Nothing," Nicky blurts out "That's Mitch Ryder. You've heard of Mitch Ryder right?'

"Oh my God. *The* Mitch Ryder? Really, you're Mitch Ryder, the singer? Oh wow. I've never been around a star before. What brings you guys here? I mean nobody ever comes in here."

I smile and slam down another Sambuca and chase it with a Heineken. Nicky's talking his ass off trying to impress the bar whore sitting next to him, while the two women smile away at each other like they won the lottery. Then the one next to me pulls her face next to mine and whispers something in my ear. Next thing I know she's moving her tongue around inside my ear and it feels wonderful. She keeps it up and runs her hand up and down my leg.

I had been through this hundreds of times before in hundreds of different situations with hundreds of different classes of women. High-class, low-class, in-between class; the only difference was location, discretion, and the use of the English language or some foreign sound of arousal.

Just like the man who had finally had enough I stand up, throw money on the table to cover the tab and announce to the gathered company, "Listen, I'm sorry to do this and I don't want anyone to think there is anything wrong with you or the way you're behaving. Honest to God, I would love to stay. You guys are fantastic but I just remembered an appointment I have to keep and I don't know why I forgot it. Maybe you were supposed to remind me Nicky, but anyway, I gotta get out of here fast." Then, just to make sure I don't hurt anyone's feelings, which has always been a tragic flaw in my personality, I ask the ear licker for her phone number. Once I get to the car I throw it out the window and head back to my apartment.

My heart is racing and there isn't anything to take my mind off of my feelings. I don't even own a television. I go to the kitchen, but there isn't any food there. I was supposed to use part of the hundred dollars to buy food and I still have some money left, but now the store is closed. I think about going to the gas station to grab some junk food but it is icy, windy, and freezing. I don't want to go out again.

There is no one to call. It is late, but if I had a real friend the time wouldn't matter. I had spent most of my life staying disconnected from people and now I was reaping the rewards of isolation. Everything was just the way I had wanted and made it.

I turned on the computer and began to type.

Chapter 1

THE OPENING QUESTION FOR THIS BURLESQUE could only be about children. Are they honestly the only thing we can make that is perfect? My soul salvation may come late but it will come because I will prove there was a time in my life when love did exist. I will prove that I did not waste it. I will prove that I served two masters at once and, unfortunately, benefited by neither. And, I will do so perfectly.

This all began on February 26, 1945. I came to earth during a great war, the Second World War. It was so intensely fought that morals and conscience were the supreme loss and sacrifice. Men were slaughtered, and brought back to the blood-stained dirt. But it was the thousands of mothers with their children, so many of them babies, whose silenced pleas and screams of terror still stream through the universe. Only they can be the righteous judges of human conduct in that war.

Deadly gamesmanship was the one-up near the end. The conflict was so bitter that entire cities surrendered only to be bombed to hell. And the innocent women and their children? They're gone now, but I haven't forgotten them. That was just one of the measures of love in the world to which I was born. But that was not a problem for me. I was an American baby. I was a Victory baby. The same God who had abandoned our enemies would now grant us rule of the world. My country would become the new Roman Empire. My loving family would be safe. There wouldn't be a mark on the map where an American citizen could not travel under the jealous and envious eyes of the world's inhabitants. We were the peacemakers.

With every factory in America up and running for wartime production and our victorious troops returning home—what was physically and psychologically left of them—my country turned its attention to post-war production of consumer goods, expansion, and the securing of borders and growth.

After receiving his honorable discharge from the Army Air Corps, my father, William Levise, Sr., proved to be overflowing with the "Right Stuff." Eventually he would sire eight children, four boys and four girls, of which I was the oldest boy.

My father is an enigma to me, and recollections of our bonding are frustrating. He was slender, good looking, and well-built; a man who was quiet and tended to hide his feelings. Occasionally he would laugh, but not often. He was uncomfortable with the beauty of the human body, as witnessed by the belt whipping he gave my sister and me when he unexpectedly came upon our pre-school exploration of anatomical differences. My father smoked, but didn't drink. He argued with my mother but didn't hit her. He let things build up and then exploded, slamming doors, punching inanimate objects, even banging his head against a wall. When you're a child you take peace for granted—until the explosions occur. His moods made me not trust him but, the few times he told me he loved me, I believed him.

My father was an only child who did not find out until he was middle-aged who his real father was. His mother, a tall, white-haired dominating figure, kept the secret from him all the way to her grave. His response to this new knowledge was to abandon the man who had raised him, and leave him alone to die in fear, confusion, illness, and poverty. I never forgave my dad for that unconscionable act. That man, my grandfather, was a short, happy Italian immigrant. He was filled with life and a ready smile, drank his coffee out of a saucer and hardly spoke English. But he loved his grandchildren as much as he loved my father, because my grandmother didn't share her deception with him either. He was simply a dupe.

When my grandmother became pregnant, my biological grandfather ran like the coward he was. Before she was showing her condition, my grandmother managed to track down and seduce into marriage a man from the same village in Italy as the coward. Having tied the sacred knot of marriage, she went to bed with my grandfather in what I can only imagine as the final piece of betrayal, and for the rest of their years together they slept in separate rooms. With a sweet mom like that lay a clue to my father's secret manner. Add to this the fact that Grandfather was a bootlegger during prohibition, and regularly changed addresses in three different states trying to stay one step in front of the law.

You begin to get a feel for the bumps in my father's life. But for me, the most intriguing aspect of his brooding character was his interest in the arts. He had attended art school and had also taken vocal lessons. In fact, it was his vocal performances on the radio in Detroit that drew the attention of my mother.

My mother, Jane Lucille McDaniel, was born in a rural town on the western side of the state of Tennessee. Her father was a horse trader and a dedicated drinker who had his own still and, apparently, got out his anger about his lot in life by beating his animals, his children, and his wife. At the age of four my mother watched in horror and helplessness as her mother caught fire from a cooking accident. A few painful days later, her mother died.

This was during the time of the Great Depression and her father quickly found a woman willing to marry a man of his great means and take on the task of raising his children. In truth, they were poor. My mother dropped out of school in the sixth grade to supplement the family income by picking cotton with other unfortunate children and adults in the thick, moist, oppressive heat and the deep black soil of the nearby Mississippi river.

Eventually there came to be five children in the family and things were looking bleak until one day, the miracle appeared. Europe was going to war and America was going to supply her every need. Like many poor Southerners, my mother's family joined the massive migration to the booming Northern industrial cities where jobs were plentiful and paid well, and life was wonderful. One of the things they didn't leave behind was her father's dark sickness. He was a short, wiry man with something to prove and one night, in a smoky, stale, beer smelling gathering, he got into a bar fight so violent his opponent plucked out one of his eyeballs and smashed it into the floor with the heel of his boot.

That is something of where my parents came from. I was told many times growing up that I didn't know what it was to be poor. Had I lived through the depression, as my parents had, may-be then I would know about hard times. Maybe. But either that bond, or some other mystical application, caused my parents to marry. When I look at their

Mitch's mom, Jane Lucille McDaniel.

wedding photograph I can see the sparkle of love in my parents' eyes. She was so beautiful and he was so handsome, and they were filled with the classic beginners hope and happiness.

Then life unfolded and reality became their truth. When America entered the war my father was called up, dashing his radio singing career into oblivion. When he came out of the war his singing career could not be revived and he had two children. He had to get what musicians and singers call "a real job." He became a parts inspector for a small tool and die maker, a job he bitterly held until his retirement. My father made several attempts at getting back into singing, but each attempt failed and he never seemed happy with that. His dream of unbridled self-expression gleefully manifested itself one winter as my sister Nina and I responded to his call and ran outside to witness his creation of an anatomically correct snowman and woman. When the neighbors complained he, once again rejected, slowly but violently tore them down.

My father died several years ago and it had a profound but controlled impact on my mother. She is now more than eighty years old and when we get together we speak only of happy times. For me, frankly, there weren't that many. My father was a hard worker who left home early, came home late, and prayed for overtime. There was never enough money and as the family continued to grow there was even less. Everyone suffered. My mother, as mothers will, tried her best to make things work, but only to the degree that my father could provide.

For years we had no medical or dental insurance and so, when I was four years old, I struggled with a high fever and hallucinations for days until the joints in my legs became swollen and I could no longer walk. I ended up with rheumatic fever and a heart murmur. That was one of many examples of a poverty I learned to fear and hate. I don't fault my parents for the poverty. Maybe I am being too critical about something I may never understand. Being poor felt empty; my parents were stretched too thin.

It is remarkable that so many people struggle with love. In reality, it seems that if someone didn't care for you, you probably wouldn't be alive. I could speak all day of people I know who have absolutely no use for love. For them it is a tool, useful only if it will help them reach their goal. Others make it the centerpiece of their beliefs and existence and end up being too vulnerable to control their own lives. One thing I will never forget though, is the calm and soothing sound of my father lying in bed, singing love songs to my mother long into the night, until we were all fast asleep.

The home I grew up in, that is to say the house I lived in from the age of four to fourteen, sat in a small seven-block neighborhood in Warren, Michigan, north of the security gates for the U.S. "army tank arsenal." A child during the Korean conflict, it became a game to breach security and dash through the armament on my bicycle while being chased by a jeep of MPs.

I was an adventurous young boy, and by the time I was five I had run away from home twice. The houses in the area were almost always wood frame with no basements and they sat off dirt streets with open ditches that ran parallel to the homes. A very active insect population also lived in our neighborhood. We moved there before developers came along, so we got to enjoy miles and miles of open farm and swampland, which was quickly bought by General Motors and turned into their technical center.

A bizarre, eclectic crowd who, with few exceptions, were culled from the debris of human failings and moral bankruptcy, peopled the neighborhood. There was alcoholism, drug addiction, violence, beating and battering, incest, adultery, child molestation, prostitution and a sense of well being that any sane person would find disgusting and repugnant. And we rarely saw the police because they were rarely called. It was all part of the game. It was as if a cheap, deranged circus had come to town on a death march to the sea of chaos, stopping only long enough to be certain the population would be forever ruined.

I emerged from that experience with a few of those characteristic patches embroidered into my life-worn quilt. The only thing in my favor was the fact that my parents still held onto a feel for the difference between right and wrong, even if it was driven by fear. In addition, I was the kind of child who carried an appetite for variety and

Nina and Mitch as young children in Detroit.

ended up befriending some of the more anchored children in the neighborhood. So, I moved back and forth between good and evil the way a chameleon experiences changes in its surroundings.

In the light of day I took on the responsibility of a paper route, but at night could be talked into attending a session of sexual intercourse between a brother and sister. I was a Cub Scout, yet found myself watching one of my compatriots talk one very poor and needy five-year-old boy into performing oral sex for a nickel and then beat him because he was choking. I attended gang-bang sessions at the house of a dirt poor, eighteen-year-old mother who had no money to clothe her five young children. But, I could never summon up the courage to vilify my acceptance of those situations. I simply didn't know there was another world to which I could escape, and I accepted my condition and poverty the way a beaten dog comes to rely on the violent abuse of its master as the hand that feeds it.

There was an instance where, at the age of eight, my teenaged baby-sitter performed oral sex on me. I liked it. She wasn't merely performing a sex act with her cool wet lips, her warm moist mouth and her tender caring hands; she was touching me and making me feel loved. There is one additional coloring that need be mentioned, and that was when I was made the prey of a soft-spoken and gentle homosexual who didn't know what any gay organization in America will readily tell you, that gay men never act on a desire for young boys.

What all this meant was that I would spend a lifetime trying to deal with a sexual dysfunction that would collapse and destroy any hope for a healthy sexual or otherwise safe relationship with another human being. The urge and need to repeatedly experience the instant gratification and inexpensive thrill of a sexual orgasm would blindly decide my priority, in even the most essential list of needs.

The poverty took its toll in many other ways, too. I wasn't able to judge the value of money. When presented with opportunity I almost always came down to a selfish determination that had nothing to do with the security and responsibility for others who might be dependent on me for protection or survival.

And love? Love being the most necessary and selfless gift we can give to another that we care deeply about? The same love that can banish our fears and heal our hurt, suffered at the hands of a world that would destroy us? Does it really exist?

I know my parents were in love. Not the kind of selfless love that comes from deep caring, but the love that poor folk, in the absence of all other considerations, use out of fear to hold on to each other to keep from drowning in a sea of desperation and loneliness.

That is my recollection of my childhood. It is not unique. There were other children like me in that neighborhood and there are millions more like us. Fearful cowards prone to abuse, and if we haven't got the guts to give it to someone else we turn upon ourselves. Those of us still alive, who are hopeful of change, wait trembling and shaking in the shadows praying to God for the courage to honorably face that one final defining moment, which will mercifully kill us or finally set us free.

As negative as that appears, it could easily be changed by a few clever strokes of my pen. My life, after all, was not completely horrible. Any person's story can be altered by the inclusion of warm memories, those flash points of hope and errant love that permeate an otherwise doomed existence. That's how it is with the poor, clinging to images so radically different from the norm that they grow out of proportion to reality.

I loved my brothers and sisters. I loved my parents. But it was a love planted in and fed from a bed of sick soil. If anything could survive and blossom into something beautiful and desirable it would be a miracle.

That is what I hate so much about the privileged in society. They proudly take for granted what the rest of us have prostituted and sacrificed our souls to discover.

Chapter 2

IT WAS A HARD STEEL CYLINDER, no more than four inches long and half an inch thick. Danny McCrary was holding it pressed vertically between his index finger and thumb. He was pressing so tightly his fingers were turning white. He held it two inches from my face, moving it back and forth, back and forth, and he told me how he had to wear gloves to conceal it in his palm. He said it would keep his knuckles from breaking. He gulped down another of the beers we had stolen from his stepfather's cache. For him, the steel cylinder served his insecurities. For me, it elevated my definitions of shock and fear to a place well beyond anything I had known or imagined. The physical brutality left me stunned and speechless.

The fight, which we used to call a rumble, should have lasted only a minute or two, but Danny was lost in a freak ascending reality as he slowly and thoughtfully drove the older boy down through his pride and humiliation. You could see the degradation take root, step-by-step, in the older boy's eyes. At first he was bemused. Who was this punk, three years younger than himself, who wanted a beating? And then, when his teeth tore through his bottom lip, he began to fight harder. He was angry. Next his eye was cut and blood streamed over his vision. He sensed his situation and fought harder but his remaining flinching eye took on a desperate look. Next, the broken nose, and a half-inch of cartilage shot out to the ground. The older boy still fought, but he was retreating. Danny pressed forward and, with an unstoppable barrage of punches, brought the older boy to his knees. Now, spitting blood and unable to see, the boy managed to cry out, "That's it. You win."

Danny drew him in with one arm and held him closely to his body. The moment took on a bizarre gracefulness as Danny methodically, again and again, began viciously bringing the hidden cylinder down upon the older boy's head. I couldn't take my eyes away. A few minutes later, when there was no movement except for an involuntary shaking, no apology or pleas to end it, and the older boy lay on the ground with several concussions, a broken nose, ruined eye, broken hand, missing teeth, severed lip, and covered in blood and his own urine. Danny said, "Let's get out of here." I looked back at the boy, and on his face and through his tear-filled one good eye I could see that Danny had taught him fear.

I don't know if it was that moment in which my cowardice chose to adhere to my soul or if it was, instead, those years of growing up in that neighborhood and gradually realizing there was no way out. But somehow it melted into my being and became, without question, a part of me.

Danny filled an extrinsic vacuum. When he first arrived with his divorced mother, and older brother and sister, it only took him a few months to emasculate the boys in the neighborhood. Since his mother, brother, and sister were never home, he had nothing but idle time. Danny savaged the streets, promoting or badgering his victims into fighting each other to the strict requirements of the mutated gamecock festival that lived in his head. If that failed, he beat them when he could catch them.

He was polite. I mean, Danny never actually went to anyone's home and said to the parent or parents, "May I see your son for a minute? I'd like to break some parts of his body." By the time his mother had found another man, Danny had already established his gang of followers, amongst whom I found myself. We eventually settled in and became single-mindedly bent on increasing our financial and territorial power at the expense of our neighbor's material and emotional belongings.

Movies, magazines, billboards, and television showed us what was available to all Americans. In fact, they made you feel un-American if you didn't possess everything they were selling. Two of the things they were pushing we had arranged to secure in abundance: cigarettes and alcohol. We then turned our attention to bigger ticket items. The gang had already amassed a portfolio of burglary and larceny charges by the time Danny's new stepfather moved in. His stepfather was a drinker, and we liked that. But I suspect the part of his new father that Danny really appreciated was the occasional hunting trip they took together. His new father had taught him how to kill.

Our early teen years were given to making and breaking the rules. Eventually, Danny went away on one of his many trips to DeHoCo (Detroit House of Correction) or some other institution for incorrigible young men. He would one day be released, get a good job at Chrysler in the boiler room, find a wife, and raise a family. I don't recall when or if the brutality and rage ever ceased because, even though I didn't know it, my life was about to make a change.

When it comes to morally responsible tenets and the spiritual ritual of boys to men, a young boy, by example—and in the absence of a loving, instructive, and caring male (whether father, part time father, or mentor)—takes what is in front of him. I was sick of it. Just sick of it. I wanted my father to be there. I wanted him to show me how I was going to survive this emotional and physical transition and freefall, the fear and brutality, the relentless perversities, the poverty. Was I wrong? Was life not as it seemed? Were we not poor, needy, and lacking in every imaginable way? Was that accidental and foreign smell of happiness on the rare misplaced wind from an existing world? Was there still, at least, some small hope, dear Father? Or, was what I saw around me all there was and all there could ever be?

My selfishness and anger only made matters worse. My mother was pregnant again. On the day of what should have been wonderful news I came to my own conclusion about the reason we were stuck in the neighborhood I despised, the reason we never had enough money, why I was embarrassed to bring my friends to my house, why I had no good clothes, why my teeth were rotting out of my mouth, and why I couldn't get a job. So, I approached my father and asked him why he didn't use the rubbers I had discovered while pilfering through his drawers. He said he had tried but he was such a bad ass he ended up blowing them off the end of his dick. He was laughing, as if he had made a joke.

I called him an asshole and he slammed me into the wall of his bedroom. This was the same bedroom in which my mother, so many years earlier, had tried through some quaint hillbilly remedy to ease the pain of infection that raged through my aching, sweating body by blowing cigarette smoke into my ears and rocking me for hours as my four-year-old mind danced from one hallucination to the next. Then, my father started punching. The only difference between my father and Danny was the fact that my father sometimes said he was sorry.

Today, gazing into my mirror at the afterimage of my father, irony bumps against genetic proof as I struggle to rid myself of my past. And yet, I don't want to throw all of it away. If I do, how can I exist? If I could discern the why, if we had known each other better, wouldn't I then, more surely than defame, defend? Such a great man. You left a hole in my heart Father, and I will not pretend to make things better. Not in a memory for or a memory of you. Life is a long, bitter road with sudden twists and turns, and no promise of the unexpected ever ending. I am sorry, Father.

In the late summer of 1959 I entered high school.

Chapter 3

IS YOU IS OR IS YOU ain't my baby? Enchantment wafts through the fantasy of my Faustian assurances as the world of high school put distance between what actually was and the promise of what was to be. Although I hadn't sold my soul, it was dirty and in need of repair. High school was "the cleaners." Not only would I now be privy to the combined knowledge of the entire civilized world but, better still, I would be thrust into a caste system where every intellectual wore the irrefutable grade of an "A+" on his forehead. This would prove to be a problem. And thus, it only took my freshman year to pacify my great expectations.

I have heard it said that desperate men do desperate things, and so I willfully drew upon my meager inheritance—desperation. My father had wanted to be an artist. He had tried to teach me but, unbeknownst to him, his failures, frustrations, and lack of confidence were always part of the lesson. My father had wanted to be a singer, but it was such a bitter pill that he didn't bother to pass it to me. During my high school experience I excelled in art and music and, with the die cast, I was now allowed to dream again. These wouldn't be the lost dreams of my childhood or my father, so softened and repeatedly rejected by the steel hymen of middle and upper class presumptions. My dreams had real possibilities in an America that appeared to be burning the furniture to feed the fireplace.

What could be of more noble sacrifice, more spiritually rewarding, more unselfish and yet, so esoteric in nature than the role of a teacher? At the all-white Warren High School, made up of working and middle-class students, it seemed we were blessed with more than our share of dedicated servant instructors. My choices of art and music had magically tapped into the best. Try as they would and as patient as they were, my other teachers could not crack my shell of indifference. They finally had to move on to more receptive students. But my music teacher, Del Towers, grabbed my attention, held it, and nurtured it long enough to allow me to grow into the only thing that proved to hold my undying love for the rest of my life. I already liked music. I was drawn to it. But Del taught me how to make my own. He showed me how to read and write music. He showed me how to perform it with confidence. And every time I did his bidding he rewarded me by raising the bar a little higher, and then gave me the tools to reach each goal. It wasn't just me. Every student in his class received the same sincere attention. It was only a question of their desire.

Music is such a natural and significant part of the American character, flowing so effortlessly, commercially, and aesthetically through inbred class differences that its impact defines who we are to the rest of the world. It is loud and quiet, and beautiful and ugly and powerful. But never, *never*, weak. Unless, of course, you want to buy it that way. Music becomes political in that it rises up as an ambassador for the culture of Western freedom. Freedom, in my musical experience, is a human right that one might die for only to have his brother or sister repaid for such belief and sacrifice by the shady dealings, greed, and unscrupulous ill will of freedom's legally endorsed "free" practitioners. Could be your neighbor. I don't know.

But, beyond the politic, the hucksters, hustlers, and dealers who peddle music, there remains at the bottom of the boiling pot, the unparalled imagination and energy of America's musical artists. Even after the opportunism, exploitation, and manipulation by the captains of the music industry, the artists' sound and music, the truth and beauty of the individual, still remain to be enjoyed. If it is indeed tragic, then the line of masochistic artists waiting and hoping to be abused and exploited is only marginally smaller than the line of sadistic handlers willing to show them the way. But that exciting world of opportunity was still out of reach for me. For the moment, I had to sharpen what tools I had because there wasn't a chance in hell of my going to college.

My embryonic musical influences included the painfully brilliant Hank Williams, whose songs my mother sang around the house, but strangely, only when she was either depressed or extremely happy. She also brought me songs she had written, and had me read the simple lyrics of her wishes. And then there were the songs my father so treasured. The big band swing, the dangerous boogie woogie, and the sterile crooner ballads. Even my dear beloved older sister Nina took me on a tour of music as she aimed to become a beatnik. She bought a guitar and wore a beret and took journalism in school until the verbose lingo and limited political reach of folk music gave way to the rebellious evolution and wordless beauty of revolutionary jazz as the music of choice for all true beatniks. I, too, fell into to my music of choice: rhythm and blues.

When summers came, time always moved more slowly, and I inevitably missed and pined for school, because I wasn't yet old enough to work. Occasionally, I found myself in Tennessee with my mother's parents. They had chosen to move back down South after her father retired from the job he held at the Burroughs Corporation, a company that, at the time, made wartime products. They had a farm near the bottom of Kentucky Lake and I whiled away the hot sticky days fishing, tending to chores, or being kicked by their mule. The long humid nights, lying next to an open window praying for the smallest breeze and being lulled into sleep by the sound of country insects, gave me a sense of security and I would drift off. It was tranquil, peaceful, and boring, and my parents knew it would keep me from the dysfunctional and criminal landscape of our neighborhood. But, if I was lucky enough to be chosen, my parents sometimes sent me to stay with my father's parents. I enjoyed that very much, but not because I enjoyed my grandparents. I had long ago figured out those dynamics and came away with few warm childish memories. I enjoyed it because they lived in the city of Detroit, which was like the other side of the planet from Warren. It was on those occasions, under the lacking supervision of my grandparents, that I was free to explore black culture first hand.

The music was more than I could ever have wished for. Artists with names like Ike and Tina Turner, Sarah Vaughan, Buster Brown, Sonny Boy Williamson, Little Richard, Jimmy Reed, Little Willie John, Jackie Wilson, Nat King Cole, Sam Cooke and the most prized of all, James Brown and his Famous Flames (and specifically his recording, *Live at the Apollo).* The Apollo recording drove me to witness two unforgettable performances by Mr. Brown at the Fox Theater in Detroit, and I studied every nuance

◆

a window to my soul

"I'm sittin' there an' over on a row of empty seats is this beautiful girl but she's really messed up. Too much drugs or somethin', an' she's just sittin' there passed out. Then this old, dirty, rumpled-up, unshaven street jerk with no teeth, long stinky hair an' filthy skin comes in an' sits down next to her. He's lookin' at her an' lookin' around seein' who's watchin' an' he does that for a while. Then he puts his arm around her an' with his free hand he undoes her blouse. Now he's feelin' her up an' she ain't movin'. He's fallin' in love an' he's gettin' excited an' his chewing tobacco that he's been gummin' to death starts runnin' out his fucking mouth just as he goes to give a French kiss. He's workin' it an' workin' it until he stops dead. He pulls his old filthy tongue outta her mouth, looks around one more time with his little rat eyes, picks the girl up in his arms an' ever so slowly walks out of the fuckin' building. Somebody's teenage daughter didn't make it home that night an' I never saw 'em again."

in an effort to commit them to memory. The lights, the choreography, the background harmonies (especially Bobby Byrd), the clothes and costumes, the sound, the players, the emotion, and finally James Brown as he worked his audience. Then, using that as the premium standard, I compared the white artists. Truly, if I was ever going to sing and make music that I could feel good about, I knew I was going to have to stay with the ethereal probes of black culture.

I had heard about a "hot little place" in Detroit, over on Woodward and Alexandrine, called the Village. The Village was a dark oasis for aspiring stars in Detroit and I was very curious about its reputation. I began hanging around whenever I could, somewhat uneasily checking things out. The slow nights, in the middle of the week, let me catch a feel for what it was and I didn't have to deal with the crowds of the weekend.

Many nights the music was no better than the memory I just shared. The two brothers that owned the Village had a pretty slick little operation. They had open auditions for house bands as often as they could. That way they didn't have to pay anybody. Unfortunately for the singers and other artists, it affected the quality of each performance but I learned to look past that as my hunger for the arcane debauchery of the joint evolved into an addiction.

Darryl was an exotic dancer there. He was a skinny young white male with a bad case of pimples, short hair, defiant attitude when he wasn't frozen with fear, bad overbite and an unspoken list of social crimes against his person that made him detestable and pathetic. I tried to be in the front row when he came parading out in his little grass hula skirt with no hips, his little grass bra with no tits and absolutely no chance of ever being able to buy any (even though you could see the drool run from his mouth as you mentioned the possibility), and finally, his real crown of thorns pushed tightly enough into his skull to draw blood.

Darryl danced eyes-closed and barefoot across the stage as his canard flew smack into the face of his twirling and desperate dreams, unaware or even caring whether he was liked or not. The audience always sat there momentarily stupefied until I, or some other patron, tossed a lit cigarette onto the stage as his non-sexy ass wiggled in our face and waited for the inevitable moment when his bare foot came down upon the fires of hell.

Eventually I decided I was ready to leave school. What was I giving up? High school football games? One night at the Village I witnessed a young man so driven by anger he hand forced a ball point pen all the way into another man's stomach. No, if it were violence I craved it wouldn't be the organized brand I got at football games. The alcoholic gatherings of my peers? At the Village they were laying out pills and powders and pot. Another state competition award for singing semi-classical music? I had come to prefer the raw, untrained, unrestrained emotion and potency of rhythm and blues.

And what would I be leaving behind at home? An evening with the family? It didn't exist. I remember when I was a child we would sit at the kitchen table, all of us, staring at the radio or some individually reserved space on the wall listening to Arthur Godfrey or *The Lone Ranger* or *The Green Hornet* and not once making eye contact with each other. It was no better when my parents purchased a TV, except we then had a plausible justification for the direction of our eyeballs. There were some wonderful programs: *The Sid Caesar Show, The Honeymooners, I Love Lucy*. Comedic. Geared to entertain, make you laugh, and communicate to a family that had never learned to communicate with each other. At least with radio we could imagine. With TV, nothing.

At the Village I began to make friends with many of the black artists. Great entertainers who might never see success but were just learning to walk, as was I, through our anticipation of anything better than what we knew. Some would go on to become stars with Motown Records, a huge worldwide recording label out of Detroit. Others, like Darryl, would swallow defeat and disappear.

I was invited to join a black group called the Peps. Because I sang my heart out I was allowed to do lead vocal from time to time. If those men knew how much confidence I gained by their acceptance of me, especially Joe Harris, they would no doubt laugh themselves silly. They didn't just let me sing, they let me into their world, and Detroit in the early nineteen sixties was a tinderbox ready to burst into flame. There was a history of precedent with regard to race relations in Detroit and none of them boded well for the future.

Many of the performances we did were for black audiences and in one instance I remember a very charming lady walking over to me and saying, "You sing so pretty and you're so light." The world was my oyster and everyday brought more knowledge. I learned how essential it was to value the moment, because it was futile to think long term. I learned if I was somebody's "boy," I was a short-term investment. I got good at spotting the unmarked police cars that held the "big four," undercover policemen who were looking for a reason. But, more telling than anything were the unmistakable signposts that outlined the disparity of laws between black and white, and the resulting damage to a human condition forced by white society to singular survival. The uninvited rage that lives on in the flesh of impotence. It was my first opportunity to challenge my racist feelings that were deeply buried beneath the innocence of a young man who believed a class war was more appropriate to his surroundings than a race war.

I needed to open my eyes a little wider. Of course we lived in a racist society. I could see it in the hesitation of my high school classmates when they refused acceptance of my invitations to watch me perform at the Village. I could see it when we drove through the suburbs and Joe Harris and Ronnie Abner from the Peps would sink down into their seats until their heads were no longer visible. I saw it in the anger of white police who stopped us, who put them in jail and let me go. I knew that whatever I did I couldn't change the color of my friends' skin and, like the other members of the Peps, I felt powerless to change the beliefs of people who fostered the institution of racism.

We weren't politically motivated civil rights activists. We were teenagers, and every time we performed before white audiences and got applause we allowed ourselves to think we were beyond the reach of that terrible American hate. Joe, Ronnie, Tommy Stone (who was also one of the Peps), and I knew it wasn't fair. We all wanted to be stars so we could somehow make up for that "something special" that was missing from our lives, and hopefully get the money we believed would insulate us from the in-justice of our times.

It was no different for Lee Rodgers, who had a local hit with a song called "Sad Affair," or Leroy Belcher with his song "Superman," or Little Bit and the Dreamers. I fell for Little Bit but she ended up calling me a dog because at that special moment of put up or shut up I chickened out. Nor was it different for any of the hundreds of young black Detroiters who over the years passed through the Village, sometimes launching a career from that building. The great performer Nathaniel Mayer with his "Village of Love" was one, as was Richard Street and the Distants.

I don't know what motivated Gabe and Leo Glantz to open that place, other than money, because they had no love for most of the entertainers. But, we all were thankful to have that stage available. In the end though, the Peps knew that no matter what hap-pened, I could never really know about their lives because I had been born white. But for that God-sent moment in my life I might still be dressed in the cloth of ignorance. I soon became confident enough and good enough to go solo.

Chapter 4

IT WAS, THANK GOD, ANOTHER GIG. I had every intention of adding it to the list of good ones I had privately come to distinguish from the sordid self-indulgence of the bad. The carefree youthful days of the Village were forty hard years behind me now. The blinding, swift complicity and love for the fame and fortune that followed was, by now, part of the historical record kept neatly in a trash bin somewhere. The rapacious, slow moving feast from that point to this was too large and tortuous to commit to film. Now I needed whatever work I could lay my hands on. Another gig in another faraway, hard to get to little town that had rocked with the entire American nation several decades prior to the irrepressible and exciting sound of my cherished string of sixties hit records. They had the money. They paid their deposit. And tonight, in the year 2001, I was still, in the minds of this audience, their "star."

"Does the smoke bother you?" the young monitor tech asked as we stared toward the stage and watched highly defined white beams of light, filled with slow floating patterns of exhaled carbon monoxide, move silently through the blackness of the auditorium. "No," I said. "Not anymore." I laughed, thinking how I wonder every day when those years of pain in my lungs will turn into something sinister and deserved. "No. It's not as bad as the fog machines. That stuff makes my throat itch. It makes you dry, you know?" I added as I wiped the cold sweat from my plastic bottled water.

"Do you still get nervous?" he asked, reacting to my irritated pacing, a result of his endless questions. "Yes," I said, lying, just to get him off my back. But it did make me think. When did I lose that anticipation? At what point did I become so greatly confident in my ability to entertain that I no longer worried about how I was going to do? Or, conversely, when did I stop caring? All those years in so many different altered states, dragging and strip teasing my weaknesses and addictions and failings before my fans, yet, somehow managing to convince most of them they had witnessed my best. In the balance? Performances so shamefully ugly that no one at all wished to recall. Blind and pointless anger over something as insignificant as fading fame.

I remember. Yes, I remember with great affection the first time I ever took the stage alone in high school. My knees were shaking and I could not open my eyes. I had held the microphone and stand so tightly there were marks in my skin. Then, when I finished singing, that magic moment of stillness and quiet, and finally, applause. In one motion it was both horrible and magnificent.

Next, of course, came the Village and my run with the Peps, but getting top billing as the solo artist had proven to be much more difficult. The shining star at the Village prior to my solo debut was a man I'll call Timmy. I had given Timmy's endorsement of me for top solo billing to management, but only after his exit. That was Timmy way of repaying me.

The first time I saw Timmy perform I was awestruck. He had complete command of the stage. No matter what was going on anywhere, in any little corner of the Village, all eyes turned toward Timmy when he walked on to perform. Many were frightened by his appearance. Some laughed and made fun. But when he began to sing, all doted upon each little breath, every exaggerated syllable, every perfect note, and he sang and danced and moved about so freely you would think that it should never be, please don't let it ever be, anything else. His energy dominated the psyche of the other entertainers to the point where nobody would, or could, follow him. He drove his audience, over and over, to ever greater heights of involvement and, mostly unnoticed, slowly disrobed with each subsequent song until finally, exhausted, covered in sweat and overjoyed with his impending triumph he ended his performance with his beloved signature song. Everyone would be drooling in anticipation. Using a drumbeat similar to the one employed by Maurice Ravel in his hypnotic composition "Bolero" he sang the living shit out of "Temptation."

> *You came*, ba ba ba bomp, ba ba ba bomp, ba ba ba
> *I was alone*, ba ba ba bomp, ba ba ba bomp, ba ba ba
> *I should have known*, ba ba ba bomp, ba ba ba bomp, ba ba ba
> *You were temp-taaa-tion*

At the very end, just as the song reached its phenomenal climax, Timmy took off his pants. The first time I saw it I burst out laughing. I was in tears. I could not believe that all of the thought and preparation for the skilled and beautiful execution of his show could, in his mind, somehow reach its zenith with so little left to show. I tell you it was maddening. I loved it. He was a freak.

While I lay in limbo between the Peps and my first solo shot at the Village, Timmy began what I now understand to be his pursuit of me. It is difficult to describe being pursued by someone of the same sex because it requires a shift in ones own perception of self and sexual identification. There I was, what I believed to be, a young man. So what did that make Timmy?

This was not the same as the build up to the oral pederasty and sodomy of my childhood at the hands of local deviants. This had an air of excitement. The telephone calls, the letters begging for a chance just to talk, standing outside my home on a summer evening and throwing pebbles at my window as I tried to shout in a whisper, "Go away," the singling out and cornering at the Village until finally I agreed to go places with him.

Timmy took me to an old casino on Belle Isle, a beautiful, quiet island respite from the city in the middle of the Detroit River. There was an old piano there and he taught me songs. I even visited his home on West Grand Boulevard and it was very much the same thing. One night after the Village, I went with him to what he described as a party. On the way there he introduced me to my first experience with Seconals, or "Reds" as they were known. When we arrived, no one else was there. The next few moments were, sadly, all about the chase and the cherry. After that, Timmy disappeared from my life forever.

Chapter 5

EVERYTHING IN MY LIFE LAY NAKED, filled with unsophisticated romanticism over any innocence that I might claim. There was fear. Bedazzled idolatry. The hunt. The capture. The hollow disingenuous eyes of the Shaman filling with flames as the impasse grew obvious. A scene from yesterday, a scene from every lonely moment I had ever lived. Just touch me. If you touch me I will know that you love me. Do you love me? Do you really love me?

I hated it. In the quiet aftermath, I thought about killing myself. I really did.

Now I had top solo billing but in street talk I had become the bitch. Much more confusing and punishing was the label "queer," and I didn't have a woman in my life that I could point to for salvation or rebuttal. I had never had sex with anyone, unless you took into account my treatment at the hands of child molesters.

When you are young—and especially in your middle teens—sometimes you are able to turn being different into a good thing. Not this time, and not in Detroit. Queers. Faggots. At least the women were safe, but watch out. If you were a man and one of those freaks came around, what would you do? You didn't want to return their smile for fear they would read it as an invitation. You didn't know what would happen, and you didn't want to find out.

I find that women are sometimes curious about male homosexuality because most hate rejection by the opposite sex. It is vanity. Such a question of sexuality is, in fact, upsetting to the natural order of things. I became desperate to find a woman. My machismo went into overdrive. The non compos mentis reality propelled me into a situation involving money that belonged to a charming, wet and sticky, bovine back alley debutante. No "Thank you" required and "No," I didn't need a receipt. I felt somewhat balanced after that.

But the memory of Timmy, oh God, that lingered for an eternity. What is a queer anyway? Should it be something unpleasant? I don't believe so. I know that homosexual men are capable of reaching love, fear, hate and joy, sensitivity, passivity, violence, selfishness, bias, prejudice, shame, regret, celebration of life and pain, compassion, creativity, discerning taste, mundane existence, political astuteness, determination, and finally a healthy sense of self bolstered with confidence through love. In that way they are no different from the "healthy" status quo. Where it turns ugly is in the presentation of their political agenda, and for a very few, their views on children.

While I struggled with that, bigger, more immediate problems began to surface. I was awakened by the force of my father lifting me out of bed and dragging me by the hair up the stairs, through the front door and, using his leg, pushing me into a kneeling position on the front lawn as he pulled my head upward and twisted it forward to face his car. Many of the neighbors on their way to work that warm summer morning stopped to marvel at the scene. The boy, dressed only in his underwear and held bowed like a tortured prisoner, and the car. The car stood there like a fantastic piece of artwork. There was a trunk, a bent hood, scraped doors, a roof and tires, but there was no front end and there definitely were no fenders. It slowly started to come back to me as my father screamed out the ridiculous. "Did you do this?" So that was the metallic sound I kept hearing on my drive home from the Village.

Mitch's dad, Bill Levise, Sr.

It was the straw that broke the camel's back. Two weeks prior, my father had gotten a neighbor to drive him into Detroit at eleven-thirty at night to claim that very same vehicle from the police car pound where it rested after I had loaned it to Ronnie from my old group, the Peps. It seemed that Ronnie didn't have a license. But, things had been building to a climax way before then.

A month earlier I had borrowed my father's car and was to pick him up at work. I arrived almost an hour ahead of schedule with nothing to do but sit in the car and wait. Raging hormones coupled with my particular sexual dysfunctions led me to masturbate so passionately that I didn't see him approaching, as the car windows were completely fogged over from my body heat. Fortunately, I had just finished, but the look of disgust on my father's face as he opened the passenger door and slid in could not stop my heavy breathing or the unmistakable smell of where I had marked my territory. I wanted to deflect his dagger-like stare and scream, "Parents can choose to have children but children can't choose to have parents," but that would not have been fair. Somewhere between my teens and the maturity of the years I am now burdened with, I began to understand and collect little sayings such as, "Teenagers: God's punishment for a few moments of unprotected sex," and "Hire a teenager while they still know everything," and my favorite, and always the one to make me rethink the gauge and powder load of a bullet, "Teenagers rule."

At some point in everybody's scheme, sacrifice has to be viewed as a measure of love. My parents had very little, but given their limited monetary resources, the fact that my mother had never held a driver's license, and my father had precious little time, they were able to involve and convince producers and record labels in Detroit into releasing two single recordings of my performances. In addition, my mother set up an audition for me with Brian Holland, the famous producer and writer at the equally famous Motown Records.

I feel awkward when trying to give my parents their due because they were rarely reliable when it came to my essential needs as a child, and so it becomes a question of how much their new-found interest and effort had been for their gratification, as opposed to mine. That also played well into my father's "second chance" at music by living vicariously through his talented, singing son. It also went a long way into relieving some of the guilt my mother felt for having so many children that my father had to abandon his dreams. Cynicism? Damned right. Don't leave home without it.

The first recording, when I was sixteen, appeared on the Carrie label. My father had befriended a black gentleman named Wade at his place of work and was initially trying to set up a deal for his own recording. Wade's wife played keyboards at a black gospel church in Detroit, headed by the Reverend James Hendrix (no relation to Jimi), who also owned the label. It was through Wade and his wife that we were introduced

Carrie Records
P. O. Box 7763
Detroit, 7 Mich.

Mar. 19, 1963

Mr. Wm. S. Levise, Sr. and Sr.
27454 Strathmoor St.
Warren Mich.

Dear Mr. Levise,

    Sincerely hope all goes well with you and family. I am
fine and is moving into bigger things of which I am happy.
I had to leave Detroit on urgent business in Greenville, S. C.
 where I am writing this letter from now.   I did not have
time to do nothing but get my things together before leaving
and I am sorry that I am late in getting you a release.   I
really would like to continue working with you and Bill Jr.
but what ever is best for you, I am in accord.   I will be
here for another two or three weeks yet but when I return to
Detroit I will have national distribution for both my labels.
I had to do some dealing to get this done but it is well worth
while.

    Give my regards to all of family and please write me soon.

                  Respectfully,

                  James Hendrix

to the Reverend. The Reverend was short and surprisingly cordial. He had a beautiful smile that seemed to say, "Hey, I just had a talk with God!"

The Reverend also had a kingly interest in rock 'n' roll but, because he did not fully understand it, preferred to keep me on his gospel label. The resulting single, on which I wrote the A side, titled "Fool for You," and he wrote the B side, titled "That's the Way it's Gonna Be," hit my psyche like a free lunch.

Unfortunately, hearing my voice on the radio for the very first time was sullied by my accidental witnessing of the Reverend handshake-passing money to the disc jockey as we left the WJLB studio. On our way back to the Reverend's we listened to our recording being played on the radio and he smiled at me with an insane quizzical grin and wondered why I wasn't going crazy. I could only stare at the passing landscape and damn myself for thinking I was anyone at all.

Once we arrived back at the "office," which was a near empty upper flat that contained a table, boxes of supplies, a bed, and on the bare floor next to it, a telephone, we began pasting album covers together. It was a hot sticky summer day and there was no air conditioning, not even a fan, and so we decided to take a break and sit by the open windows next to the bed. As we sat, the Reverend slowly began running his trembling fingers with their sharply manicured and polished nails up the length of my leg. His eyebrows were pointing down in a frown but he still had that crazy, toothy smile. I silently rose to my feet and walked down the stairs to the street. I asked myself over and over again why only men kept coming after me. It was depressing.

I returned to the Village where at least, among other things, I was a "star." I also began showing up at Thelma Records on the corner of Grand River and Grand Boulevard, hoping to get a contract with Berry Gordy's ex-wife. That didn't work out. I failed the audition with Brian Holland at Motown Records because my writing skills weren't equal to my singing ability.

It was shaping up to be a really bad winter when a musician friend of mine from high school called and mentioned that his parents were taking him to Florida in a few weeks and asked if I wanted to go along. He said I needed to have a hundred dollars. I knew I couldn't ask my parents, and as I stood in the outer lobby of the Village preoccupied with thoughts of money the most incredible thing I could imagine occurred.

Behind the concession stand was a very pretty Jewish girl named Susan Bilsky. She had been working there with her friend Bobbie Segal for a few weeks and every time I came out to the lobby on a break, the two were laughing and having fun, trying to keep the men and boys at bay. I never dreamed of speaking to them because it was clear to me that everyone thought I was a faggot. But unbelievably, Susan said hello to me.

From then on, I stopped to talk every time I saw her. I couldn't say she was my girl but it made me angry and jealous when other guys swarmed around her, especially when it was a guy I knew, because I was certain of his motive. Even though I wanted to take her to bed, I was still reeling from the fact that she had said hello to me.

Over the weeks, as we talked, I mentioned how disappointed I was at the prospect of not going to Florida when, out of the blue, she volunteered the money as a loan. That was so cool. But I missed a subtle little magic in our exchange, and it flew right past me because how could I have known or even suspected that when I turned eighteen Susan would be my wife. Sweet Jesus, what was I thinking? She was a Jew by birthright and religion. I was the mongrel lineage promise of America leaning toward Italy, religiously baptized Methodist, occasionally raised Baptist, and converted to Catholicism by a sparky little Jesuit because I did not want to spend another empty, impoverished Christmas without the sensual rewards that lay within the opulent grandeur of the Catholic Church.

Jew. It played into every racist and hateful prejudice I had learned in my childhood, but for that matter, so did hanging out with and befriending blacks. Not for the last time would the poison of my past come back to haunt me.

I thanked Susan and headed to Florida.

Chapter 6

CERTAINLY WHILE TRAVELING IN SOUTHERN FLORIDA, but even before, I became aware of the backward gentile hearsay and long list of hates directed toward Jews. It did not help matters when every angry stereotype with regard to Jews seemed to find a face in Miami. It was another form of racism and discrimination that made me very sad.

As I lay on the beach with my friend Joey Kubert, totally surrounded by what I jokingly thought of as the "evil Jewish hoardes," the only crime we could discern being committed was the future burden on the health care system as it would come to struggle with an epidemic outbreak of skin cancer.

I thought about my Jewish girlfriend, Susan. Susan wasn't rich and neither were her parents, Jack and Belle. Jack was a truck driver and had, at one time, owned his own newsstand in New York City. Divorced, he married Belle, gave birth to beautiful Susan and lived in Oak Park, Michigan, right across the street from Oak Park High School. And here I was because of her, in love with the warm sun, the soft white sandy beaches, the warm rolling waves, the smell of the salty ocean water, the pleasant breeze, the swaying palm trees and the memory of the snow and cold from twenty-four hours before. Yes, it was my first winter visit to Florida and there we were, myself, Joey, and the Jews, all saying a prayer of thanks to the genius of Carl Fisher and his legacy, the dredge. But it would have to end. I didn't like that part.

It was, more than anything, my jealousy and distrust of the wealthy that drove me to the obvious. I did not hate Jews. I hated rich Jews. In fact, I hated all rich people. It is tacitly understood that if you hate rich or wealthy people and you are poor, you are undoubtedly envious, and probably stupid and lazy as well. It is interesting, how hate works. In America, something can be hated and still be allowed an escape mechanism through which you can change the negative energy into something positive. However, there is justifiable cause to balance and seek resolution in your favor for more precisely identified targets and issues—if you can prove your case.

That is why it is essential to know and work from the premise that extremely wealthy people do not think of themselves as people. They think of themselves as gods. It was for me, unfortunately, the gods themselves that eventually pissed me off. But it is "so American" and it makes you rethink the twisted genius inherent in the founders of our country. Those brave, daring, and courageous men, mostly successful business men and wealthy plantation and land owners, a number of whom were slave

◆

a window to my soul

The defamation and ridicule, when left to the imagination of a common Southern population that still held distaste for "Yankees" in general, only heightened the evil perception of Jews. Jews were all seemingly rich, "obviously" from the bounty and wealth acquired by their greed and shameful abuse of poor, stupid, working class fools. The implication was that Jews were rude and arrogant, complaining and manipulating, skilled at pulling new interpretations of constitutional law from the belly of the constitution, abusively litigious, dripping with gold and odd fashion, attached to Cadillacs, and all speaking with, what I later discovered to be, a New York accent, even though they came from all over. One of the locals joked that we had traveled so far south we were north again.

It was another ten years before I stumbled upon a copy of the book Mein Kampf, *where Adolf Hitler carried these disgusting hatreds to an elevation that was profoundly insane. According to Hitler, Jews would direct the evolution of mankind through their cunning self-serving agenda. They would control the world monetary system, cause countries to go to war for their own material gain, (say, that does sound reasonable if you're in the arms industry) and never have a "real" allegiance to any country because they were, and would forever be, desert-hopping nomadic misfits who suffered under the delusion that their God was a real-estate broker. Why else would Jews be driven from and persecuted by so many, and yet set up shop in each new home with an ease of transition that could only come from a stubborn, single-minded purpose and insidious practice. In America,* Mein Kampf *implied, the "chosen ones" controlled the media, and thus, public opinion. Wealthy Jews bought members of Congress and owned them. And Hitler's last complaint? By following the dictates of a punitive God in the Old Testament, whose words were written by Jews, they had killed Jesus Christ. My question is: why did it take the world so long to realize that Hitler was fucking insane?*

owners and indentured servant keepers, who in one brilliant catharsis were able to proclaim that which they had no right to, that which was incredible and hypocritical, that all men are created equal.

There was the key, the lie, and the promise in one neat little package. There were no other words available that would allow those men to start their own country and, at the same time, have the blood and sacrifice of the commoners around them. After all, who would physically protect those beautiful words? Yes, the commoners would be their "equal." Smooth, to say the least. And promises would be made and broken. But, off in the distance somewhere was that long shot chance that you, a commoner with bold initiative and hard work, could rise up through the class distinctions and become one of the American elite. All you needed then and now was money. Well, I bought it. I decided right there, on that marvelous Florida beach, that I was going to be rich.

First, I would have to destroy my hatred of the wealthy. Given the fact that I was going to one day be living next door to them, it simply would not do to have ill feelings toward them, since I was certain they would welcome me with open arms.

While Joey and I were in Miami, many fortuitous events were in the making. Cassius Clay, whom I respectfully refer to as Muhammad Ali, was going to box Sonny Liston. This was important to me because I loved the sport of boxing. Before I was old enough to make myself intimately aware of the sport, I knew three things about it. My father had told me that Sugar Ray Robinson had beaten him up outside a Detroit library while showing off for two of his pals; most of the fighters, the really good ones, were Italian; and everyone was always looking for "The Great White Hope."

I recall sitting outside one summer night, listening to the first Floyd Patterson/Ingemar Johansson fight on a little transistor radio. I savored every second of it and surrendered my imagination to the ringside, dodging the lurid sweat and the spattering sacrificial blood while sitting next to the announcer as he tried in vain to be heard above the screams and cheers and jeers of the drunken, impassioned fans. He coughed from sucking in the smoked filled air but, in spite of the winner, he called the fight just right. "Peek-a-Boo" Floyd was already past his prime and, even to a young teenager like me, you had to know he must have badly needed the money.

I wondered if there would ever come a young champion that I would be able to more closely identify with. Then came Ali. "I am the greatest," he would say, so proud and sure of his place in the world. I wanted that cocky confidence and strength. Then he would say, "I'm pretty, and I'm smart," and he was not just empowering young American blacks with his theatrics and bombast, he was giving young men of every color all over the world a simple but absolutely necessary piece of life called hope.

One of the most cherished moments in my life came decades later as I sat right next to the Champ, the man who had helped repair and shape some of my life-view at such a critical moment, and we shared a banquet "birthday" meal together while covertly watching a boxing match on my hand-held TV, hidden discretely between ourselves just under the table, as the speakers, one after another, droned on and on with their praise of, and birthday wishes for, Muhammad Ali.

Muhammad Ali and Mitch Ryder watching TV.

But just as interesting to me was the impending arrival of a group of British musicians who called themselves The Beatles. Joey and I maintained the customary Detroit contempt for British invaders and reasoned that, if they could be successful making music, so could we. I told Joey about three white boys that had come through the Village as an auditioning back-up band and how nicely and easily they were able to perform the rhythm and blues that I loved so much. And because we secretly admired The Beatles, we might be able to blend the two styles into something new. In the beginning, most of the new wave of British rockers were doing cover versions of American black music anyway.

When we returned from Florida I called up the white boys from the Village and we settled into rehearsals at the home of Johnny Badanjek, the drummer. Johnny was one of the most gifted and powerful rock drummers to ever breathe air. At the time, he was using a bass drum that was half the size of his parents' house and he was always messing with those crazy calfskin heads. Jimmy McCarty, the lead guitar player was equally talented, extremely fast and probably the most serious musician of the group. Earl Elliot, the bass player, relied more on sensitivity and taste than attack, and when Joey was added on rhythm guitar you had a group of teenagers, fortified by self-awareness, that were begging for a crack at the British. For now, we were called Billy Lee and the Rivieras, but this same group would eventually become Mitch Ryder and the Detroit Wheels.

We started playing church dances, bar mitzvahs, record hops, little teen clubs—anywhere they would let us set up. Our show brought all of the best elements of our combined musical knowledge to a hybrid state that had not previously existed in white boy Detroit. We put together a new sound and our fans showed their appreciation by filling up venues that held thousands of people. We were so hot some of the Motown Records recording artists were opening for us. This from a group of young men who had yet, with the exception of my first solo recording, to see a recording studio or their eighteenth birthday. The only thing missing was the hit record and, as if by cue, my father stepped in with the money.

The record label was Hyland Records and the accompanying publishing arm was Xyland Publishing. Apparently the "big" record label needed some of my father's hard earned cash to make the project work. Side A was written by me and titled "You Know." Side B was written by Jimmy and me and titled "Won't You Dance With Me."

The next step was to get the record played and that effort led to our big break. There was a disc jockey at WXYZ radio named Dave Prince. He had met my parents and all of the boys, and had seen our show and liked us. He even played our record, but it did not do well enough to become a hit. He had a contact in New York City, but felt we could strengthen our position by putting together an audition tape and arranging a showcase performance.

Dave captured the interest of a successful record producer named Bob Crewe, who was swimming in hit records, and because of Mr. Crewe's involvement we were slated to open for the British group, The Dave Clark Five. The engagement was going to take place at one of the nicer venues in Detroit, the Masonic Temple, which was

---

Mar. 19, 1963

TO WHOM IT MAY CONCERN:

Release is hereby granted to Bill Levise, Jr. from under recording agreement dated May 5, 1962. The above mentioned artist is
now free to record for any other firm he desires without any interference from Carrie Records or myself. It is understood ####
that all previous recorded masters, tapes and songs shall remain
the property of Carrie Records and any subsequent royalties or
 earnings due will be fowarded to above named artist when recieved
by us. We grant this release upon the request of artist with
regards

Sincerely,
Carrie Records

James Hendux

COPY   1.

XYLAND INTERNATIONAL Publishing Co.

            Standard Songwriter's Contract
            _____

        This Agreement made and entered into this   27th   day
of   June   , A.D. 19 64 , by and between XYLAND INTERNATIONAL
Publishing Company, a Michigan concern, with offices at 237 Pasadena,
Highland Park, Michigan, hereinafter called "Publisher," and;

    William S. Levise, Jr.   of   27454 Strathmoor, Warren, Michigan
    James W. McCarty   of   19394 Caldwell, Det. 34, Michigan

    ***********************   of   _____

    ***********************   of   _____

    ***********************   of   _____

    ***********************   of   _____

jointly and/or severally (hereinafter called "Writer(s)");

                    WITNESSETH:

        In consideration of the agreement herein contained, and of
One (1.00) Dollar and other good and valuable consideration in
hand paid by the Publisher to the Writer(s), receipt of which is
hereby acknowledged, the parties agree as follows;

        1. The Writer(s) heregy sells, assigns, transfers, and delivers
to the Publisher, its successors and assigns, a certain heretofore
unpublished original musical composition, written and/or composed
by the above named writer(s), now entitled:

    "Won't You Dance With Me"
    _____

including the title, words and music, and all copyrights thereof,
including but not limited to the copyright registration thereof,
NO. EU-825187 May 12, 1964   , and all rights, claims and
demands in any way relating thereto, and the exclusive right to
secure copyright therein throughout the entire world, and to have
and to hold the said copyrights and all rights of whatsoever
nature now and hereafter thereunder existing and/or existing under
any agreements or licenses relating thereto, for and during the
full terms of all of said copyrights. In consideration of the
agreement herein contained and the additional sum of One ($1.00)
dollar and other good and valuable consideration in hand paid

by the Publisher to the Writer(s), receipt of which is hereby
acknowledged, the Writer(s) hereby sells, transfers, and delivers
to the Publisher, its successors and assigns, all renewals and
extensions of the copyrights of said musical composition(s) to
which the Writer(s) may be entitled hereafter, and all registrations
thereof, and all rights of any and every nature now and hereafter
thereunder existing, for the full terms of all such renewals and
extensions of copyrights.

2. The Writer(s) hereby warrants that the said composition
is his sole, exclusive, and orgional work, and that he has full
right and power to make the within agreement, and that there exists
no adverse claims to or in the said composition. The Writer(s)
hereby futher warrants and represents that he is not a member of the
American Society of Composers, Authors, and Publishers, the Songwriter's Protective Association, or of any other society or
association which requires as a condition of membership the assign-
ment of any of the rights herein set forth has been directly or
indirectly made to Broadcast Music, Inc., or any other person,
firm, or corporation whatsoever.

3. The Writer(s) hereby warrant(s) the foregoing musical
composition is new and orgional and does not infringe any other
copyrighted work and has been created by the joint collaboration
of the Writers named herein and that said composition, including
the title, words and music thereof, has been, unless herein otherwise specifically noted, the result of the joint efforts of all
the undersigned Writers and not by way of any independent or
separable activity by any of the writers.

4. In consideration of this agreement the Publisher agrees
to pay the Writer(s) as follows:

(a) In respect of regular piano copies sold and paid for
at wholesale in the United States of America, royalties of;

_3¢ (THREE CENTS)_____ per copy;

(b) A royalty of _3¢ (THREE CENTS)_ per copy of dance
orchestrations thereof sold and paid for in the United States of
America.

(c) A royalty of _50% (FIFTY PERCENT)_ of all net earned
sums received by the publisher in respect of regular piano copies
and/or orchestrations thereof sold and paid for in any foreign
country by any foreign publisher.

(d) A royalty of _$10.00 (TEN DOLLARS)_ for each use of the
Lyrics and music together, in any song book, song sheet, folio, or
similar publication containing at least five musical compositions.

3.

(e) A royalty of _50% (FIFTY PERCENT)_ of all net receipts of the Publisher in respect of any licenses issued authorizing the manufacture of the parts of instruments serving to mechanically reproduce the said composition, or to use the said composition in synchronization with sound motion pictures, or to reproduce it upon so called "electrical transcriptions" for broadcasting purposes; and of any and all net receipts of the Publisher, from any other source or right now known or which may hereafter come into existence.

(f) For purposes of royalty statements, if a composition is printed in the United States, as to copies and rights sold in Dominion of Canada, revenue therefrom shall be considered as of domestic origin. If, however, the composition is printed by a party other than the Publisher in the Dominion of Canada, revenue therefrom shall be considered as originating in a foreign country.

(g) In the event that the said composition shall not now have lyrics, and lyrics are added to the said composition, the above royalties shall be divided equally between the Composer and the other writers and composers.

(h) As to "professional material" --Not sold or resold, no royalty shall be payable:

(i) Except as herein expressly provided, no other royalties shall paid with respect to the said composition.

5. It is specifically understood and agreed that the intention of this agreement is not, and the Composer shall not be entitled to receive any part of the monies received by the Publisher from the American Society of Composers, Authors, and Publishers, or any other collecting agency from which the Publishers shall receive payments for use of said musical composition in all countries of the world.

6. The Publisher shall render the Writer(s), as above, on or before each August 15th covering the six months ending June 30th; and each February 15th covering the six months ending December 31st, royalty statements accompanied by remittance for any royalties due thereunder.

7. Anything to the contrary notwithstanding, nothing in this agreement contained shall obligate the Publisher to print copies of the said composition or shall prevent the Publisher from authorizing publishers, agents and representatives in countries inside and outside of the United States from excercising exclusive publication rights and other rights in the United States in said composition, provided the Publisher shall pay the Writer(s) the royalties herein stipulated.

4.

8. The Writer(s) may appoint a certified public accountant who shall upon written request therefore, have access to all records of the publisher during business hours relating to said composition for the purpose of verify royalty statements hereunder.

9. The Writer(s) hereby consent to such changes, adaptions, dramatizations, transpositions, editing and arrangements of said composition, and the setting of words to the music and of music to the words, and the change of title as the Publisher deems desirable. The Writer(s) hereby waive any and all claims which they have or may have against the Publisher and/or its associated, affiliated and subsidiary corporations by reason of the fact that the title of said composition may be the same or similar to that of any musical composition or compositions heretofore or hereafter acquired by the Publisher and/or its associated. affiliated and subsidiary corporations.. The Writer(s) consents to the use of his (their) name and likeness and the title to the said composition on the music, folois, recordings, performances, player rolls, and in connection with publicity and advertising concerning the Publisher, its successors, assigns and licensees, and said composition, and agrees that the use of such name, likeness and title may commence prior to publication and may continue so long as the Publisher shall own/or excercise any rights in said composition.

10. Written demands and notices other than royalty statements provided for herein shall be sent by registered mail.

11. The Writer(s) hereby expressly grants and conveys to the Publisher the copyright of the aforesaid composition, with renewals, and with the right to copyright and renew the same, and the right to secure all copyrights and renewals of copyright and any and all rights therein that Writer(s) may at any time be entitled to, and agrees to sign any and all other papers which may be required to effectuate this agreement. And the Writer(s) do hereby irrevocably authorize and appoint the Publisher, its successors or assigns, his attorneys and representatives in their name or in his name to take and due such actions, deeds, and things and make, sign, execute, acknowledge and deliver all such documents as may from time to time be necessary to secure the renewals and extensions and the Writer(s) agree upon the expiration of the first term of any copyright in the aforesaid composition in this or any contract, to do, make, execute, acknowledge and deliver, or to procure the due execution, acknowledgement and delivery to the Publisher, of all papers necessary in order to secure to it the renewals and extension of all copyrights in said compositions and all rights therein for the terms of such renewals and extensions.

large, but not large enough to take away from the intimacy of our well-rehearsed stage show. And where The Dave Clark Five were going to come out and play their hits and stand there looking British, we were going to entertain. This would be very risky given the mindset of the young teenage female audience.

We got a sense of what we were up against as we waited in our dressing room. The streets below were full of young, rabid, anything-that's-British-will-do, fans. We opened our dressing room windows and, without showing our faces, stuck a hand out the opening, which then set off a small riot in the streets below. We did this repeatedly, and with each ensuing riot and scream we became angrier about the nonsensical hold over our girls that the British enjoyed in America.

When we finally hit the stage all thoughts of boundaries, fair play, and decorum went out the open windows and we performed as if we would never, ever have another chance like this again. We stole the show and Mr. Crewe was so pleased with our initiative and courage—but even more so with our raw talent and potential—that he offered us contracts. We were pleased with ourselves and came to realize that we had broken the invisible barrier that the British mystic had temporarily laid over the land of Detroit rock 'n' roll. It also sent a message to England that said if you are going to play in Detroit you had better bring something different from what you had planned for the rest of the country.

Joey and I smiled at each other and thought about Florida. I think Joey was about as close to being a friend as I ever had. I really didn't have anyone else and so I shared what I could with him. It was a little awkward because of our very different upbringings. He came from a middle-class background. He had an older brother, Dave, and his mother and father reminded me of Ozzie and Harriet, the television family that was afraid to show the world how it suffered. Joey's father was in real estate and played the piano for relaxation. Apparently he was, at one time, a musician. They weren't wealthy, but they never seemed to be wanting. Joey's family lived in a very nice, neat, clean brick home with well-kept grounds, and every time I saw his mother she looked as though she was ready to go to a dinner party. Joey always dressed in nice, bright, fresh clothes and was able to easily laugh at the world.

One time Joey and I were sitting outside a store near his house, just hanging out, when another boy from the neighborhood, very much like Joey—well dressed and good looking—walked past. I still don't understand what started it but when he came out of the store he and Joey began to have a discussion about whether or not they should fight each other. I felt as if I had been transported to a different world. They were talking about where to fight (so as to avoid damage to their clothes), who was going to throw the first punch, how long they should fight, and I felt myself going into a state of mind I would only be able to compare at a later date to the use of LSD. Back in my neighborhood, if you hadn't already been sucker-punched, the fight would have just about been over. But they talked a little while longer and then it started. I think Joey threw the first punch, but whoever did, the fight was over at the first sign of blood. Then they shook hands and said goodbye. That kind of stuff freaked me out.

I liked Joey mostly because he didn't care what was being said about me down at the Village. He was only interested in what went on between us, and that was a respect I had never gotten before. I allowed myself to dream and believe we had a friendship. A true friendship. The kind of friendship that can grow and blossom past modern aphasia, where every little raised eyebrow or quick little wink spoke volumes of understanding between the friends, thus engendering courage and calm through belief and trust in each other. One of those friendships in which you swear to die protecting each other, even though you held serious reservations. But that was not what I had with Joey. We were uncommitted pals.

Chapter 7

WE WERE FORTUNATE TO HAVE MOTOWN Records in Detroit. As each new talented artist from that incredible "hit factory" blazed up the music charts, our pride in our city's name went with it. Motown, short for motor town, as in General Motors, Ford Motors or Chrysler Motors, meant automobiles. Not only had we put the country on wheels, we were giving it the musical soundtrack to drive with as well. Those were magical days and our little group, Billy Lee and the Rivieras, was just one in hundreds of young Detroit area musicians and singers who knew that, thanks to Berry Gordy, it was now possible to have success on the world stage. Well, maybe.

Along with subtle elements of racism comes the ability to sleep through painstaking intellectual self-analysis and then, suddenly, make itself evident to the host. With that in mind, how can we equate the hunger young, white rock 'n' rollers from Detroit have for symbolic representation from a successful, hit-making artist from their own race to a latent form of racism? It is difficult, but not impossible, especially when speaking of Detroit, because for years Berry Gordy wouldn't touch white artists.

Look at his roster. When he finally got around to signing white artists, word was that he would tie up the best of them in contracts and then sit on them to keep the artist from the marketplace. From the inception of his successful company to the first hit record from one of his white artists, a period of at least nine years passed. So whatever help whites were looking for it clearly was not, for one reason or another, coming from Motown Records. Sometimes, in conversation with other musicians, Berry Gordy was referred to as a "reverse racist."

I personally did not see it that way. In fact, one night at a club in Detroit a few years after I had gone to New York City, I had a conversation with Berry and he invited me to join Motown. Of course, I had already made a few hit records at that point and

Carrie Records   2925 Hendricks St. Detroit 7 Mich.
May 5, 1962

AGREEMENT:

1. We hereby employ the personal services of *Bill Levise, Jr.*
    as a singer for the purpose of making phonograph records for sale and
    profit.

2. Recordings will be made at recording sessions at such places and at
    such times as we may designate. A minimum of _6_ record sides shall
    be recorded during the period of this contract. We shall have the
    right of selecting the compositions to be recorded.

3. All monies advanced to you by us, including session cost and other ex-
    penses, will be charged against your royalties when earned.

4. You warrant, represent and agree that you are free to enter into this
    agreement, that you have not made and will not make any agreement or
    undertaking with any other person or firm for the purpose of making
    phonograph records in the past nor during the full term of this con-
    tract and that you are not obligated to anyone deriving rights or in-
    terest from that would interfere with the carrying out of this agree-
    ment to its full intent and purpose.

5. The term of this agreement shall be for _2_ years beginning at the
    date thereof. You grant us the option to renew this contract for
    another _2_ years upon all the terms and conditions contained here-
    in. Such option shall be exercised by written notice mailed to you
    not later than ten (10) days prior to the expiration of the terms
    of this contract.

6. For the rights herein granted for your personal services, we shall
    pay you a royalty of .03 (cents) upon 90% of all records sold at
    wholesale in the U.S.A.
    For all records sold at wholesale outside the USA, we will pay you a
    royalty of .03 (cents). Payment of these royalties shall be made
    quarterly on or about the first of each of the following months -
    Jan. April, July, and Oct. together with a statement showing the num-
    ber of records sold and paid for preceeding each quarter.

7. All recordings and records and reproductions made therefrom together
    with the performances embodied therein shall be entirely our proper-
    ty and we have the right to make records by any method and deal and
    sell in the same under any trade name or label designated by us.

8. After the necessary signatures, this agreement is binding between
    Carrie Records and *Bill Levise, Jr.* who resides at
    27454 Strathmoor in the city of *Warren, Mich.*

    Artist _William Levise Jr._ By _James Hendrix_

    Witness _Joe Arnet Robinson_

    William S. Levise Sr.

possibly he had not heard that Brian Holland, his top producer, had rejected me three years prior. Or, perhaps he was only joking.

Another thing to consider, especially form my point of view, is how we go about picking our heroes. I fail to see any difference between a young black man admiring and wanting to emulate Lou Gerhig, and a young white man admiring and wanting to emulate Jackie Robinson. And if it is true in sports entertainment then it should very well be true in musical entertainment.

In the late 1990s I sent a CD of my music to a black-owned record company. It was rejected without being heard because the black executives said I was "just another white boy trying to rip off the black man." I responded by stating that I chose my heroes carefully. With love and respect, I learned and was inspired by them, and the highest tribute I could make was to try my best to integrate their teaching into my style.

That worked for me, but I also understand that some proponents of the careful and never-ending debate over the black American experience could become defensive and accusatory, given the history and means by which black contributions to popular culture have evolved. Especially in music.

Let us use, for example, the "black face" of Al Jolson—a white man who covered his face with black make-up and tried to sing and sound black. Nothing subtle about that. So, let us take away the black face. You still have a white man trying to sound black. I find that offensive as well. But finally, let us take a white man whose history, social and cultural experience, style and personal choices all come together in his voice and he is then perceived to sound black. That is where racism becomes elusive.

It is tragic that, even today, young, good-looking white boys are packaged and sold to a targeted young white girl audience and one of the most desirable attributes to their talent is their ability to sound black. You may as well just come right out and say, if you were to borrow from the lengthy past on this issue, "We like the music the Negroes make but we don't want our children, especially our daughters, to be around them."

I believe that music can heal. I believe it knows nothing of racism, and I believe it is given and taken as an expression of love. Having said and meant that, the boys and I were on our way to New York City where the hunger that was so deeply felt by our young white rock 'n' rollers in the Detroit area would now be satisfied, along with the rest of their American counter-parts. This was because we were only months away from exploding onto the music charts with our own little home-grown style of Detroit rock 'n' roll. And best of all, we would become ambassadors of good will for our beloved native city as we were now to be called Mitch Ryder and the Detroit Wheels.

But before that could happen, we had to leave our families and friends, our contracts had to be signed by our parents—as none of us were legally old enough to have that responsibility—and we had to pretend we were not afraid.

Chapter 8

WHEN I SAY WE HAD TO pretend to not be afraid I don't know that I was speaking for anyone but myself, and the type of fear I was feeling was more an uncertainty over the future than anything else. We knew we were good. We had a ton of self-confidence and, for the most part, my fear was kicked to the curb under the pure adventure and excitement of my first visit to New York City. But, Susan was pregnant and we had chosen to get married which, in a more innocent and responsible time, seemed the only thing to do. The feminist cry of "my body is my temple and I shall worship as I will" had not yet been clearly articulated. There were abortions, but not the mind boggling, insane numbers we have come to know today. And some were very dangerous, but they were a far cry from abortion upon demand, repeatedly, over and over.

In any case, Susan was pregnant, we married, and I had to make sure I could support my new family. It was a lot of pressure for an eighteen-year-old. I remember thinking at the time, when the boys and I boarded the train for New York City and Susan stood on the platform as the train slowly pulled away, that she was beautiful. I tried to imagine what our baby would look like and, as we waved to each other and she grew smaller and smaller, I determined that he or she would be beautiful, like his or her mother, and I wasn't going to let my child go through a childhood like the one I had survived. But sixteen hours later, when the train pulled into New York City, paternal muse had grown smaller and smaller and the adventure had begun.

It was not as if we had started somewhere in middle America, with its chaste knowledge of sophisticated big city intercourse, and slowly worked our way from hamlet to village to town to Mecca. No, we had pretty much gone right from an auto-body shop to the greatest party on earth, and we didn't have a clue.

Chapter 9

NEW YORK. IT IS SAID THAT first impressions are lasting ones and when we stepped out of Grand Central Station, stretching our necks upward to just barely see the sky, our smallness made even the wind-blown New York street trash look more honest and important than the everyday common-place litter on the weed-lined streets of Detroit. Around us lay the ultimate phallic monument to men who would be kings and we were being invited to sample the power of thousands of men, living and dead, whose dreams, even in failure, were greater than anything we dared imagine.

In the outer extremities, such as Detroit, we had men of vision and power and drive who created their own monuments. But New York, as far as I could tell, was the living, beating heart of the matter and the depository museum of a greatness our Detroit boys had somehow been denied access. The Detroit power brokers had apartments and homes here somewhere, but that was only about money. What they didn't have was their blood mixed inextricably with the paint on the Manhattan canvas.

New York City was the most exciting thing I had ever seen. I honestly did not know how to act. Should I try to act important, or should I just try to blend in with the general population as they raced by around us, unaware of the magic unfolding by the second? Suddenly Earl, the bass player, woke me from my dream and we began loading three taxicabs with enough equipment and baggage to cause a small bemused crowd to gather long enough to bring a smile to their faces. Hello.

On the long taxi ride to our recording company, I began to hear voices and see strange visions, as the landscape and city blocks became a blur and I entered an hallucinatory state.

The stares I now saw were not the blank, vacant stares of mindless wandering. Was this going to be a revolution? Will we stumble upon justice? My weak and abused immigrant cousins came from the world community running, crawling, scratching, and clawing. They wanted only the promise of shelter from a life that had already brought them to their knees. All they wanted was enough compassion to allow them to once again dream. But, their predators knew too well how big the pool of pickings would be. There was more than one god at practice here, and Paradise had many addresses. I had already begun to master bringing my eyes down to the floor, but I secretly held on to the beginning evolution of my dreams. In that I found the embryonic search for fame.

For me, fame presented itself as "Genius, Inc.," and the man who would radically offer up a cracked prism, a brilliant color kaleidoscope of New York fame and excess, first appeared before me as less than a pure socialite talent. His name was Bob Crewe. Within the hush of this marvelous secret world beneath my feet, creeping along like a slow moving mud slide, were the underworld and gangster connections that were so much a part of the New York music scene.

But, before I begin my tell-all journey through New York City, let me share with you an impression I proclaimed in the writing of this book. Unbowed and with right-eousness about my scorn for my enemies in the music business, I have been, until now, silently waiting for them to die choking on the vomit of their own larcenous victimizing. Their evil and perverse manipulation tortured what was, in the beginning, one of the most innocent and beautiful earthly loves I have ever known, my music and my song. What I brought to those confessions was the essence of my being and the vulnerability of trusting in love. Because this was a conceptual element that was vacant in their own lives, they chose to overlook my good side and focused on what they fanatically em-braced, the bad. They saw me as an arrogant, disrespectful, ungrateful punk who had the nerve to challenge their authority. It was the anticipated response of a paternalistic, inhumane, and fear driven establishment.

I, no doubt, will be waiting a long time. However, the days turn into years and one by one men do turn to dust.

And now, ladies and gentlemen, the story. This is my Big Apple experience from 1964 until 1968 with a brief revisit from 1971 until 1973.

The first order of business was to meet with our producer/ manager/ publisher/ legal advisor, Bob Crewe. When we arrived at his offices, after taking our clever taxi-driver's "out of towner" extended and costly tour of Manhattan, I was impressed to find Crewe's offices in the same building as Atlantic Records. Atlantic, compared say, to Columbia Records or RCA, was the relatively new competition. It had begun out of the trunk of a roaming vehicle that scoured the distant rhythm and blues enclaves of the Southern United States in search of raw black talent at a shamefully and disgrace-fully discounted rate. It's original parents were members of the Ertegun tribe, a Turkish affair with excellent taste and a deep love for the soulful creations of America's descendants of slaves.

As we entered Mr. Crewe's offices, I recalled the last time I had seen him. He had come to my parents' house in Michigan as they acted out the Detroit version of Mom and Dad artist management to secure their signatures on the contracts he would need to make us all stars. At that time he was subdued, polite, conservative, and business-like.

Now we were ushered into his Manhattan offices that overlooked Broadway and what was approaching us was a prototype for a good-looking, shamefully engaging, un-leashed, flamboyant screaming queen, the likes of which we could only have hoped to see in some B movie with weak distribution. He slowly looked us over with the gazing manner of a belly-full wild animal that regrettably identified the meal it neither had time nor appetite for. He then small-talked his way through a greeting the way an extremely busy man might talk to his children after Mom unexpectedly dropped them off at work. We were hypnotized.

We were then sent off to what was to become our home, a rundown hotel a block off 71st and Broadway in a section of town locals referred to as Needle Point. Our home was called The Coliseum House. There were two people at the desk when we checked in: a gimpy doorman who dragged his leg when he walked, and a skinny, un-attractive girl. As the lonely months came to pass she would take on a new aura, mysteriously becoming much more pleasing to the eyes of the band. As hard as I try to remember, I swear I never saw another guest there the entire time of our stay, which lasted well over a year.

Up an elevator—which moaned, bumped, and rattled—we came to a jerking stop. Our foot-dragging doorman then slowly led us down a dark, musty hall until we came to an old door with at least seven different coats of paint. I knew this because the door was chipped enough to reveal all seven colors. Behind that closed door was our sanctuary: one living area with a couch and a table, one bathroom, and two bedrooms with two beds in each. There was only one working light in each room, which was fine, as the cockroaches liked it that way. Johnny and Earl shared one of the bedrooms, while Jimmy and I shared the other. Joey slept on the couch in the main room with the understanding that we would all rotate for couch time. Yeah, right. It didn't matter. We were a group and we had come here to conquer.

Jimmy McCarty, our guitar player, liked to play records late into the night and because of our close proximity, I was subjected to his addiction. He favored jazz guitarists at the time and after listening sessions usually came practice sessions. Many nights I sank into a deep sleep with the sound of his great talent surrounding me. It is ironic that today he is one of the premier blues guitarists in the world. Jimmy liked to argue just for the sake of arguing, which made for many lively discussions between the two of us, but it was hard to stay angry with him because of his appearance. Jimmy was, and still is, a tall, slender good-looking man with a full head of hair. But, his particular kind of tall and slender always reminds me of a newborn giraffe standing up for the first time.

Our neighborhood became the place to explore on weekends. We preferred weekends because there were fewer people to deal with. The city was quieter then, too, except at night when tourists came over for the club action and shows. We sometimes visited the Hudson River and watched the floating garbage, or traversed the weed infested and littered cross streets as we struggled to keep our balance trying to find a flat spot on the blacktop. That particular part of the West side reminded me very much of the condemned buildings in Detroit, where people lived but nobody cared. It helped ease our homesickness.

As a group, we had no money and we were very bored. Then the call came to do a gig; it was going to be our first gig in Manhattan. Finally the decks of playing cards were thrown away and everything became much more serious.

We were given extended bookings in Midtown Manhattan at the Metropole, on the East Side at Basin Street East, and in the Village at the Eighth Wonder. The Metropole had a weird dynamic in terms of the entertainment. It was there that the band and I got to meet famed trumpet player Dizzy Gillespie as he performed on the very stage we stood upon. It was both a thrill and an honor. Then there was the night Gene Krupa, the great drummer from the forties, was doing a solo thing. Everything was going okay, but you could see in his eyes that he was so disgusted with his career being brought to such low depths that he had decided to get drunk. Sure enough, about two songs into the set he made a move forward, lost his balance and the whole drum set, including Gene Krupa, came tumbling down about seven feet to the floor. I was still years away from understanding the role of the faded star and the various ways of dealing with that. I felt sorry for him as he lay there, not wanting to get up.

My favorite of the three places was owned and named after an old leather-faced, weatherworn but sociable, dyke with a gutteral laugh and twitchy trigger-finger anger, Trude Heller. Trude was the mother of Joel Heller, who owned the Eighth Wonder. From time to time Mr. Crewe would send some of his society friends and business contacts to catch the show. We always knew when such an event was about to occur because there would suddenly come a burst of activity, chairs and tables were moved around, and fresh white table cloths came out along with the rare emergence of Trude from the unknown place of her hiding.

It was an exciting time to be in the Village, with all the artists at the different clubs and sometimes, after our show, we could walk a block or two and catch someone like

Bob Dylan doing an acoustic act, or some nice jazz or blues. There was a lot to choose from.

The Basin Street East gig also carries memories for me. Our band did a few turns as a house band backing up the stars. Mostly I just sat around while the band backed up different artists, and I got to do my show with the guys as the opener. One time I personally saw to it that Mr. Bo Diddley was served his barbecue ribs before each performance and wondered at his ability to leave the sauce on his hands and still play his beautiful guitars. I liked his Flying V with the tiger fur, sauce-stained, lining.

One night a loud and boisterous gentleman came in as if he were crashing a party. I hadn't dreamed that a homosexual could be so outwardly macho and physically menacing. Apparently the Marlboro Man had been alone out on the range just a wee bit too long. He decided he liked us and insisted we call him "Uncle Charlie." We did. What was up with that? Back in Michigan we thought faggots talked with high voices, walked like women and bent over on command—or struggled to suck you off—and here's this guy and he's got fight scars all over him and he's taking over the place. These New York queers were a different breed.

More often than not, after our shows we all gathered for the subway ride to The Coliseum House and the safety of our rooms where we traded our "star" demeanor

for the raucous frivolity of unsupervised teenagers. We sometimes set up an amplifier in the window and broadcast warnings to the mostly Puerto Rican neighbors of an impending space alien invasion, or went to the roof and papered the streets below with the latest versions of our aerodynamically correct invading space ships. But the opium-like suspended time factor was wearing off, and after months of such behavior things were beginning to get more depressing.

We hadn't been home for months and the reality of our situation was beginning to sink into our young minds. We had no money and there was never enough food to quell our teenage appetites. I had lost the sense of being a star in the manner we had all enjoyed back in Detroit. New York was clearly not going to be as easy to conquer as we had first imagined. In a moment of self-pity, I surrendered to the advances of a waitress at a nearby restaurant. It was the first time I had cheated on Susan and, as if by some kind of karmic payback, I got the crabs. I freaked out, shaved myself and did the whole "God, please forgive me" thing until everyone was sick of hearing it. We were all unhappy with our situation. We avoided calling back to Detroit unless it was an emergency, because of the outlandish cost of the telephone.

I, for one, felt very disconnected and was ashamed for many reasons. I thought we were failing. I found myself thinking more and more about Susan and our unborn baby. We were all dealing with crazy emotions and we weren't really drinking or doing drugs yet. That would come later. I became lonely and depressed and, like all of us, was wondering when we were going to begin recording records. There had been very little communication between Bob Crewe and us.

Then the telephone rang. It was Bob and he wanted to know if I would join him for dinner. Naturally I was excited, because it meant we finally had some movement, but I would have been blind not to see the disappointment on the faces of the band. That evening we had been arguing about how to share a can of pork and beans for dinner and I was being singled out for preferential treatment. It was the first notice that I would be considered and treated differently than the band. It was the planting of a seed. But more importantly, it was the plan laid bare, and we refused to accept it at face value.

Mr. Crewe lived in a beautiful complex on Central Park West called The Dakota. This is the same building that John Lennon lived in and would be murdered outside of some years hence. On this day, there was a smartly dressed green and gold uniformed doorman at the gate entrance—which was quite different from the occasional passed out bum that graced our entrance—and he escorted me to my destination. I had never been in the home of a wealthy person and the opulent furnishings, smooth fabrics, high grand ceilings, deep rich marble, detailed wood moldings and carvings, woven tapestries, exotic plants, and discreet lighting were overwhelming. There was soft music floating through every room of the home, and then we went to the dining area to be seated.

Now, with my mind not distracted by the pre-emptive strike of decadent ambiance, I got my closest look yet at the man who would make me a star. I suppose energy would be the most apt word to describe Mr. Crewe. Whether he was talking, walking, or smiling, he was alive with energy. I believe he smiled the entire time I was there. He carried himself in an effeminate manner and I could not take my eyes away from his gaze.

It was a fine meal. Extraordinary. Apparently it was a meal he had put together out of things that were "just lying around." There was a lot of pointless talk and laughter and the mood was relaxed. There were no drugs, however, Mr. Crewe had one glass of wine with his meal. In the back of my mind I couldn't help think of the boys and the can of beans back at the hotel. I was trying to make sense of it and at the same time ease my guilty conscience about why I alone had been invited.

We returned to the living area and Mr. Crewe began to engage me in a slightly more thoughtful and serious conversation. We spoke of music and artists and my dreams and desires, great performances I had seen and he shared his views on the same. It was all very polite and I felt as if I had made a good impression, in spite of the fact that I was in way over my head. You have to understand that, at the time, Bob Crewe was a real player in the music industry. In addition to producing, he either wrote or co-wrote the hit songs "Sherry," a number one single for The Four Seasons (fronted by Frankie Valli); "Big Girls Don't Cry;" "Walk Like a Man;" "Bye, Bye, Baby (Baby, Goodbye);" and Frankie Valli's solo hit, "Can't Take My Eyes Off You."

Finally the evening came to an end.

On the long walk back to the hotel, as the neighborhood became increasingly worse with each passing block, I wished I could someday have what I had just seen. Not anything Mr. Crewe held out or represented. Just the kind of material wealth he had access to. I could give those things to Susan and she would know I was a success. My malleability was beginning to drip down my leg, as was my compulsion to have that which I had not earned. I began to walk faster. I became anxious about what to tell the boys when I got back to the hotel because I knew they were going to want to hear everything, and I began to edit out things I thought might make them jealous. How stupid of me. Mr. Crewe hadn't even mentioned the band. Nor had we spoken of recording or anything else they might want to hear. This was going to be a disaster. Well, we were still all in this together. I stopped walking and slowly turned my focus back on the band and said to myself . . . wow, here we are. New York.

Everyone I had talked to over the months, from the trash man to the store owner, agreed that for what I was trying to do, New York was the place. But the chances of success as opposed to the probability of failure were not in my favor and most people here, like everywhere else, were simply trying to survive. So what secret promise would it take to make someone want to die trying to survive in New York City?

While I waited for that answer I began an entertaining observation through which I watched the futility of the attempts the wealthy employed to balance their egos against their fake humility and gratefulness. New York City, because of its symbolic value and name recognition benefited from the term "great city" in the same manner Washington D.C. enjoys its symbolic crest as a "bastion of freedom," while not having to look more than a few miles in any direction to see the not so pretty side of the democratic experiment. It is a facade made credible by the numbers. Is New York different from Detroit? Yes, but only because it has the cheapest to most expensive food on the menu.

Chapter 10

THE PROBLEM, AS IT WOULD BECOME clearer over the length of the relationship with Bob Crewe, was the fact that this successful music maker represented an age and philosophy in American music that had only recently begun undergoing—and was not responding very well to—great changes. These changes were occurring as a result of a relentless onslaught being promoted by the British money hounds. If we were to give proper credit to the British music industry, it would have to be for their uncanny opportunistic instincts and an undying love for American culture. After all, when you live on an island the only thing new is whatever washes up on shore. So, in terms of music, it was the British beachcombers that instigated the regurgitated "new" sound of the British invasion.

The Brits began their exploitation of an America that was smothering under the gloom of a presidential assassination, a quicksand foreign war in Vietnam, an increasingly violent civil rights struggle, and a conservative mind-set that was falling under its own weight. That is why, when they did appear, the British were such a breath of fresh air. It wasn't about their music. In the beginning they were all doing covers of American artists. But then, just to make the trail a little colder, they began doing covers of what had been, until then, largely overlooked black American recordings. I have to marvel at their pious declarations and justifications. The British claimed it was a response to the undeniable racism being practiced in America. They were simply giving credit to artists who were shunned because of America's racist practices.

Wow! I had to go back and look, but I discovered that the British had such strict immigration policies in place at that time that they hadn't given themselves proper credit for that day in the future when the "Empire" would come home to roost on the peaceful, loving non-racist soil of Great Britain. Weren't these the same British who had subjugated entire continents of people who were not white? Of course they were. And wasn't that going to be a special day for "Great Britain" when the Empire's people of color came home to collect that which was promised them? Yes, indeed it was. But, it wouldn't be financially or morally prudent to face that truth just as you were waging a campaign to spank Americans for being so naughty. So, they would eat their invitation. Given the fact they were stars simply because they were British allowed their egos to test the lyricism of their inherent arrogance. A thousand and one little Shakespeares were born.

Bob Crewe had established himself as a minor singing star on the American landscape as Bob Crewe and the Crewcuts, and had already done the same early on as the producer of the hit recording "Silhouettes" by the Rays. He was in the middle of Frankie Valli and The Four Seasons and had done Freddy "Boom Boom" Cannon, amongst others, when he ran into me. Bob had structured his business in such a way that he controlled any and everything having to do with the music and the artists he produced.

There were exceptions of course. For example, I was somehow aware that the contractual arrangement he had with Bob Gaudio, the musical brain behind The Four Seasons was different. But, for the most part, Mr. Crewe held all the cards. He either wrote or held a piece of the songs used by his artists and, in one case I know of, attached his name as a writer by coupling two different songs that had been written and published by others.

Bob's office complex was very much like the old Tin Pan Alley, where a series of small cubicles stuffed with pianos or other instruments, would-be poets, dreamers, and the occasional real writing talent of individuals who wanted a piece of the still-blossoming fruit called rock 'n' roll, toiled away everyday searching for the next big hit. All of the music appeared on his record labels, or was licensed out, and he held management, recording, and publishing contracts wherever he could to ensure no one would steal from him.

To guarantee such a thing he placed his brother, Dan Crewe, in charge of his business affairs. Dan was gay, but was hiding behind a heterosexual marriage. He was an ex-Navy man who had slick administrative skills. This was necessary because Bob had no control when it came to spending the millions of dollars he recklessly went through in his days of success.

What was most important, though, at that precise moment in time, was that Bob Crewe was a "star maker." This wasn't necessarily bad if you ended up being one of his stars, but it was a nightmare if you only ended up having one hit with him. When I began to work with him, Mr. Crewe was powerful enough to cause Andrew Loog Oldham, manager of the Rolling Stones, to transfer American administrative publishing rights to the Rolling Stones catalog to him for a short period of time. It also put Keith Richards and Brian Jones in the control room at the time we were cutting our first hit record, "Jenny Take a Ride."

But that is a leap ahead. Right now I need to step back and talk about those mysterious transformations in the relationship between Bob Crewe and myself, not only as it affected my music, but how it impacted my marriage to Susan.

I often tell my daughter Dawn that the decision to leave her, her brother Joel, and her mother was the only thing I have ever regretted in my life. That is the truth. In a way it is ironic because during the time I was with Susan and the kids, it was in show business terms really the beginning and the end. So in a strange way Susan witnessed the birth and death of a "star." Unfortunately, she was spared the part that counts: the struggle to survive and go on living.

I was first allowed to visit Detroit for a few days when Susan was around seven months pregnant. We met at her Aunt Betty's, who lived on Grand Boulevard near the very train station that had taken me to New York. Aunt Betty was quite the opposite of Susan's mother, Belle. Belle was kind of step back and take a look, but Betty was all about loving life to its fullest—and dancing. She loved to dance, and she liked me very much. Susan and I tried to put together a plan about where to live, but we didn't have the means to carry it out. So I flew back to New York to begin recording.

Bob Crewe truly did believe I was an amazing white talent with an ability to transcend the color barrier through my interpretation of black American soul and R&B. I believed that as well, and so the very first recording we tried was an up-tempo R&B ballad called "I Need Help." Jimmy McCarty was the only Wheel invited to play on the track. I'm sure he had mixed emotions about that, considering the other boys were sitting on the bench. I did too, but we still hadn't figured out the grand plan that was twirling around in the mind of "Genius, Inc." and so everyone was a bit uncomfortable. I did, however, love the recording and the performance. It was a flop. Bob claimed it was because we released it at the very same moment John, Paul, George, and Ringo released their movie and song called "Help." There may have been something to that.

But now I had to rush home to be with Susan, as she had given birth to our baby girl, Dawn Michelle Levise. I wasn't home very long on that visit, but I was there long enough to understand that a miracle had occurred. I didn't hold Dawn much because I didn't trust my reflexes with such a delicate little baby. Now, with a lifetime behind me, I still remember exactly what she made me feel as I held her next to my heart. It was the first time in my life that I even pretended to know what love might be. She was me, and she was Susan, and she needed to be kept safe. The memory melted warmly into my blood as I rushed to return to the airport. I had to get back to New York quickly to begin another recording session.

I was again invited to The Dakota, once again alone, but this time not to be evaluated. This time it was to meet a man who would make a big difference in how I perceived the business of music in New York City. I would, during my time with him, be sheltered and protected and pampered during the yet-to-come grooming process. His name was Alan Stroh and he would become my manager.

We again sat immersed in pleasant surroundings but this time it was Alan who asked the questions and Mr. Crewe who observed. Alan was funny and a free spirit, but clearly not the same creative personality and energy that resonated from Mr. Crewe. Alan was, however, a man of confidence and a different sort of creator. He was a dreamer who needed to channel through someone.

The most noticeable thing about the two of them was the fact that they were both overtly gay. We were listening to a recording that Alan wanted me to hear. It was the beautiful voice of Aretha Franklin out of Detroit. But it wasn't the Aretha the world would come to know. This was powerful stuff, but it was inaccessible. She was at that time still with RCA, but they didn't know what to do with her power. That wouldn't come until she moved to Atlantic Records.

Suddenly, a horrifying scream came from the kitchen, and then another and another. You could hear scuffling and the sound of crashing pots and pans and plates being broken. We were all alarmed. I ran to see what it was and as I entered the kitchen the struggle ended. In the silence and amidst the blood I saw that Mr. Crewe's imported pet Jaguarundi, a wild mountain cat from South America, had killed his two Siamese cats for infringing on his red meat dinner. At first I was amazed at the carnage, and at the feat itself because Siamese cats are known for their aggressiveness as fighters, but then I became even more amazed at the shrieks and cries of hysteria that came flying from the mouths of Mr. Crewe and Alan Stroh.

Rather than trying to calm them down, I decided to head back to the hotel and tell the band what had happened. I assumed that when you are really wealthy you lose all common sense and respect for life. I wasn't too uncomfortable with that. It reminded me of the neighborhood I had grown up in, but the incident left a bad taste in my mouth.

What I was unaware of were two essential elements. One, Bob Crewe had already made his decision to make me a star through his and Alan's connections. And two, the process, to which I was oblivious, had already begun and the hype machine was marching through the ears and homes of all the important people of the day who were successful in the music business and on the social scene.

While I was in New York, through the generosity of her parents and what little money we had, Susan was able to get an apartment for us to live in in Detroit, even though I wasn't there.

By this time our Stea-Phillips recordings had begun at the Stea-Phillips Studios. These are the same sessions mentioned earlier that were attended by a couple of the Rolling Stones, and were live recordings of songs we performed in our gigs. The sound was terrific, what with the two-story high ballroom ceilings of the studio and the natural echo. Our band had come up with the idea of doing medley songs in our set as a way to keep playing without having to stop. However, the idea to combine "C.C. Rider" with "Jenny Jenny" by Richard Penniman, whom you may know as Little Richard, was the brainchild of Bob Crewe. On the playback everyone agreed, including the two Rolling Stones, that we had a "hot" recording. The sessions were long, but we were able to compile nearly an album's worth of material. We were then sent back out on the road.

Bob Crewe knew how to use his energy to promote his properties, and had installed in his office one of the first technical marvels of that time. He set up a dedicated telephone line designed specifically to transmit a recording he could play for the person on the other end of the line. The signal from the recording went directly into the telephone transmission without exterior sound. But, every once in a while, Bob picked up a connected line, broke the signal and screamed words of excitement and encouragement to the promotion man or radio station he was calling.

This was to work them into a frenzy of "I gotta have that!" He screamed out things like "Don't you love it?" "Isn't that great?" "I love it, I love it, I love it!" He snapped his fingers and was all over his office dancing about and jumping up and down like a wild man, very much the same as he was with us in the recording studio as he tried to inspire us to excitement.

Those early hits we made couldn't, as good as the band was, have had the element of alive insanity contained in the grooves without Alan's personality inside the studio. I don't mean in the control room. I mean actually in the studio, during the recording, flying about like a man possessed.

We had taken an extended gig in up-state New York in a town called Massena, which lay off the St. Lawrence Seaway. We bought BB guns and spent our days going to the dump and picking off rats. At night we did five sets, forty-five minutes each, and had Sunday off. It was a grind, but somehow Earl Elliot, our bass player, managed to find a girlfriend and that pissed us off. One less gun at the dump. Then we got called back to New York to finish a few more songs. This time it was a different studio, but it was the entire band again and everyone felt positive.

Just as we were feeling like a group, I was again invited to The Dakota where something very special was about to occur. I was picked up by a mysterious man with long hair on a Harley motorcycle and driven to Columbia Studios, where I was quietly ushered into the control room and allowed to witness Bob Dylan working on *Highway 61*

Revisited. I can't explain it at all. It was an honor that still baffles me and I certainly hadn't acquired the credibility to be there. My self-confidence had not yet proven itself worthy of such an event either. Whatever message Bob Crewe was spreading about the abilities of his next star was beginning to scare me because Bob Dylan was already a giant. More than anything else, I wondered if Bob Dylan knew I was there.

As the summer ended we found ourselves playing a naval base in Newfoundland, where I actually died from a mis-read prescription for my annual shot of penicillin, a carry over from my days of rheumatic fever. I awoke to see a football helmet and felt a strong pain in my chest where a doctor had rushed from the football field to beat me back to life.

Then, as it grew colder, near the end of fall, we returned to Massena for the grind once again. We didn't know it, because we were in such a remote part of the world, but "Jenny Take a Ride" was coming up the charts. Then a call came near the end of our engagement. It was a call that would change my life so completely that, as it may

have now become apparent to you, I still may not know fantasy from reality. But the reality on that most perfect of nights was the fact that we had to leave the

Mitch and Alan Stroh

next day to do a gig near Pittsburgh, Pennsylvania at a place called The Little Red Rooster because "Jenny Take a Ride" had entered the top ten there, and was bursting into the top ten in Detroit, San Francisco, Philadelphia, and quite a few other major cities. But for us, the shocker was the fact that we were being paid for fifteen minutes on stage what we made for the entire week doing six days a week, five shows a day.

An artist's very first hit record is more a curiosity than a statement. It is a debut into a world so different from normal that it bends time and space around it. One has to wonder where such a terrifying power comes from, how is it kept under control, and who controls it? But that is only from the perspective of someone on the outside looking in. If you're in the business, the first hit record, especially coming from an independent label as ours was, is filled with enormous possibility. Not the least of these possibilities is financial gain, and every gamer involved switches into high gear and straps themselves in for the ride because every facet of your being is rushed into a measure of time a million times faster than anything you have ever known.

Chapter 11

SUSAN AND I TOOK TO MARRIAGE and parenthood quite naturally and even though we were young (we were both about to leave our teenage burdens behind us), we were happy and proud. It was nice to have the support of our families and we felt, for lack of a better word, adult. It showed in our caring for Dawn, in each other, and the way we assumed our responsibilities. My family concentrated their pride more in my career than my little family, and even though Susan's parents and Aunt Betty were bragging about my career too, they cared more about Susan, the baby, and me as a good father.

It is one of those memories that you can't let go of. I was in our apartment, the Wagon Wheel Apartments in Royal Oak, Michigan, having not been home for very long, and Susan and I were awakened by the sound of the clock radio going off at seven-thirty A.M. to the sound of the band and me playing "Jenny Take a Ride" and the disc jockey screaming, "If this doesn't wake you up, nothing will." Our record had just hit number one in Detroit. We had done it. That unbearable separation of almost a year had finally begun paying dividends. On top of that, the band and I had left The Coliseum House in New York for good and we were all back home feeling secure and basking in the glory of success. Two weeks later the recording entered into the history books as our first top ten recording in the United States.

Susan and I purchased our first vehicle, a small blue rear-engine Corvair convertible, which a consumer advocate later titled "unsafe at any speed." Gone now were the early days of dating and going out with mostly Susan's friends, because now we had to trade that anonymity for a more difficult proposition. We still saw most of her old friends when I was in town, and she kept in close contact with her friends when I was gone, but new friends were introducing themselves into our lives and we weren't prepared for that aspect of budding fame.

The way I had wished and prayed for fame was suddenly irrelevant when the object of my prayers began to reveal its definitions and demands. We were still fans and consumers of our musical heroes, and neither of us had been capable of making an immediate jump into the persona of the famous. We did a lot of things together in the beginning, trips to visit relatives, shopping for groceries and baby clothes, going for rides in the car, the zoo, taking Dawn here and there, going to Kentucky to visit my dear sister Nina, visiting friends of Susan's, cooking and eating meals at home, even going to an occasional movie. Stuff like that brought a modicum of stability to my life and I loved being around and watching my baby daughter develop. At this point in time, she had not yet begun to walk.

As I said, that first hit record is important and New York slowly, under the guidance of Alan Stroh, started to control time and space in such a way that it would not immediately shock my senses, but let me know that I was expected to make myself available for exploitation. Since we only had one top ten, no one knew for sure whether we were a fluke or something to watch out for. With all of the intrusions, Susan and I still felt together as a family, and she herself later said that during those early years I was a good father to Dawn.

My time was now being divided between home and family, and touring. Sometimes we rented a vehicle and a trailer and did Midwest dates, but we were also put on a couple of Dick Clark Caravan of Stars tours. Those were different. We played big coliseums and arenas because we were part of a package show and were exposed to way more people than we would have been as a solo headliner with one top ten record. In those early days we set up our own gear and traveled to parts of the country that we never could have dreamed of going prior to our good fortune.

Earl Elliot, the bass player, assumed the role of road manager, which he traded off with me. I was acting as road manager the night we were supposed to perform two shows in St. Joseph, Michigan. Between shows I went to a trailer near the stage to get paid. In entering the trailer, the DJ who promoted the show greeted and paid me, while the spineless disc jockey who emceed the show alerted state troopers that he had seen a loaded .38 Special handgun in my briefcase. I was taken away in handcuffs through the thousands of teenaged fans and brought directly to jail.

Because of my status as a major star on tour with a schedule to keep, we were able to get a judge to hear my case immediately. During the arraignment, I was stunned to see the judge was so drunk he could hardly take his seat at the bench. It turned out that his wife had died the afternoon before and he had drowned his sorrows in a bottle. It was for this reason that New York was able to get the incident quashed from my record because the only judge who could free me was drunk when I was arraigned. Turned out I didn't even have to produce any documents regarding the gun.

I later learned there was a small riot when fans learned I wasn't going to get to play the second show. And to let you know, I had purchased the gun legally in Texas, and it was legal in Michigan. But, it was against the law in Illinois, where the disc jockey was from.

Back in New York City, Bob Crewe flew me in to do another session as a solo and came up with a fantastic R&B ballad called "Takin' All I Can Get." It was such a good song and my performance was so emotional that Aretha Franklin, who had by now switched to Atlantic, was considering doing a version of it. But again Mr. Crewe had miscalculated the public's appetite for a solo Mitch Ryder. He wasn't even close to throwing in the towel, however, so now he had to try to keep the momentum of the group going and take us out of that mediocre territory called "the one hit wonder."

We went back in the studio to do several more cover tunes and add to the growing vault of recorded material being collected. It has been noted that, in the approximately two years and four sessions the band and I were together in New York recording, Bob Crewe managed to turn those sessions into the release of five albums of covers and originals, with the sixth album being the monumental disaster "What Now My Love."

The song he chose next "Little Latin Lupe Lu" was interesting as a single because it had been released just three months prior by the Righteous Brothers, and our version went higher up the charts than theirs, landing safely in the top twenty. It was clear to anyone paying attention that the group and I had a certain sound that was connecting with the public.

The sessions that I worked on with the band took place at three different studios, and much of the solo stuff that Mr. Crewe did with me was recorded at Bell Sound Studios. When I made these trips into New York, as was happening more frequently, I stayed in a hotel and visited Mr. Crewe at The Dakota.

The Dakota intrigued me because it was clearly prime Central Park real estate, but the stuff that went on in Mr. Crewe's place betrayed the general notion that people of wealth comported themselves in a low profile, conservative manner. I don't know if Alan was also living in the cavernous apartment, but every time I visited he was there. The cultural swings that were taking place in America at that time, I was convinced, had found birth either in The Dakota specifically or New York City in general.

One day Alan attempted to have sex with me but ended up damaging me so badly he went, driven by shame and guilt, to Tiffany's and bought me a watch that cost several thousand dollars.

Alan now got down to the business of getting me a booking agent. He chose Frank Barcelona at Premier Talent, a place where I met Ritchie Nader, who later became a promoter of note. I ended up having sex with almost every one of Frank's female secretaries, to the point that Frank begged me to leave them alone.

I think what happened was a reversion back to my earlier reaction at the Village in Detroit after the incident with Timmy. I didn't believe I was a homosexual, and so I went about proving my manhood and satisfying my perverted sense of sexuality, as learned in my childhood neighborhood, by having sex with as many women as I could. It did not occur to me that I was cheating on Susan because I wasn't in love with any of the women I bedded, and I truly missed Susan and Dawn.

My way of trying to solve the problem was to fly Susan to New York where we began looking for a place to live together. That would at least keep me out of trouble in the place where I was spending more and more time. We looked at a few places, but everything that seemed safe to our Midwestern sensibilities and safe for our daughter was too expensive. So, for the moment, I brought Susan and Dawn to New York when I was able.

Alan, in addition to taking the band and me to California for the first time to do a show in San Francisco and carrying on about "White Rabbit," a psychedelic acid rock song by Jefferson Airplane, also began the task of making the connections we needed for the future. We did a lot of TV appearances, which required going to L.A., and I remember running into some of Susan's friends from Michigan State University on that visit. That was because Michigan State was playing in the Rose Bowl that year. Her

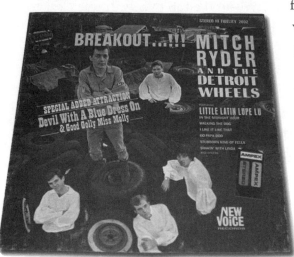

friends were nearing graduation and Susan would have been with them if she hadn't given up her university studies to marry me.

Alan took us to a clothing store on Sunset Boulevard and dressed us up in the outfits we wore on the cover of the albums that featured "Jenny Take a Ride" and" "Breakout." Later, most of the band and I rented some motorbikes and did a tour of the hills, where I had an accident and damaged my hand. That's why I appeared on Dick Clark's TV show with a bandaged hand. I remember looking at the other two set positions while we were waiting in our stage performance area and watched the fabulous Paul Butterfield Blues Band. Then we did our thing.

I also remember a Dick Clark show from Philadelphia earlier that year when I made eye contact with a curious Paul Simon as he stood next to Art Garfunkel. Both were staring in wonderment at the mighty Mitch Ryder. We were now meeting and performing with artists whose records I had purchased, not stolen. Wow!

In addition to the booking agency, Alan signed me to the Connie De Nave Agency for publicity. I thought it was funny because one of their other clients was Dave Clark from the Dave Clark Five, whom we had destroyed in Detroit to earn our contract with Bob Crewe. I began a friendship with one of her secretaries, which eventually turned sexual, and then into a fascination for the two of us.

The next thing to occur was a key part of the question as to who broke up the group. Apart from Bob Crewe's early signals about which direction he was leaning, the United States government made their move and sent draft notices to my dear friend and Dawn's godfather, Joey Kubert. Then they repeated their plunder of the Wheels by drafting Earl Elliot. Earl decided to make his own choice, as opposed to the government, and enlisted into the Marine Corps. Joey was pissed off, frightened, and sad. Here we were, finding success and having our teenage dreams realized when he was asked to put his life on the line. I talked to Joey, told him I would see what I could do to involve Alan and Bob in pulling strings, not knowing that in less than a year Jimmy McCarty and I would both receive our draft notices.

Joey had heard that the Army would not take you if you were a drug addict, so he began shooting up so as to leave tracks in his arms. It worked, but in the meantime we had to keep a working group out in public and we replaced Earl on bass with Jimmy McCallister. Instead of hiring another guitarist we brought in a keyboard player, Jerry Sherida, who was with the band for a few months before he got his draft notice. Jerry chose to buy several pounds of marijuana, lock himself in a motel room, and call the police on himself so he would have a criminal record and be refused by the Army.

And that brings me to another argument over our lovely British Invasion specialists. Not only were they loved by our girls simply because they talked weird, but they also weren't decimated by the draft in America. How can you compete with that?

As the year I was twenty neared an end, Jimmy, Johnny and I went into a session that produced the single "Devil With a Blue Dress On." Carmin, the bass player from the group Chicago Loop, another of Bob Crewe's projects, and Gary Knight, a writer and cool keyboard player from Bob's stable, were also there. We had a friend from Detroit named Denny, who was begging us to help him get a contract with Bob Crewe. He supplied the very high falsetto screams on the track. The record became our second gold recording and stayed in the top twenty with three different trips into the top ten over a three and a half month period. It was a winter soundtrack for the nation and now things were really changing in our lives.

As the recording started to fade, Jay Silverman, our promotion man in Detroit told me he had never seen anything like it, except for The Beatles. And since I was about to turn twenty-one, Bob Crewe finally gave me a solo contract. As far as I know, no new contracts were offered to the remaining Wheels. In exchange for the signing, I asked for and received a fifteen thousand dollar advance, which I used as a down payment on a home for Susan, Dawn and myself in Southfield, Michigan. I had accomplished something I had never imagined. I had lifted myself up to middle-class.

But things weren't quite right because, other than the signing advance, neither the Wheels nor myself ever received any royalties or money, and in fact, never received an accounting the entire length of our relationship with Mr. Crewe. Every penny I had in my pocket was my share of what we earned on the road, and that was only 50 percent of what was being paid. I laugh about it now because it is so unfunny, but I remember

Frank Barcelona meeting with me one day and advising me to save my money. Well, at the time, who cared? I already had more than I was used to having and life was wonderful. Another reason to resent my poor working-class roots. Besides, Bob Crewe and Alan Stroh both loved me. They wouldn't let anything bad happen to me.

Susan and I loved our home, but now I was asked to devote more time and energy in New York City. I had just been named Artist of the Year by *Cashbox* magazine, one of three magazines that competed for the top spot as the recording industry's authority on record sales, chart position, and artists on the American landscape. There were countless interviews and photograph sessions, and even more recording with Bob Crewe. On top of all of that, before the New Year was over, what was left of the Detroit Wheels dissolved completely.

Jimmy and I had a difference in opinion about the direction of the group from the beginning. First of all, the very day we decided to go professional back in Detroit, the boys wanted to have a singular name for our group and I, remembering what my mother had told me about having your own name so you don't become part of a faceless, ever-changing cast, hung tough to Billy Lee, and they finally settled for the Rivieras.

Even though the original band was skilled at playing R&B they wanted to hang around the rock 'n' roll flagpole while I set my goals on competing with my R&B heroes and doing the music I loved. Yes, I was aware that our hits had come from the group, as opposed to my solo work, but I was also aware that the group was no longer what we had brought to New York. I wanted to compromise and add an R&B horn section, while Jimmy wanted to keep it "pure."

That was not enough reason to break up the group, however, it fit in nicely with Bob Crewe's plans to create a star who could do a slick, safe show in Las Vegas for six or seven months at a time. Besides, he had much bigger plans for me and those plans didn't involve nurturing our remaining group into a self-sustaining model, as most of our British competition was doing. There was a divide in the remaining group that Bob Crewe exploited, but there was also a divide and a building resentment on my part about how my career was going. It manifested itself in the area of songwriting.

My very first recording was a song I wrote and at this point in my stardom with Bob Crewe I had to fight to get a B side for a love song to my daughter, Dawn. He said, "First of all, we can't call it Dawn because The Four Seasons already had a hit with a song called 'Dawn.'"

Not sure where I stood, we compromised and called the song "Joy."

Chapter 12

MR. CREWE SEEMED TO BE ROLLING in cash, and he came to purchase what he called the "triplex" It was the top three floors of a building on Fifth Avenue and 67th—about as high rent as you could get. He said he had purchased it from Tony Bennett for around two and a half million dollars. Every floor had its own balcony that overlooked Fifth Avenue and Central Park East. The interior decorating had to have cost an additional million dollars. It had its own private elevator to the first floor and from that point on I was given a bedroom and access to all areas when I was in New York. My bed had a mink bedspread. The triplex was where my education about the road to superstardom began. And, there was a lot of educating going on because at least a third of my time was now being spent in New York City, while I divided up the remainder with Susan and Dawn in our new home. Plus, there were personal appearances, which were becoming increasingly numerous.

I was staying at the triplex so much that the maid asked me what I wanted to eat as she made out the week's menu. Mr. Crewe had also brought in a young man named Billy that he was guardian to. Billy wanted to be a saxophone player and many mornings that's all you could hear. He was a big, muscular young man and kept a weight set in the triplex. He also provided sex to Mr. Crewe as part of his agreement with Mr. Crewe to keep him from going back to prison. Alan chose a young man named Lenny who provided the same services for him.

There was a kangaroo-skin couch on the main floor where all kinds of people passed through. Once I arrived to find Stephen Stills (of Crosby, Stills, and Nash) deep in conversation with Mr. Crewe on the dead kangaroo. Another time a very perplexed and fearful Seymour Stein was there. Stein was at that time employed at *Billboard* magazine and was trying to figure out some damage control for the Federal investigation into "bullet fixing," a term for falsely attributing chart positions to recordings so as to increase their sales and radio exposure. He later went on to a big career with Warner Bros. Records and was a co-founder of Sire Records. Artists, producers such as Shadow Morton, whom Mr. Crewe said would be great if he could quit drinking, and socialites of every stripe . . . the place was never dull except on holidays. On holidays the city was dead.

The triplex was also the place where Bob, Alan and I first listened to "Strawberry Fields" by The Beatles, and correctly guessed it was the prelude to what was to become "Sgt. Pepper." It was the place where we sat transfixed listening to a recording by a young Stevie Winwood performing "I'm a Man" with the Spencer Davis Group. It was the place where I came in to find Bob Gaudio working on more Four Seasons recordings. And there were many, many parties.

The address, the access, and the company kept made me feel important, and in a way I was, because Bob Crewe was driving me up the ladder to superstardom. Publicity dates were arranged with other famous artists so I would look to America as an already established star of unequaled proportions. Millions and millions of recordings were being sold under the name Mitch Ryder and the Detroit Wheels but all the time I was in New York stoking the machine, the boys were back in Detroit waiting for the next dictate to come down from Mr. Crewe.

On one of the vacation weekends Mr. Crewe decided to take me to Connecticut to visit a man named Morris Levy. Morris eventually wound up in prison for the way he did business, and was rumored to have something to do with the murder of a policeman. But at this point in time he and Bob Crewe were fast friends, and while the two of them went to discuss their private business I was given a tour of their beautiful mansion by Morris's wife, who was probably the most physically attractive women I had ever laid eyes upon.

Another holiday weekend took Mr. Crewe and me to see a home in Connecticut that Dan, his brother, had purchased. There was a huge fight between the two of them because when Dan arrived, Mr. Crewe had almost completely taken down a wall with a sledge hammer in an attempt to help his brother reshape the interior. Unfortunately, Dan had not been consulted. It wasn't much of a fight, at least not the way I was used to them, but they were doing some serious homosexually inspired notions of physical damage to each other.

The triplex was also the very first place I did acid (LSD), but it was controlled and we had a licensed doctor in attendance to monitor our reactions. I recall walking into Central Park that weekend and feeling wonderful. As I walked, I came upon an acquaintance and friend, Michael Bloomfield, a talented guitar player I had first seen at the Dylan sessions, and then again with Paul Butterfield. When the band and I were on the road Michael had approached me about being the singer for a new group he was putting together for Columbia Records called The Electric Flag. I turned him down. On this day, though, he appeared distressed and stood in a tortured stance on an open field in the park as he sang tortured lyrics. On closer inspection he was actually foaming at the mouth. I said hello and he acknowledged me, but he was either having a bad trip or was on some really bad speed.

Alan decided early on that it was very much in my interest to go to England. Those frequent trips began right after the initial success of "Jenny Take a Ride." One time, Susan and I met Alan in London and were escorted to the residence of Lionel Bart. Lionel was a beloved character and artist who had risen from a lower-class background and who created a timeless musical called *Oliver*, which was based on the play *Oliver Twist*. The musical was a fixture on the London stage scene for many years.

Susan and I were guests at Lionel's a few times, but I also stayed there on several of my solo visits to England. On this particular trip, after awakening from our jet lag we went down from our bedroom to the living area where Alan was sitting with Lionel. Everyone was focused on Lionel's brand new color TV, rumored to be one of the first in all of England. On that first trip it was arranged for us to visit the legendary (at least in the minds of the Brits) shopping area, Carnaby Street. Whoopee!

Fashion? Why not? It proved to me that the English were gifted at performing private wet dreams in public. But that didn't have any effect on the way Lionel and Alan and I felt about each other. I'll never be able to say Lionel was a fast and true friend because, over the years of his fame, thousands of entertainers and famous people would be guests of Mr. Bart. I did, however, think of Lionel as special, particularly his gift for music, because later on he was the only person I knew in music who could answer The Beatles "Sgt. Pepper" with any comparable creativity, authority, and genius. It was a release of his own music on Polygram Records which, if it had been promoted and his fame was not considered passé, could have stood the same test of time as the release The Beatles had.

Another great memory was coming into the main room at Lionel's to find him working with legendary composer and lyricist Leslie Bricusse as they attempted to collaborate on lyrics for "Talk to the Animals" from Dr. Doolittle. But the biggest surprise was going into Lionel's bedroom to say good morning to find him shooting up liquid methedrine.

Susan and I not only enjoyed the trips to England, but also trips to the Bahamas and Portugal. We were a family, but on those long trips Aunt Betty and Susan's mother, Belle, took care of Dawn. There were times when I missed my daughter so much that I packed a little bag for her and the two of us ventured out on the road together for a short trip here or there. When we were home we sometimes had friends over for a party, but we were mostly stay at home people who enjoyed the few blessings life afforded us.

One of my favorite memories of my daughter was when I tried to teach her to shave my beard. She always watched the morning ritual until one day I asked if she would like to try it. I lathered my face and gave her the razor. That was the last time that occurred. Another of her favorite things was to wake up Daddy, and she did this by taking a running start toward Susan's and my bed, leaping as high as she could, and coming down firmly on my resting stomach and sleeping body. How can you not love that? There was not one thing about my life with Susan and Dawn that I did not miss when I was away. For me, they represented life the way I thought it should be. Safe, comfortable, and filled with love. I am getting ahead of myself but it is so easy to do that when I want to gravitate to the good memories.

Lionel Bart

I was in New York City between hits and Alan sent me to a woman who taught me the social graces and responsibilities I would need in the presence of the upper class. Things like the correct way to chew your food or hold a fork, all the way up to making polite conversation. In addition, I was sent to another woman, someone famous whose name I don't recall, and began taking acting instruction. All of these preparations were being charged back to my royalties and I had no control over who, when, or where. I do suspect, even though it's way too late to prove, that the Crewe brothers were charging these things back onto royalties for the Wheels, as well.

On my second trip to England, since Lionel already had a house full of guests, I stayed at an apartment that someone told me was owned by Sammy Davis, Jr. It was there that I was given an advance listen to the *Sgt. Pepper* album, and I was also introduced to Robert Stigwood, manager of the Bee Gees. That trip also took me to residences of other famous British musicians and was orchestrated by Alan to make my face available to the British music scene. But the theme that never ended was the absence of the Wheels. They never made the trips.

Back in America I was being introduced to wealthy families who lived on Long Island. In fact, the band and I were hired to play a few of their private parties. Vera Swift was one who comes to mind. She was, at the time I met her, newly divorced from

the head of the huge Swift Meat Packing Company. We had already established ourselves with kids when we stole the show away from The Young Rascals on our first
"Murray the K" radio show, but now it was more about our managers making connections, paying off debts, or creating a buzz that would go from the street all the way up
to the penthouses and mansions. As far as the road work went that year between
"Devil" and "Sock it to Me, Baby," it was light in comparison to the amount of appearances I faced after the breakup of the group, and so I spent more time at home
being a father and husband.

That year Susan and I had a birthday party for Dawn, partied with friends, sat at
home, and occasionally smoked hashish. It was strictly recreational and was considered
the thing to do then. Given the fact that I was a star, it was almost expected. I hadn't
turned into a drinker of habit, even though my Italian Grandfather got my sister Nina
and me drunk on wine or beer when we were little and he baby-sat.

It was a quiet life but I do remember visiting with Susan's friends, Howard and
Elaine Segal. Howard was the brother of Bobbie Segal, Susan's girlfriend from the Village, and he pulled out a copy of a record he had just bought by a group called The
Electric Flag. I laughed to myself, knowing that I had been offered the role of singer
for the group, but saw no reason to explain anything since I was still a few hits away
from what would prove to be "the end of my career," as would be stated by an angry
Bob Crewe two years into the future from this place and time.

So here we were. Susan, Dawn and I had gone from an apartment to a house, and
I had traded the Chevy Corvair for an Oldsmobile Toronado. I bought a motorcycle,
moved into an upper middle class neighborhood, bought a new Cadillac, and then a
Chevy station wagon for the dirty work (such as groceries, flowers, and all such menial
tasks), hired a nanny for Dawn, foot patrol security guards, and was extremely grateful.

All of our neighbors were professional people, or the wives of such. The man
who built our home had built one for himself a few doors down. He was the developer
for each of the homes near us. It wasn't lost on me that all of our friends—everyone
I worked with in music, my good friend Wally Schwartz (from whom I have purchased
every vehicle I have owned since 1967), and with very few exceptions the community
we were living in—were Jewish. It hit home one day when I received a letter from *B'nai
Brith* soliciting a contribution. They probably thought my birth name of William Levise
couldn't be right, so they changed my name to William Levine.

Oh well. I had to get Dawn to Hebrew school. I was being a good father and husband, but you can't count on that for a safe marriage when you are famous, because
one day our next-door neighbor, who had an eighteen–year-old daughter, came to visit
me when Susan had gone shopping. Once she was in the house, she quickly made me
aware that she had no underwear on and would like sex immediately.

That was just one reason for both Susan and me to fear the future. We knew nothing of fame as a practical matter. In the end, Susan proved to be the one with more courage. My fate had yet to be determined, but she was the person she appeared to be and not the seed of a transitory illusion, as was I. Her fate was written in stone, and she knew there would be many days and nights when loneliness would be her companion. Susan was brave and strong and responsible, and was a loving parent whose sacrifices were met with those same qualities.

Where were those things in my life? Where were those qualities that would ultimately be the only parts of our existence to define our worthiness and legacy as parents and human beings? I didn't know. What I knew for certain was that I was chasing stardom, and in the beginning of that journey nothing else mattered at all, except success. I was without question a star. But how big a star was what Mr. Crewe wanted to know.

If I had to pick a moment in time that demonstrated I had found happiness it would have been my time with Susan and Dawn, and eventually our son, Joel Matthew. We were a young family blessed with good health, a little money and some success. I remember looking into Susan's eyes and I could tell she had a notion as to the meaning of love. I, however, was having a hard time dealing with the very same subject she so easily seemed to embrace as the natural progression of things. It was as if she believed we would truly and forever be in love if we only had the chance to become familiar to each other.

My fixation was a bit more complex and confusing and had very little to do with the love we needed to survive. But now, with the sorry benefit of hindsight, I know that my choice of priority on that issue stands foolishly alone as a monumental mistake. If you grew up as I had, with no mentors or role models to guide you to maturity, and instead stood alone your entire life in an open field greeting every fallen object from the sky that bounced off your head with a "what the fuck was that?" only then can you understand how difficult my responsibilities were.

I began at the age of nineteen in trying to make a marriage work. The question that plagued me concerned my ability to hold on to what we had with regard to success and ask myself, "how much of what I had was I responsible for bringing into being, and how much belonged to Bob Crewe?"

Was my self-esteem so battered that I could dare imagine he could make a star of anyone? Was it that easy?" Was it as easy as picking from the enormous litter of young men who wanted to become stars? Something, at least in this instance, told me I had played a part in this success and I recalled what my high-school vocal instructor, Del Towers, had said about my being extremely talented. I decided it wasn't all about Bob Crewe. It was at least about the two of us, and a good deal about the band.

Being a star was only important for what it could bring into my life and all of the attendant changes therein. I wasn't taking myself as seriously as some of my more successful and more intelligent peers in the business. No matter how well I performed, or how beautifully I sang, I hadn't been the one down in the trenches with the lawyers and accountants hammering out the deals. This was all out of my control. I was simply along for the ride, and I often thought that my fellow artists who were paying attention to such details were being paranoid. My ego was maturing on style, as opposed to substance. As long as the hit records kept coming, I was safe from the ill will of an industry that, by nature, was insensitive and exploitive and whose executives were, for the most part, angry and bitter at having to suffer the childish abuse of so many of their client victims.

Chapter 13

THE FIRST GLINT OF SUN WAS just about ready to tear apart my eyes as it approached the crest of the hill we had staked out to park on. I had gotten out of the limo to take a piss before it became too light outside. I looked back at the limo and David Rudnick, our driver, slowly rolled down the power windows and a huge mushroom of pent up cigarette smoke billowed out into the fresh Long Island country air. The music from the radio was too loud with the windows down. Somebody would notice us. David turned off the radio and I watched with amusement as the bent coat hanger antenna on the beat up Cadillac limo jerked and twisted its way back into the fender.

We hadn't been sitting on the hill that long and we were beginning to sober up. A few hours earlier, at the conclusion of another boring middle-of–the-week Manhattan night, David Rudnick, club owner and artist manager Steve Paul, a few others and I had hatched a plan. After several large bottles of alcohol—to tide us over on the hour and a half drive to this mansion on Long Island—we began to make our move. I didn't know any of the principles, or the victim. I just knew that at three A.M. it sounded like a pretty neat idea.

Steve Paul's Scene was one of the hundreds of trendy clubs that popped up in Manhattan and for some months, or hopefully years, would be the hip place to mingle with a never-ending cast of famous, rich, and accomplished stars, most of whom were none of the aforementioned. Steve was so genuine and politically astute that he was now working on a few years of "hipness" with his club, and the reputation was well established. So what were we doing here outside this Long Island mansion about to kidnap actor and comedian Alan King's son as he left for school? That was the question I asked as I slid back into the limo. As near as I could tell Steve was having financial problems. Thank goodness wisdom finally prevailed and we quietly drove away.

The impassive nature, abandoned self-awareness, grandly delusional and corrupting effects of my fame were starting to take their toll on me. I wasn't going into a downward spiral, because I still had a couple of hits in front of me, but I would carry this lovely behavior with me for many years after the hits were over.

There are some people, a small few, who make the necessary adjustments in life to accommodate fame, but I wasn't one of them. I was extremely happy to be famous, but beyond that, I believed whatever power I held, away from Bob Crewe, was mine and under my control. I also didn't consider myself addicted to drugs because I didn't use them on a daily basis, but when I did use them, it was usually in excess. I also didn't believe I was trying to suppress unpleasant feelings, because I had long ago buried them.

What I didn't realize was that in the great emotional upheaval of my childhood, all of my feelings were covered over as an adult and I felt nothing at all. Nor, because of my star status, was I made to suffer any immediate consequences for my actions. I had become a star and a zombie, so therefore I began taking on the airs and attitudes befitting a man of my great station. I didn't become a prick or an abusive asshole. I became a fool.

I began spending more and more of my free time in New York City, instead of going home to Susan and Dawn. In New York I could hang out with names and people I could only read about, had I not become a star. Besides, there would be plenty of time for my family after I had made all of these great connections and had many powerful friends. My favorite place to frequent was, of course, Steve's place, and I often got up and jammed with other visiting artists.

Steve's place was like a circus. Tiny Tim performed from time to time, coming on stage with an old wrinkled brown paper bag from which he would pull out his ukulele. After each set he never hung out with us. Instead, he grabbed the train back to his mother's place then turned around and returned to do the next set. It was some kind of weird phobia he had.

One night Jimi Hendrix came in, as he had quite a few nights before. On this night I fully expected to sit with Jimi and quietly have a drink, as we had before. But, this time he asked me to go with him to his hotel room for a preview of his new album, *Axis: Bold as Love*. What a great talent! We listened to the entire album on a very elaborate sound system. Jimi had mixed it so sound moved around the room in an early conception of quadraphonic sound. I thought it was one of the coolest things I had ever seen. The best part was that I couldn't believe that Jimi wanted my opinion. In addition to such special treatment I had the feeling Jimi thought well of me because when the time came that Jimi decided to break up "The Experience" he asked me to come sing with him. Me, being the fool I was, said no.

Another night I jammed at a club where Stephen Stills and Neil Young played guitar and bass. I played drums and Otis Redding sang while Brian Jones, founder of the Rolling Stones, sat transfixed in the audience with a woman on either side. I arrived to hear a pre-release for Sly Stone's "Thank You (Falettin Me Be Mice Elf Again)" and was offered as much cocaine as I could handle from a family size container that was once filled with Pond's Hand Cream.

I watched the triumphant entrance of The Doors into New York and had to hide from a fight afterward that Eric Burdon, founding member and vocalist for The Animals, referred to in his first autobiography. In England I attended the coming out party for the British band Procol Harum as they performed their hit "A Whiter Shade of Pale." In one of the booths sat The Beatles, all dressed in their Sgt. Pepper uniforms. I walked downstairs to the toilet only to find huddled in a corner and playing an unplugged electric guitar the great Eric Clapton. And, I sang with rock guitarist Jeff Beck at a club when Rod Stewart was his singer.

Despite the company I was keeping—and my star status—I lacked confidence. I felt I was living a lie. Perhaps it was a latent psychosis or an uninvited monkey on my back, or maybe just the silent turning of the worm. Whatever it was, it gnawed at me constantly. I wanted to grow as an artist and I pleaded my case to whomever would listen that Bob Crewe was stifling my creative freedom with his ironclad control. All around me it seemed my fellow artists were making their own music and I just wanted a fair chance to prove myself.

But then strange shit would happen, like hearing Jimi Hendrix do a cover of "Hey Joe," or for that matter Jimi's cover of Bob Dylan's "All Along the Watch Tower," which he performed at the New York City Center for the Performing Arts, with Bob Dylan and me and the rest of the world watching in awe.

The drugs, the women, the rumors, and my street fame and behavior were out of control to the point that Mr. Crewe and Alan were becoming concerned with their investment. But, I continued on. Somehow it got back to them that I had spent several hours in the back of a Manhattan bus with the drummer from Sly Stone's band circling the city, unable to remove our white powdered faces as we sat paralyzed for the afternoon. Neither Alan nor Mr. Crewe wanted to see me busted for drugs, or sleeping with trashy women, so they arranged a special meeting.

It was a two-part plan. The first part was to get me back into the studio and keep me on the road as much as possible, and the second was to find a person to occupy my interest while I was in Manhattan.

I was introduced to a young socialite from a wealthy family in St. Louis. Her name was Sarah Smithers and her family's fortune had been created on a foundation of bar soap. Sarah's father was a diplomat who did a lot of work in Europe, and her brother was, at the time I met him, in the military. As I recall, it was the Air Force. But the mansion in St. Louis was occupied by, and the family was run by, the grandmother. She was the one who was clearly in control of the family fortune.

Sarah was a girl who could have easily been a model, except for her near-sightedness, which led to many unfortunate collisions. She was a close friend of Keith Richards's girlfriend, Linda Keif. She was also a real blonde, not the kind that half the young women in America were becoming.

Sarah calmed me down and took the wanderlust away. I almost stopped going to my old haunts altogether. We began seeing people and going to events that I considered a weird cross between outrageous and touristo. We went to museums, strolled in the park, and many times just stayed at her brownstone on the upper-east side conversing over music and literature. We dined with Salvador Dali and his wife at The Plaza and, while Sarah conversed in Russian with them, he and his wife's hands accidentally connected under the table while each groped for my leg.

Sarah was clearly upper class and well educated, but she was the black sheep of her family. She existed on an extravagant allowance that only the wealthy can afford their children. It was a new world for me, this calmness and order. It wasn't that Sarah was incapable of being a wild woman, because she was that and more. It was the way she prioritized events and life that removed the chaos. When we were together we wanted to be away from the madness of the Manhattan trendsetters, whose world we now frequented only out of necessity.

Sarah shared another piece of important common ground with me. She had an insatiable desire for sex. Sarah said she loved me, but I was unable to share that love with her because I was still unwilling to abandon Susan and Dawn. Sarah's family had me investigated, and even after they made her aware of my private and financial situation, she held fast to her love for me. She persisted in trying to make a home for us in Manhattan. I was on the very edge of destroying my family forever when I reached out to Alan for help, which was ironic since he was the one who had introduced me to Sarah.

As those days slowly passed, I was getting closer and closer to the superstardom that Alan and Mr. Crewe had worked so hard to achieve. Then came the release of "Sock it to Me, Baby," our third top ten recording. When you threw in this additional top twenty hit, we were becoming very familiar to the public. Along with that came a higher degree of recognition within the music business. My booking agent, Frank Barcelona, had arranged a deal with Hasbro Toys to market a Mitch Ryder doll that was accompanied by a floppy version of "Sock it to Me, Baby."

Back in Detroit, Susan and I went shopping at a retail store and bought a few Mitch Ryder dolls for keepsakes. I settled into family life and fortunately for me, Sarah was not the kind of person to deliberately cause disharmony in my marriage. I believe she was leaving it up to me to make a choice over the future direction of my personal life, and at that time I felt confident that I would eventually leave my family for her.

It was around this time that Alan, under Bob Crewe's direction, created a plan to break up Mitch Ryder and the Detroit Wheels. One needed only look at the cover of the album to understand what was coming. In previous albums, the covers were images of me—and the band. On the cover of the album that featured "Sock it to Me Baby," was an image of me alone with the band appearing on the backside. The shift in attention was not lost on the band. Plus, they hardly ever saw me except when we were on the road, and the sessions were now being recorded mostly without them.

Beyond that, Jimmy insisted on keeping the group pure in the sense of its line up and I, now more than ever, wanted to increase its size to include my beloved R&B horn section. Under Alan's direction, a plot was developed in which I would walk away from the Wheels while on the road. We had spoken to Johnny, the drummer, and he agreed to come along. Jimmy and I already disagreed on the matter, so it was pointless to ask him again. Joey was lost in a world that was destroying him physically, and our bass player, Earl, didn't seem to care about much of anything except his girlfriend, who was the daughter of a well-established music business boss in Detroit by the name of Harry Balk.

Early, like thieves in the night, Johnny and I made our departure as the band slept. But just as we were leaving the hotel, Johnny backed out. The years of manipulation by Mr. Crewe, the degrading humiliation of the band members, the loss of two of the original members, the constant bickering between Jimmy and myself, the well-meant intrusion of my peers—all of it had finally paid off. I was alone. I breathed an uneasy sigh of relief, but I was afraid and ashamed. The next day I did my scheduled appearance backed by a group called the Vagrants, featuring Leslie West on guitar. He was one of the most underrated talents in our fair land, but came with a personality that had to be handled like a tube of nitroglycerine. After the gig I thanked him, but it wasn't over for Leslie and me. We would bump into each other again under much different circumstances six or seven years down the road.

The day after that, Alan and I, as we had planned, went to Baltimore and began auditioning horn players, and then went quickly back to New York to put together a rhythm section. It was well established at that time that the best horn players came from Baltimore or Memphis. We began rehearsals in Mid-town Manhattan and slowly the show came together. It was a mutated representation of what I had been striving for, but I threw myself into it thinking I would change things to how I liked them out on the road, away from Alan and Bob Crewe. Alan had brought in Jamie Rodgers, an accomplished Broadway choreographer who had done the choreography for *West Side Story*, to teach me basic dance steps that built into a dance routine that I performed throughout the show. He also taught the entire band a variety of steps they were to perform while they were playing. There was a stage set and expensive custom-made suits for me to wear during the show, and the band had to be fitted for tuxedos with sequined lapels and patent leather shoes.

Lionel Bart

One day a man arrived with a make-up case for me that was so large and professionally equipped it appeared to have been stolen from a Hollywood film studio. A bus was acquired to transport us, and Frank Barcelona went about putting together a tour that would not be equaled the rest of my career. I think when that tour started I only had fifty-nine or sixty days off the entire year. But before it began, Alan thought it would be fun to do something special to relax—something along the lines of the quiet before the storm.

We flew over to Lionel's, Susan and Alan and me. Once there, we were invited to attend a party in the English countryside that was being thrown for The Beatles, who by this time were as big as they would ever be. The trip through the countryside was very mysterious, and deliberately so. We were provided with a map, which had substituted visual images for geographic locations. It said things like, "travel along in this direction until you come upon the girl with kaleidoscope eyes. . . ." And sure enough we eventually came upon a beautiful barefoot maiden standing alone in the middle of a grassy field in the open country dressed only in sheer silk, flowers all about her and in her hair, and eyes the size of small moons. It went on that way, clue after clue being taken from songs on the *Sgt. Pepper* album.

Finally, we came upon a huge farmhouse and in the drive was parked the colorful paisley Rolls Royce that carried The Beatles. I soon found out there were only a few Americans invited, and probably no more than thirty people all told. Susan, British singer Lulu, and Cynthia (John Lennon's wife) were the only women there. The party would officially last for three days, but we only stayed until the afternoon of the second. In the main room was a massive walk-in fireplace where people gathered. People also gravitated to an upstairs living area because there were two bedrooms there. In short, it was a large farmhouse lying on the gently sloping English countryside and everything was in its summer beauty. Throughout the house were large bowls of joints and hashish, and acid was available by request.

We settled in and after awhile I took Susan to an empty chamber room that held a grand piano. We were so excited. The Beatles! Oh my God, the fucking Beatles! All of them were there, except for Paul, who was visiting a girlfriend in America. Inside the room Susan and I sat at the piano and amidst the excitement I began to calm us by starting to play a song for Susan. The door to the room suddenly opened and in walked George Harrison and his publicity agent, Derek Taylor. We hadn't been introduced yet and as I rose to greet them Taylor said, "Get the fuck out of here, I want to use the piano." We got up and left without saying a word.

Maybe Alan was right. Maybe I did lack the confidence I needed to become the superstar they were shaping, but how would anyone act if one of the gods of their age wished you to be gone from their presence? Susan went to talk to the other women and I, visibly shaken, walked into the main room. Sitting alone in front of the huge fireplace was Ringo, who was staring straight ahead and wearing a frown. I reasoned he was not having a good time, so I approached him because I felt the need for a kindred soul and I thought he might as well. I wasn't there for more than thirty seconds when a beastly person came rushing toward me and chased me away.

I was beginning to feel very depressed. There I was, rejected by two of the gods of that century and the acid was now putting me onto a bad trip. I don't think I could have felt any lower than I did at that moment. Alan and Susan were nowhere in sight so I walked away slowly and took a seat at the other end of the room but still in front of the huge fireplace. I stared into the fire, asking myself what I could have done differently that would have made them like me. I wanted to kill myself. But, as the gloom and paranoia slowly took hold a miracle appeared. A human figure appeared before me and spent the next hour repairing my psyche and covering me with words of encouragement and love. The miracle was John Lennon.

I wish I could remember more about that hour, but drugs have kept many of the details at bay.

Susan and I were later attacked again by Harrison, who was clearly not pleased with what he termed "plastic people." Alan took exception in my defense, and Lionel began to get involved. The politically astute decision was made to leave the next afternoon, but I never did forget the core of love that saved my life the night before in the being of John Lennon.

Chapter 14

RETURNING HOME, DROPPING SUSAN IN DETROIT, and going on to New York City was starting to take an energy I didn't know I possessed. There were photo sessions, interviews, a major tour to begin, and the next two moves by Mr. Crewe that indicated his obsession with the creation of what was becoming a monster to my way of thinking, but was really only the same old superstar he was bent on achieving. He once told me that he was going to make me into the star he never was allowed to be because he was "too pretty for them."

He had now, probably because he was always in need of enormous amounts of money, sold me to Paramount Records and created a new label for them called Dynavoice. Gone was my old label of New Voice with Bell Records as the distributor. Mr. Crewe needed to grow and he was driven by a great degree of talent, and a desire that burned at him every moment of the day. The way he carried on about his nemesis, the larger than life now-legendary producer Phil Spector, I thought maybe that was it, but Bob Crewe was, in those days, the most prolific and creative producer on the scene. The problem was the scene was changing, and that was something he couldn't control.

Alan managed to get me signed to the William Morris Agency in Hollywood for a year-long contract in which they would, with the help of my movie agent, Bullets Durgom, find the right vehicle to bring my "exotic" look to the silver screen. I was totally unaffected by any of it at first, because Mr. Crewe had convinced me it was the natural evolution of a star with my talent. It was probably more like him rolling the dice and saying let's see if we have a winner. In addition to that, he now began the work—the long costly work—of creating the *What Now My Love* album.

For my part, I was to begin my first tour with my big band and I was so pleased the city we would begin in was Detroit. It was the same Detroit that had given me to the world. The Village, The Norm Ray Band, The Tempests, Billy Lee, and Billy Lee and the Rivieras. The performance would take place at the University of Detroit Field House. I knew all of the Wheel fans would be there. That was a given because as far as radio play was concerned, Bob Crewe had recently put out a record called "Too Many Fish in the Sea" by Mitch Ryder and the Detroit Wheels, which settled into the top twenty, even though the group had already broken up. But I was confident in my belief that my love for R&B would rule the day.

It was time to take stock of my life and my career. In my personal life I was clinging desperately to the notion that I was a good father and husband, yet everything about my behavior in New York went against that lie. My fame allowed me to come to a con- clusion about women that cheapened them and made me believe that any man could have the most beautiful women in the world if they had fame, money, or both. I also started to believe that homosexuals who used their bodies, fame, and money to trade, sell, or buy sex ran the industry I served. This belief was reinforced by conversations in Mr. Crewe's home about frequent vacations to third world countries where young boys could be had for the asking.

I had come home briefly from a tour to be with my family and was astonished to pick up a Detroit paper and see the announcement of my father's return to the stage. It didn't surprise me to see he was attempting a comeback; he had done that a few times through the years. What astonished me was the fact that he had, for the first time and without my knowledge, chosen to use my stage identity and was billing himself as "Papa Ryder." I chose to overlook what he had done because my parents were also sadly reaping the rewards of my fame. Their inordinate amount of attention toward me was having a disastrous effect on my brothers and sisters, who were essentially being left out in the cold. If I thought my childhood had been rough and neglectful and want- ing for attention, I could only guess the price they were being made to pay, as my parents were being transformed as surely as I was . . . and not for the better.

On the musical front I felt very alone. Bob Crewe told me not to worry and pla- cated me with his dreams of where we were headed. Alan, whom I trusted and felt safe with, was becoming weird and distant. Then the bombshell dropped. Bob fired Alan. I immediately became afraid for my future, because Alan alone understood my desire to not only write my own material, but also be one of the great R&B singers of my time. Now he was gone and Mr. Crewe wouldn't tell me anything about where he had gone to or how to get in touch with him. If Alan needed me to defend him I was more than willing, but I could not find him anywhere.

When these traumas hit, whether it was struggling with drugs, sexuality, Sarah, Susan, finances, or anything at all, the place that became the safest for me was the road and the show. But before I could escape to that, Mr. Crewe had one more bit of news for me. My movie career was now going to be handled by a woman named Gladys Markowitz.

During this time I also tried (and to some extent succeeded) to do a good deal of charity work and sponsorship for charitable causes. It was a "feel better about myself" kind of move, but even if it was for selfish reasons, good would come to those who benefitted from it. I became "The Prince of Hearts" for the American Heart Association. Then I flew to St. Louis to meet with Danny Thomas to talk about raising funds for a new hospital he was creating called St. Judes. I performed for our Marines at Paris Island. I lent my name and image to fund raisers for a multitude of diseases. There were many causes a famous person could support. At that time in my life I still cared, and I took pride in being able to help. That would change. Eventually.

What would soon become my entire world was starting to take shape now. Everything around me seemed crazy and warped, except for the performance. The time on stage. I suppose that non-performers would see it just the opposite. They would say the stage was make believe. A fantasy. While it wasn't the real world, it was the only thing I could trust, because I could control it.

I took on a ten-city tour with one of my heroes: Wilson Pickett and his big band. It was just as important symbolically as it was musically because of the horrible race relations in America at that time. It also gave me a chance to go toe-to-toe with one of the men who belonged to a club I was desperately seeking admission to, the R&B masters. We packed mixed audiences into large arenas and the tour was exciting and successful.

One night I was sitting in the front of Wilson's tour bus talking to one of his players when Wilson came through the door. He said hello to me then pulled a handgun from his coat and began firing at his drummer in the back of the bus. He cursed with every bullet fired and then, having emptied the gun, turned to me and casually said goodnight as he walked off the bus. My ears were ringing as I spun around to find the drummer curled, shaking and in tears, but alive. I never found out why Wilson did that.

With the help of my musical director, Jimmy Loomis, and his wonderful arrangements, I started to turn the Bob Crewe Las Vegas eyesore into something of a big band R&B review. We had Howard Bloom on bass; Johnny Siomis, who came over from Chicago Loop and later worked with Peter Frampton, on drums; Frank Invernesi on keyboards (Frank was an ardent golfer); and Doug Rodrigues on guitar. The horn section featured Andy Dio on trumpet and J.D. Crane on trombone. Robert Shipley was on baritone sax. Jimmy Loomis on both alto and baritone sax I would rather forget. It was a well-trained band, but because of the short lived existence of the collaboration, I did not consider it one of the four bands that were major players in my musical and personal life.

I called my brother Marc, who was singing locally in Detroit, and asked if he would like to join me as a part of the show. The only problem was he would have to leave high school. Marc had a wonderful voice. It was clearer and more polished than mine, and I felt he could do very well as one of the opening acts for the review I was building. I found with my loneliness and separation from the Wheels and my little family of Susan and Dawn, being on the road for what seemed like forever became more bearable with an immediate family member with me.

To make the review complete, Wilson Pickett pulled a fast one and offered to help by giving me two members of his show. Naturally I was delighted. Not only would I get a good strong female opener, but I would also get her talented husband to handle emcee duties. When I think of Wilson Pickett (or the Wickett Pickett as he was called and spelled it), I think about his stint with the Ohio Players and his performance of "I Found Love." I also remember him as the man who introduced me to the Apollo Theater in Harlem. But now I could also think of him as the man who dumped one of his problems in my lap.

As my show evolved and grew larger over the months, so did my newly acquired opening female singer. I let her stay until Wilson said she could no longer perform, and then she and her husband thanked me and walked away. Wilson wouldn't have a pregnant woman on his tour and I discovered I would.

In spite of such nonsense, my brother and I were having fun and the show was looking and sounding good. My spirits were once again lifted but the bitter feelings between the Wheels and me continued. Jimmy wasn't one to sulk, so he joined the group Cactus and did something I had yet to do, and that was to be an artist on a national record label. Atlantic Records. Paramount Records, where Bob Crewe was now working me, had not yet achieved legitimate credentials in the music industry. They had a wonderful reputation as a film company, but not in music.

To top off the band, which we dubbed Spirit Feel, we acquired a carry over from the last days of the Wheels, road manager. Ray Reneri. Ray cared about me in a way that was special. I mean the guy actually cried when he recognized the way people were trying to take advantage of me or hurt me. But he was not the protector Alan had been, and his position and need for the job dictated his keeping quiet on most major decisions.

And then there was Romeo, my bodyguard. I had picked up Romeo, a former bodybuilding champion, from a gig we did on Long Island at a place called the Action House. I was exiting the stage after completing my show, and was preparing to be mobbed and torn apart as usual when this huge man grabbed me. Within seconds, I was safely in my dressing room completely untouched. I hired him on the spot. Romeo was so grateful. Due to the generous salary I was paying him, Romeo was able to move his mother out of their unsafe neighborhood and put her in a nice hotel in lower Manhattan.

Another gift I acquired from Long Island was a new drummer whose playing I liked named Liberty Devito. He went on to back up Billy Joel, which was interesting because Billy Joel and I would, at one point in the future, both be signed to Paramount Records, but that was a few years down the road.

Back at the triplex, Mr. Crewe was working on the creation of the "make it or break it" album *What Now My Love*. He was also trying to find a replacement manager for Alan, and a lot of big names were being tossed around. Marty Erlichman, Barbra Streisand's manager, was one. Jerry Weintraub, who would in the future manage John Denver and also become chairman and CEO of United Artists film studio, was another. Things were still okay between Mr. Crewe and me, but there was a constant friction as we settled into the recording of *What Now My Love*.

Mr. Crewe attacked the project as if it was going to be the defining triumph of both our careers. At last he would produce the music that would carry me over the threshold of super stardom and in one fell swoop be vindicated and reborn at the same time. Mr. Crewe was putting everything on this gamble and became more involved in this particular project than any other I had witnessed. He was extremely emotional about it and drove me to the heights of my singing abilities.

The record was a lavish production with beautiful string and horn arrangements by Hutch Davies. This was on top of my physically and emotionally draining vocal performances of classic ballads from a different time and place. I did not like the concept of the classics, but because I was a professional, I gave as strong a performance as I could. I still trusted Bob Crewe's commitment to my talent, but it felt as if we had become disconnected.

That was one side of the album. The other side was filled with hard-hitting rock classics and performances of the best studio musicians available. Guitarist Michael Bloomfield, keyboardist Barry Goldberg, and drummer Bernard Purdie were amongst the seemingly cast of thousands. We had developed a fortress mentality, and Mr. Crewe was very secretive about and protective of the raw tapes. At night, he brought them to the triplex, where in the past he trusted them to the engineer. We labored with the project for months. During this time he was invited to appear at the Grammy Awards in New York City and insisted I attend the event with him. I had no desire to be there and told him as much. I didn't feel comfortable with it.

I declared I had nothing to wear and he went into his closet, which was the size of a double-wide trailer, and threw a tuxedo at me. He was insistent. I tried on the tux and realized it was five sizes too big, and again said I would not go. He wanted to be there with his little fop on a leash and I suddenly realized that's just how he viewed me.

I was like his boy toy, or his puppy. I also realized that was pretty much how the industry viewed me as well. I was in shock. I lay down on the bed without another word and refused to go.

I thought about how I viewed myself balanced against the new reality that lay next to me. The sex moved without passion and there it was. I was a whore for yet another bitter night without a clue to the chemistry, attitude, or drive that defined homosexuality. I thought I was finished with it. It was a mistake. I came up with a thousand reasons as to why I wasn't gay, and ran to Sarah.

The single from the album *What Now My Love* miraculously made it to number thirty on the *Billboard* charts. I stared at the album with pictures of Bob Crewe looking adoringly over what seemed to be my entire career, and I snapped. Sarah replaced me on the telephone to radio stations across the country when I became too exhausted from the effort. She explained to program directors that the album was not a good representation of my musical direction or beliefs, and asked if they would be kind enough not to play it. I believe it was that, more than the break-up of the Detroit Wheels, that led to the beginning of my decline, but all of the historical criticisms I have read simply say it was dreadful music.

Now the situation with Mr. Crewe was strained to the limit. He demanded to know what I wanted and expected from him as my producer. He didn't know I had secretly recorded almost an entire album's worth of funky, hard-edged R&B originals over the last few months, every time I went to Detroit. Even if I only had two days at home I booked one of the days in the studio. From the first day he showed me his intentions for *What Now My Love* I began my own covert recordings.

Chapter 15

THESE WERE HEADY TIMES TO SAY the least as I adjusted my psyche to attempt a movie career. I hoped that whatever it was that convinced Bob Crewe I was a gifted performer would also be a factor in the world of film. I wasn't a pretty boy, so that ruled out all of the beach party movies. Besides, right before Alan departed I got a glimpse of the direction that was charted for me, and it was exciting. Alan and I had an appointment to meet with noted director Otto Preminger.

I remember going up the elevator to Otto's office door and walking through only to find a long, red carpeted hallway running the length of an entire city block. One walked in for the appointment and started the long city block walk toward the small distant figure sitting at a lone desk at the other end of the building. With every step, the figure slowly grew larger until you were finally standing in front of the great Otto himself. It was rumored that by the time you had made the walk he was able to determine, by watching your body language and approach, whether or not he liked you. I have to say, it was an interesting experience.

Apparently Otto liked me and I was flown to California for my first screen test. It was for Warner Brothers and Gladys Markowitz was now in charge, but strictly for movies. Of course I tried to lay her. My test was for a movie called *The Wild Bunch* and Sam Peckinpah, the esteemed director, personally showed up to direct my test. These were big roles I was being tested for, but my dedication to the art form was vacant, to say the least. I had the opportunity to speak with a few actors who had devoted their entire lives to acting, and beyond their jealousy, they tried to make me understand how fortunate I was. It was lost on me. The night before the screen test, instead of focusing on my possible new career, I had a girl I wanted to screw fly in from Detroit and I stayed up all night doing just that.

Back in Manhattan I spent a night with a classy, well-to-do socialite at her Upper East Side townhouse that overlooked the East River. There, she cautioned me that, "a gentleman never asks a lady for a blow job." The next morning, after being let out through the servant's entrance, I was rushed to a meeting. This was a second meeting with an accountant, lawyer, and the director of a new film called *In Cold Blood* that was written by Truman Capote. It was down to me and one other actor, Robert Blake.

I was beginning to get discouraged at the near misses until I finally landed a lead role with American International Pictures. They had broken Steve McQueen and were into a lot of sci-fi horror films, but it was still the break I had been looking for. I was truly pleased with myself and felt fortunate, but the truth became, as it had so many years before when I watched money change hands to get my first record played, too hard to swallow.

American International would give me the role but only if their music publishing arm, Liberty Records, could own the soundtrack with my performances. Naturally, Bob Crewe refused to give up his music rights, even if it meant stopping my acting career, and I became disenchan-ted and bitter. I told him it would only be this "one time," but he would not let go for a moment. It was money he desperately needed, and it was also his false pride.

With the failure of the *What Now My Love* album, Bob's desperate release of old Detroit Wheels tapes, the fruitless year and a half pursuit of a movie career, the endless stream of female sex partners, the neglect of my wife and daughter and the never ending live performances, a deep pall descended upon my spirit. There were still opportunities available, it's just that there were too many omens in the air and I was tired. Very tired.

Mr. Crewe now finally allowed me, because he was clueless, to begin producing a band called The Illusion. We produced one single together and I allowed them to open some of my shows. Mr. Crewe also decided to let me produce the A side of my next single. It was released on Dynavoice and called "Ring Your Bell." He and Paramount made no effort to promote it, and the only radio station I know of that played it was the same station I had started my career on, WJLB in Detroit. And, that airplay was only through the efforts of my friend, disc jockey Frantic Ernie Durham.

It was clear that Mr. Crewe had tired of me, yet he would not let me go, so I again ran to Sarah. Sarah hired an attorney for me with her own money and we began trying to remove myself from my contract. Once Mr. Crewe got wind of it, though, everything changed overnight.

Every access to my own money was frozen by his attorney. Even though I had no manager at that point, management commissions were still being deducted and stowed away somewhere. The fifty percent deposits that were being held by Premier Talent were no longer available to me, so I had to keep my little dream afloat on the road with the remaining fifty percent I picked up the day the show played. And the bookings were beginning to wind down. There was still time to do something, but it was hard to focus on business when I was forbidden to talk to anyone while litigation was pending. The final punishment came when I was no longer allowed access to the triplex.

I was headlining a show at the Paramount in New York City and opening for me were The Who, Eric Clapton with Cream, and Smokey Robinson and the Miracles, among others. In the public's eye I was at the top of my game. I performed my usual magic, leaping into the audience, getting my clothes ripped off, and exciting little girls, but when I sat backstage in the shadows and watched the other performers I began to realize that my time as a headliner was nearing an end. It was okay that the situation was sad and confusing, but what made it unbearable was the fact that I had to continue on while the collapse took place around me.

Out of the choices I was presented—for I had no control during litigation and Mr. Crewe's powers remained in place while I was in legal limbo—I decided to sign a management contract with Robert Fitzpatrick. Mr. Fitzpatrick had a huge roster of artists, every one of which he promised his personal attention and direction. It was a far cry from the one-on-one attention and management I had come to know with Alan

Stroh, and I felt neglected. I had to make appointments to talk to Mr. Fitzpatrick. This only served to add to the estrangement I felt all around me.

Mr. Fitzpatrick was associated with Robert Stigwood, manager for Cream, Eric Clapton, and the Bee Gees. Susan and I flew to England for a meeting with the two of them and arranged to hold the meeting at dear Lionel Bart's house. Susan was deliberately left out of the meeting, where Mr. Fitzpatrick and Mr. Stigwood assured me that I still had a promising future. But, both went out of their way to persuade me that I should divorce Susan, which would allow me the proper disposition for my continued career pursuits. I think if I had believed I was gay I might have taken their advice, but my reaction after the meeting was to take Susan to an upstairs bedroom where we conceived our son, Joel Matthew. I didn't mention the hurtful part of the meeting to Susan and I made time for us to be together before returning home. Then I went back to New York and rejoined Sarah.

I took the big band to England, hoping to get something started there with the help of Robert Stigwood, but we weren't allowed to perform because of an immigration snafu that required the exact same number of British musicians to go to America at the exact same time. I attended a party hosted by The Who guitarist Peter Townshend, and was interviewed by the British press whose only repetitive question was, "What is it like to sound black?"

Peter tried to convince me to take Jeff Beck back to America with me. I had no doubt that once there, Jeff would leave me and try to start his own thing, but I entertained the idea. I had already jammed with Jeff in England at a small club where his singer was so intimidated by my presence that he stood at the rear wall of the stage and sang the entire set with his eyes closed. His name was Rod Stewart. So, I asked Jeff if he would like to come back with me and he seemed interested until I asked what size tuxedo he wore.

I thought it would be interesting to see whether or not my brother Marc could handle someone like Stigwood, so I arranged for him to spend the evening at the country estate. The next day my brother told me he spent the entire evening being chased about by the old queer and that "Stiggie" begged him for sex and even attempted to rape him. I figured my brother would, under his free will, decide if he wanted that lifestyle, but I was infuriated when I heard of the attempted rape.

Robert Fitzpatrick had arranged the big band and me to be the entertainment for a Schlumberger family party. This family's money came from extensive oil interests. The guest list included, among many notables, Generalissimo Franco, Premier of Spain along with two truck loads of troops; Grace Kelly; and "Hank the Duece," a.k.a. Henry Ford II. Susan and I enjoyed a little of Lisbon before going into the hills to the winter home of the oil baron.

Right away I had an argument with the lady of the house because she wanted to hide our speakers behind thick velvet drapes. She said they were ugly and I told her that her guests would not be able to hear us if she had her way. People, no matter what station in life, are pretty base and at the end of the evening nearly everyone was drunk and acting foolish.

I remember sitting at a bar in Manhattan with another wealthy Portugese national, Jamie Matheus, of the famous wine concern out of Portugal. Jamie was crying on my shoulder about how difficult it was to be wealthy, but not famous. I advised him that I thought it was more difficult being famous and having no money. At least that evening we could still both laugh about it.

I returned home and was to have a meeting with Mr. Fitzpatrick, at which time he was going to listen to the album I had been creating while being put on ice by Mr. Crewe. I fully expected a private meeting where we could talk about his thoughts or criticisms. That would allow me to make changes where need be. Perhaps what happened next was due to my ignorance of the artist's responsibilities in regard to product, seeing as how I had spent my successful years being steered by Mr. Crewe.

In any case, Mr. Fitzpatrick said to bring my album and meet him at a trendy club on the East Side. We met and he asked me to select any song from my album. I selected one, which was a basic R&B tune that had not yet had a final mix, because I was expecting feedback from my manager. Fitzpatrick had the DJ play the song for the entire gathering of patrons and then followed it with "Street Fighting Man" by the Rolling Stones.

I was embarrassed for many reasons, but the biggest embarrassment I felt was my ignorance of how the game was played. It was like being tossed from a speeding car onto the freeway and having to survive being hit by the onrushing vehicles. Another fact that was lost on me was the change away from the music I so loved. My album was what I considered to be an R&B triumph. The truth of the hour was that it wasn't only Mitch Ryder doing R&B that the public no longer craved, it was R&B in general that had now lost favor with the record-buying public. The meeting left a permanent scar on my ego.

The months passed slowly and Premier Talent released me. Mr. Fitzpatrick was now supposedly in charge of getting bookings. I had an English road manager at this point named Brian Condlifte, and we slugged away at the road with a sense of doom and sadness. It seemed as if every passing week one or another member of the crew or the band had to be let go.

Back in Detroit, Susan and I began to look for a more affordable home. She was sticking by me. I don't know if she was aware of my endless infidelities or not, but she was doing her best to keep our family together. We had to let go of the nanny and I traded the Cadillac for a small Opal GT sport car. We looked at a number of places, but it was heartbreaking to have to lower our standard of living.

The public had no idea any such problems were in our lives. They continued to believe I was a homegrown success story. Back in New York a lawsuit I had filed had made it to the New York Supreme Court . . . and I lost. My mistake was suing to be released from the contract as opposed to suing for stolen royalties. Sarah and I parted. I left Fitzpatrick and came home to Detroit.

I was totally defeated but still had some gigs on the books that had to be honored. The band was now reduced to four pieces: drums, bass, guitar, and keyboards. We did a gig in New Jersey and after the show I sold everything I owned. I took the money on one desperate gamble that I might be able to fly to England and convince Stigwood to help. It was coming up on Christmas and when I arrived I bought a train set for Joel while I waited for the appointment. I was feeling hopeful, but when I arrived at the office early and waited the entire day until they had to close, it was clear that "Stiggy" had washed his hands of me.

A young couple took pity on me and allowed me to spend the night at their home until my plane left the next morning. As he and his girlfriend lay together, I lay on a makeshift bed on their floor and spent the night jacking off.

Although it seemed like a flash, that magical run at stardom lasted more than five years. Now I was broke. Completely.

Some quotes from Bob Crewe:

"I always thought that Mitch would become a big movie star because he has such looks and magnetism and I just kept envisioning him on the big screen."

"I just loved him . . . he was very special."

"Could it be I ingested or snorted up too much cocaine? Mmmm, yeah, probably. Like fourteen million dollars went down the drain."

"My brother made me a deal with Motown to save my ass."

This last quote was speaking of his sale of publishing rights, which were divided between Motown, and eventually, Morris Levy.

"I sold my triplex for like $385,000."

So, here I was in Detroit without a penny and neither the Wheels nor I had ever received any royalties the entire time we were with Mr. Crewe. At one point I had an accountant estimate that the band and I had been ripped off for over seven and a half million dollars.

What a great business.

Chapter 16

FEAR RULED THE DAY, AND IN my mind it felt as though the years had been condensed to minutes. My friend Salvador Dali, the acclaimed artist from Spain, stated in an issue of *Circus* magazine, where he graced the cover wearing a jacket I had given him as a present, "Mitch Ryder, big big star and now nothing."

That is what it felt like. I looked around our house, which Susan had struggled to make into a real home, and sat for hours thinking about better times. I smiled and remembered the time in our master bedroom where I had fainted at my son Joel's briss. I was looking at the glass of red wine I was holding for the toast just as the rabbi snipped and the warm red blood of my son began to run. There were countless moments of contentment that had gotten set aside for a later day because I was much too involved in my career to cherish and respect the moments for what they were when they were.

In 1968 I was at the height of my career with millions of dollars being made from my talent, and yet $29,695.88 was my total personal income. I admit that was a good income for 1968 but hardly a "star" income. My lack of education, guidance, and protection did not exist to the degree required to keep me safe. I began to panic.

In the filing for 1969, my income decreased by almost half, and there are two different addresses on the filings. These two documents represent my deepest disgrace and cause for regret that is with me even today. In these two years, in my early twenties, I was challenged to stand as a man and I failed. My cowardice prevailed and I ran from everyone and everything looking for a place to hide. During this time I lost my case against Bob Crewe in the Supreme Court of New York State. I was also in federal bankruptcy court in Detroit. But the most damaging was my appearance in divorce court against Susan.

Prior to these events becoming final, I looked for a way out of my financial problems. Susan and I were still living in our beloved house when I befriended one of my local promotion men, Larry Benjamin. As the money slowed to a trickle, I went to Larry for help. I wanted to know if there was anyone in Detroit who might serve as my manager, since I was terrified by the notion of being in New York. He said he did and made an appointment for me to meet Barry Kramer, whom you'll soon learn more about.

Months before this occurred I made up a prospectus to try to get local moneymen to invest in my own production company. I had taken on a partner named Sammy Kaplan, but Sammy, unbeknownst to me, was not considered a good risk by the moneymen and the deal fell flat.

There were no jobs, there was no money, and collection people were calling all the time. My fame bought me some breathing room but without a solution to the unpaid bills, time was running short. I insisted that Susan give me a divorce. She did not understand why. In truth, neither did I, except a selfish, unloving survival notion told me I could not support a family. I lied to her and told her I was no longer attracted to her. And, I admitted that I had been steadily unfaithful. I told her whatever I had to, to make her angry enough to give me the divorce. Our son Joel had just begun to walk. My God, what was I doing?

I look back and try to justify my abandonment of my family by pointing to the absence of love in my childhood, but that doesn't wash. I was afraid, and instead of clinging tighter to my family, fighting for what I knew was right, having the courage to love unconditionally, and ask for help from those who loved me, I chose the way of the coward. Perhaps it was because I didn't know anyone loved me. Even more terrifying was the idea that I didn't love anyone.

Susan found a little home in Southfield where she would go on to raise our children. She still lives there today. She also had to go on welfare and other state aid because any money she received from me was not enough either in amount or frequency to be of help. I was allowed to live with Larry Benjamin. Larry had just gotten a divorce in which he declared to his wife that he could not stay in his relationship with her because he was gay. And so he was. But he was also into an unstructured lifestyle. He was dealing drugs, mostly cocaine, and got involved in part ownership of a professional boxer. Larry's particular manifestations revolved around young boys and Bentley automobiles.

I got to sleep on the couch and as I had just moved in, hadn't had time to figure out what his life as a single was like. I found out rather quickly, though, because one night I said goodnight and went to sleep fully expecting to be undisturbed. I always slept in the nude and so it came as quite a surprise to awake from the haze of the sleeping pills Larry had given me to help me sleep through the uneasy times I was facing, to find myself uncovered and taking sitting space away from the twenty or so persons who had arrived at Larry's invitation to enjoy loud music and plenty of drugs. Up until that point I thought there was a limit to how depressed one person could be.

Larry finally took me to meet Barry Kramer. Even though I had absolutely no ties left to New York, New York felt they still had ties to Paramount Records, and to me. After taking the bath they took from Bob Crewe, they wanted to recoup some of the small fortune they had been talked out of. Paramount gave me an ultimatum: record with Jeff Barry in Los Angeles or record with Booker T. and the M.G's in Memphis.

The subsequent album, *The Detroit-Memphis Experiment*, became what I considered the high point watermark coming as it did in the middle of my despair. I had sacrificed, to a degree, my relationship with the Detroit Wheels to pursue rhythm and blues, had cut my own R&B album of original compositions to assert my independence from Bob Crewe, and now was being presented an opportunity to record an album with the premier R&B group in America. It didn't matter that I did very little writing for the album, because it came as a surprise and we had a small budget. Booker T., Steve Cropper, Duck Dunn, and Al Jackson, Jr. Life doesn't get much better than that. And that recording, along with my fearful swirling brain, was what I took to the meeting with Barry Kramer.

Barry Kramer was a local Detroit boy with national intentions who had a love for the written word and a soulful desire for money. This was the late nineteen sixties and hippies, drugs, love, and peace were about to bring the status quo to its knees. Barry was going to be intentionally near the front of the movement by capitalizing on his representation of that culture through an alternative magazine he called *Creem*. The password became "Boy Howdy."

Barry was a short man who was naturally high-strung and nervous, and who chain-smoked more than a cowboy on the range during breeding season. When he was still a child, his father suffered a fatal heart attack while playfully lifting Barry into the air. When they hit the floor, Barry had to struggle to break himself free of his dead father's grasp. Barry's eyes were green and cold, as if this unexplained hurt was forever trapped behind them. He had a great sense of humor, but unfortunately it only showed when he was stressed and angry.

I discovered many years later that Barry had photographed some of my publicity shots in New York. The infamous swimsuit collection, to be exact. What made that shoot important is that back in the day I was having difficulty getting on the covers of the teen magazines. I was discussing this fact with Connie my publicist when she said, "To be frank, you're just not pretty enough."

At that time, Bob Crewe would have done anything to attract the teen mags, and that was a big difference between his expectations and mine. The last thing I wanted was be on a cover of a magazine. But, the shots with me in various styles of swimwear were taken anyway.

The *Creem* offices were in a mostly abandoned three-story building in a seedy section of Detroit on the Cass Corridor near Wayne State University. It was the perfect location for Barry's embryonic, youth-oriented publication. Before he was finished, he would have a magazine that threatened to rival the fabled West Coast rag, *Rolling Stone*. Barry Kramer was all about business.

Larry and I walked through the broken glass and empty, dust-laden barber chairs of the vacated beauty/barber shop on the first floor and up the stairs to Barry's office. I don't know exactly what made Barry decide to take on my resurrection, but I was very relieved when he did because I was at the end of my rope and couldn't bring myself, for any reason, to go back to New York. I don't believe Barry, or even Larry for that matter, sensed how desperate and insecure I was about being Mitch Ryder.

Bob Crewe had told me I would never be a star again, and I had managed to make many enemies before I left New York. Sadly, I didn't realize at the time that paybacks to powerful people in the music business were an option I could enjoy. On the back cover of *The Detroit-Memphis Experiment* I took a written swipe at Robert Stigwood, calling him "an old ass I once knew." That, along with what I said about him personally, his relationship, and the manner in which I left his partner, Robert Fitzpatrick, would all come back to bite me in the ass down the road.

But, here and now in Detroit, what happened in New York didn't seem to matter. Here, I was a star. I still wouldn't have to try very hard to get laid. I hadn't been in Detroit much up to this point, so fame continued to have it's totally unbelievable effect on the female population. Had Detroit been unforgiving, this place in time most likely would have ended the Mitch Ryder story, but being divorced and broke was something that was overlooked as the name marched on.

One of the biggest problems Barry faced was the fact that he now had to divide his energy and attention between the two different entities he controlled. I remember very well the initial displeasure of the *Creem* staff upon the announcement of my arrival, but beyond their displeasure there was curiosity as to how Barry, whom they admired, was going to pull this whole thing off.

One of the first people I met was the magazine's chief photographer/layout man/graphics specialist, Charlie Auringer, who over the years has revealed himself to be a genuinely nice man who had occasional bouts of binge drinking. At the time I met him, he had an insatiable desire for young beautiful girls who, when asked what they did for a living, would all tell you they were models.

But the real uncut jewel at *Creem* lay hidden in the walls of the building at Cass and, if the wind was right, you could here him cursing his Viking gods for abandoning him to the presence of a certain evil force named Mitch Ryder. His name was Dave Marsh, and he was *Creem's* head music critic/music editor/spiritual guide.

I've always wondered about critics. I mean, what causes them to be born? What was their childhood like? When all the little boys and girls were playing out their fantasies and dreams of what they wanted to be when they grew up how could you spot the ones who wanted to be critics? Did they say to themselves, "I want to pass judgment on something and I'm going to make it something I most likely will not know shit about," or did they simply come out of the womb complaining? Were they picked on excessively? Were they nerds? And most puzzling is the question of historian impotence. Is an historian, in this case music historian, the kid who collected the most records? Is that how they qualified themselves? I suspect that in most cases budding critics envied beyond reason the power of those who could accomplish that which they could never summon the courage to attempt. I also enjoy the notion that music critics believe they somehow protect the public.

Back to Dave. He was born in Michigan and had taken massive amounts of LSD so as to be rejected by the draft and the army during the Vietnam War. His flashbacks scared him enough to seek the truth so badly that he ended up a fucking genius. Brain damaged or not, the guy could write and his written critiques, buoyed by flashbacks, would scatter so many elements of his subject's music that the law of averages could only produce the truth about the artist.

Dave Marsh was taller than Barry but smaller than me and he spent way too much time trying to figure out how to kick my ass. He was fun to watch, all skinny with his long, stringy, drowned rat-like hair, and I looked forward with great anticipation to his manic outbursts. One time, after I had put together a band and was taking a break from rehearsal, a great crashing noise was heard and I looked out the window to see broken glass and an innocent typewriter scattered all over the sidewalk and street three stories below. Apparently, the volume of our instruments was interfering with Dave's ability to concentrate, and so he tossed his typewriter through one of the huge plate glass windows that covered the front of the building.

In his early career there, before he made an international name for himself, his talent was the only reliable fuel that kept everyone at *Creem* warm. Barry wrote as well, and in the future many more good writers would work for *Creem*, but David . . . he was Mark Twain's cynical, illegitimate, genetic missing link.

Chapter 17

I FOUND MYSELF MISSING SUSAN AND DAWN and Joel. One day while she was working at the job she took out of necessity, I went to her house and cleaned the kitchen. I wanted to surprise them with a perfectly ordered and magically cleaned house. I looked around the small home Susan had created and I fell to my knees buried in self-pity and sadness. I wished I was still making good money, but that money was the reason for all our suffering. It was a pitiful exhibition and I obviously didn't get it at all, but I walked through the small house looking at my children's toys scattered about the rooms and their little clothes lying about and deep in my heart I still wanted to be a part of that. I picked up the clothes, folded them, and held them to my face. I missed the safety of a family, my family.

I spent the afternoon straightening and cleaning, as if somehow making up for the neglect and irresponsibility I had shown them. It brought back the coldness I had felt as a child and I began crying again and feeling sorry for myself but now, looking back, I clearly see the impact of my own parents' neglect.

The next time I saw Susan, I begged her to take me back. I had hurt her so deeply she refused; she was not a fool. Maybe too trusting, but certainly not a fool. She knew it was impossible for me to miss something I never had and she set about devoting her life to raising our children.

Susan was not a heartless person and she allowed me to have open visitation, because she knew what my business was like. If I were to spend any time at all with our children, she would have to be as liberal as possible. I had hurt them and myself so badly, and became so uncomfortable with the ugliness of that truth, that I created a place for it deep within myself where I vowed to bury it and to never go back to it again.

Back at *Creem*, I had gone in early to set up for the day's rehearsal and was walking around the offices for no particular reason when I bumped into a strikingly beautiful university student who was home for the summer and was doing some intern work. We spoke briefly and played with a litter of new kittens she had discovered. Of course I took her name and number. Kimberly Priest. What an odd last name I thought. That's just what I needed right now . . . a priest. She left, and I carefully looked around for Dave Marsh in the same manner that Peter Sellers always looked for Cato in the Pink Panther movies. Only then did I cautiously ascend the stairs to the rehearsal room to await the band's arrival.

◆

a window to my soul

Privilege, as granted by birth, is a condition of peril in a democracy. Here, the gatekeeper must never become tired or, for the slightest of moments, suffer distraction. Materialism is the balm that cools the heat of ensuing rage when the mirror casts no reflection at all. The soul-denied dancers, beautiful in their self-confirmation, move to the music of a very small band.

Freedom, blessed freedom, could you be so common that I might fill my lungs with you and still gasp for the breath of life? Were it not for my good fortune in deliverance and sweat filled blood by your hand might I perish as well? Where lies the reason of desire while massed against your walls lie beggars and thieves waiting to hear the first break in your will? Your weakness so immediately reinforced in reversal by endless contributions of the perfect few. I shall pass a plate of collection that will be filled with your tokens and commerce of fear. Then, and not sooner, shall sleep be of peace.

The hands of labor both are the backbone of Detroit and the covenant with my past. I have sat next to the wealthy as their insipid needs found a desperate voice, only to be retracted and apologized for at the approach of daylight. I have tasted the potions and powders used by the bored, frustrated children of means and could find no doctor to heal, no crime or cure as the elements seeped out through opened wounds. I have listened in disgust to their jealous affirmations of my fame. They always return to the safety of their transparent dwellings wounded, and regretting having tried to pet the monkey.

Chapter 18

BARRY KRAMER COULD READ PEOPLE LIKE a gambler could read an odds sheet. He knew that if he were to have success with me it would have to be without my knowledge. *The Detroit-Memphis Experiment* had been sold or assigned to Dot Records, and they were releasing the first single, "Sugar Bee." Since Barry's plans regarding my direction were not yet complete, all he could do was sit back and wait for the results of the record company's promotion. All the while he was formulating a strategy that would have some relevance to the contemporary record buying public and, at the same time, keep my desire alive. The path of least resistance was to re-form Mitch Ryder and The Detroit Wheels.

All around us, the gate the Wheels and I had opened those few years earlier, the gate that said, "All right all you little white boy rock 'n' rollers from Detroit, now it's been proven. You can come from Detroit and become national stars," was wide open. Now, every major record company was flying in to sign up every band that could stand up. During this time Bob Seger began his long-fought battle to achieve his due. Ted Nugent rose up to claim his share. The Frost, SRC, Third Power, The Rationals, The MC5, Tee Garden and Van Winkle, Iggy and the Stooges, Cub Coda and many, many more from Detroit also tried to get their share of the pie.

The gate had been opened, so it wasn't going to take long for Barry to realize that Mitch Ryder and The Detroit Wheels, as commercially viable as the name might have been for a short fix, was not going to do it. It was going to take a complete transformation and re-introduction to get Mitch Ryder into a competitive space. Besides, Johnny Bee (Badanjek) would come back but Jimmy McCarty wouldn't. Jimmy had become a member of the group Cactus and had success beyond the Mitch Ryder connection. He had also recorded for a major label, something that none of the rest of us had done.

Earl Elliot survived Vietnam, came out of the Marine Corps, and put his bass guitar away for good. He retained his love of art in spite of the Marines and was beginning to direct his life to a place where he would be happy and prosperous. He had a distinct talent for floral interior decorating design, and went on to achieve great success with it. He was an entrepreneur who later became an import/export student. He also opened a gay bar in Detroit. Earl, it was suggested, was happier to stay away because he hadn't had the chance to experience fame beyond the initial hit recording and therefore hadn't truly been bitten. Barry and I debated the merits of having Earl rejoin and decided not to ask him.

Joey . . . now that was a different story. Joey Kubert was a strong-willed person, but when you mainline drugs it is possible to become weak very fast. He had gotten hooked enough to stay out of the army but then had to sit on the sidelines, a practicing drug addict, as he watched his group score hit after hit without him. It was eating him up. We cautiously approached Joey with the intent of rejoining the band and he swore up and down he was no longer using. Sadly, he wouldn't last. In the original group he had played rhythm guitar and now he was being asked to play lead, which he wasn't very good at. We decided to bring in a second guitar to do leads and Joey's precarious ego was so damaged that he left. We blamed his decision on the use of drugs, which was ludicrous because we were all doing drugs. Of course Joey was doing the horrible heroin, while we were only doing marijuana, hash, speed, downers, and LSD. Blame is the last resort of self-denying liars.

This was a time of great confusion in America as millions of people bought into the ideals of the "drop out" hippie culture. But the train kept rolling, and soon enough it seemed that everyone owned the required trappings of psychedelia and had learned how to flash the peace sign. In the music business world of the new counter-culture, record company vultures ate their same old meals but with a new set of clothes, a ready supply of drugs and long hair. It felt as if any recording group that was inclined to promote drug use through their music or persona instantly became stars.

FM radio replaced AM and there were no longer three-minute limitations on the length of the songs. Bob Dylan had seen to that. The quality of the artistry on many of the recordings slipped from time to time as the artist struggled to remain coherent while their brains struggled with each particular drug. However, as the level of consciousness rose so did the lyrical messages, and artists found a relevance to the new culture in much the same way as the previous generation had when they brought forth their rebellion. It was a pity that drugs had to play such a large part in the scheme of things.

Kids rebelled against the restrictive mind-set of their parents and left home to join the pilgrimage to the "hip" Meccas of the counter culture where they found themselves broke, in some cases, and at the mercy of predatory street people or semi-conscious well-wishers.

Communal living appealed to many white kids, not because they had an overwhelming desire to become communist-like, but because they didn't feel safe enough to make it on their own. Some hip icon that promoted the intellectualism of natural choice, screamed out for sexual liberation and many people threw their rubbers and birth control pills out the window. College kids had the added bonus of bringing about liberal change, which was, in many cases, funded by their unsuspecting parents.

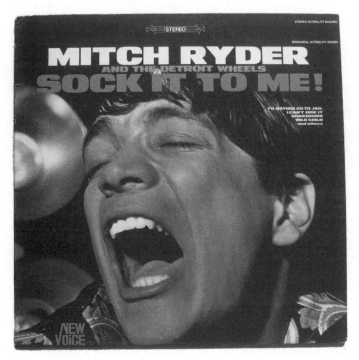

Smoking pot became the new national pastime and entrepreneurs scuffled frantically to keep up with the will and desire of the people. Detroit had a place called Plum Street that became the place to go for "authentic" hippie supplies. It was the "peace love" generation.

Most of this came about only a year or two after the assassination of Dr. Martin Luther King, Jr. It meant very little to most white kids in suburban Detroit, except to make them even more suspicious and afraid of blacks, after having witnessed the riots and Motor City burning on television. I was in Detroit during the riots and I remember being diverted away from the city by an armored tank as I cruised in my Cadillac Eldorado. To quote Bob Dylan, this car was, "a good car to drive after a war."

The only legitimate protest white kids seemed to embrace was the war in Vietnam, for which I had gratefully received a dependent classification because of Dawn and Joel. It was against this backdrop and the aforementioned situations that Barry Kramer worked his magic.

I was visiting an outdoor music festival in Detroit and as I walked toward the entrance a young, good looking, skinny, long legged woman with a briefcase ran right into me. She was full of life and had an engaging smile. It was Kimberly Priest, the girl from the office who had the kittens. My desire for her was so intense that I wanted to get her away from the other performers to a place where I could persuade her to be with me.

I asked her to come to the *Creem* offices with me but she said, even though she would like to, she had to work with the booking agents at the concert as part of her summer internship. The only thing left to do was to become bold, so I told her if she didn't come with me right then there would be no second chance. Fortunately, none of the performers at the concert had yet eclipsed my fame and as we drove back to the office my new single, "Sugar Bee," came on the radio. She might have been star struck but I knew I wanted her, and we made arrangements to meet at her parent's condo while they were out of town.

Kimberly had one more year of study at Michigan State University, which happened to be Susan's school, and to my surprise and the complete shock of her parents, she dropped out to live and work in Detroit. Kimberly got a place in the city and was sharing it with a girlfriend named Sandra who worked for Barry Kramer at *Creem*. I moved in, but Kimberly eventually lost her job and could no longer pay her share of the rent. It is the time honored question . . . what do you call a musician without a girlfriend or a wife? Homeless.

I went into the hospital to have my appendix removed and returned to the relative inactivity of Larry's apartment for my convalescence. There, I was interrupted by an offer, four days out of surgery, to appear in Puerto Rico in the middle of a Detroit winter. Naturally I took the offer and with Kimberly in hand and five day old stitches in my lower stomach, we headed south.

Kimberly was unintentionally deceived into thinking that, because of my new recording on the radio, my flamboyant manner, and the sudden trip south, this would be the exciting, glamorous showbiz world she had anticipated. Boy was she wrong. *The Detroit-Memphis Experiment* died quickly—not because it was a bad recording, but because it was out of fashion.

When we returned from Puerto Rico we found an apartment in Royal Oak and began living together. If the two of us had been clean and sober most of the time, she might have been able to better judge my situation and leave me for someone a little more promising, because I don't think either of us were in love.

Barry was still assembling the puzzle pieces and kept the band on the road as much as possible, and I insisted Kimberly stay on the road with me. The band rule was that there could be no women traveling with the band, so I circumvented that by traveling in the back of the equipment truck with Kimberly. It was the dead of winter and we had to drive to Kansas City. We brought some blankets and pillows, made a space for ourselves, and tried to keep warm. We could hear music from the cab where the two roadies were smoking pot, listening to tunes, and enjoying their heater. We were freezing in the trailer with the equipment. It was about twenty degrees outside with a blustery wind, but I was obeying the band rule.

Then, as we had frozen our way to the Kansas border I felt the truck make an un-scheduled stop. It only lasted a moment and we began to move again. Our little area was on the wall of the trailer that was attached to the back of the cab and I could hear laughter, but more important, I heard a female voice talking and laughing. I became incensed. Kimberly was freezing in the back of a truck hour after hour and the two asshole roadies were picking up hitch-hiking whores and treating them to drugs, a free ride, and a warm heater. I began to beat on the wall of the trailer, but the loud music and moving truck made it impossible for them to hear me. Or, maybe they didn't want to hear.

I looked around as Kimberly held a lighter, since we had no light in the back, and I found a microphone stand. I unscrewed the extension from its base, took the metal rod and began beating against the forward wall behind where the party was taking place. I rammed it over and over again, each time imagining what I was going to do to the two assholes who had picked up the road bitch and left the star's girlfriend in the back of the truck to freeze. I hit the wall so many times that I tore through the sheet metal. Finally the truck stopped and they came around back to open the trailer. The road dog disappeared and Kimberly was allowed to finish the trip in the cab with the heater. I stayed in back, smoked a joint, and was relieved that I had been able to give my precious love the respect she deserved. I couldn't give her money.

When we loaded our equipment truck for long trips, there were large stacks of *Creem* magazines to be dropped off at various locations along our route. Barry had not yet made his distribution deal with Curtis Distributors in New York, so this was the way he shipped some of the magazine without having to pay mailing or freight charges. We stayed at cheap little motels that never had telephones or candy machines that worked. Charlie Auringer sometimes accompanied us as road manager and magazine distributor. It was a seemingly endless journey that saw quite a few personnel changes in the band and had an air about it that suggested the same kind of tedium and fruitless movement I had experienced with the Wheels on our initial stay in New York. We didn't know if or when we were going to record, and there was very little money. We lived al-most as beggars, but at least we were able to keep a roof over our heads when we ar-rived back home. Then, at last, Barry was ready with his plan.

My hair had grown below my shoulders and I had grown a mustache to augment my bell-bottom jeans, worn out shoes, and raggedy t-shirts. I looked like a bum. Actu-ally, I couldn't afford any better. Kimberly had an equally depressing wardrobe but, be-cause of her magnificent body, no one seemed to notice. She also kept what we called "straight clothes" that she used for her work as a Kelly Girl temp worker. We struggled for money but it never became an issue. In fact, it fit right in with the counter-culture view of materialism and the anti-establishment mood of the times. Still, it hurt the day the repo man came to take away my car. I didn't want to be embarrassed, so I went down to meet him and give him the keys. He laughed as he pulled away.

Clearly, these were not the gravy years of my tenure with Bob Crewe, and I spent more than one night trying to reconcile thirteen records on the charts, three top tens, two top twenties and several top forties—millions upon millions sold for what? A fifteen thousand dollar advance for the house Susan and I had briefly owned. Meanwhile, the *Detroit Free Press* wanted to do a cover story on me for their weekly entertainment insert. The rough-looking cover picture pretty much said it all.

In a rare lucid moment, I willed myself to believe I was young enough to overcome this situation and establish myself back onto some sound financial footing. So, I turned my attention to the band, which was now known as Detroit. My self-esteem and confidence had been so shaken by the years in New York, and our current situation so devoid of monetary security, that I no longer felt like the "singular star" of the past and so I chose, in my weakened state, to simply become a member of a group. I was running from Mitch Ryder. My idea was to contribute equally to a project and share equally in its returns.

Paramount saw things differently and changed the name from Detroit, to Detroit featuring Mitch Ryder. There ended up being four different singers who did solos on the album, and that made me happy. The recording itself was put together piece-meal, because of personnel changes in the band. Boot Hill was our original keyboard player but was replaced by Harry Phillips. Other changes were with guitar and bass, and the final recording ended up having two different groups of musicians from many different sessions. Barry talked Eddy Kramer, the engineer and co-producer for Jimi Hendrix, into coming to Detroit to listen to and mix some of the early tracks, but ultimately the production fell into the hands of Bob Ezrin. John Sauter and Ron Cooke appeared on bass, and Ray Goodman had been cut to make room for Mark Manko and Steve Hunter on guitar.

The photograph on the back of the *Detroit* album showed us, left to right: J.B. Fields, John Badanjek, Harry Phillips, Dirty Ed (Oklazaki), Steve Hunter, Ronnie Cooke, and me. One of our roadies, I forget who, sat in the passenger seat of the car. J.B. was our spiritual leader and a member of a Detroit motorcycle gang called the Renegades, whose clubhouse was on 8 Mile. For many years 8 Mile Road served as a dividing line for the races in Detroit. The photograph was a bit intimidating in a time of cultural peace and love. Actually, it was scary. We looked more like a motorcycle gang filled with bad intentions than we did flower power hippies.

The music, though, was powerful. We heard stories about Aerosmith playing our recording as they flew from one city to another in their private jet. We, however, were struggling to stay alive in spite of our peer admiration. The band Detroit soon changed.

We picked up a young guitar/keyboard player from Colorado named Brett Tuggle who eventually made a good name for himself in L.A., but only after he left the Mitch Ryder school of insanity.

One day I personally accompanied Mark Manko to clean out his older brother's apartment. In an attempt to collect money, his brother had been murdered by drug dealer "friends." We couldn't get the blood out of the carpet. It wasn't long after that when I stood by Mark as he buried his baby brother, who had shot himself in the head while sitting in a bathtub full of water. His poor parents discovered the red water as it fell over the edge of the bathtub and throughout the house.

That group was the most violent group I had ever been exposed to. But, none of the players looked at themselves as violent, even as we adopted a biker code and philosophy that drove our lifestyle for the next two years. In a way I look at Barry's introduction of that band into the music scene the same way I now look back on the movie *King Kong*, except there was no love interest. The music was powerful because it was filled with naked hate, frustration, attitude, and desire. Every note played by every whacked out, freaked out, high as a motherfucker band member contained energy no mortal could ever summon. They wouldn't even know where to begin looking. And

*The band Detroit, minus the wheels. L-R: J.B. Fields, John Badanjek,
Harry Phillips, Dirty Ed (Oklazaki), Steve Hunter, Ronnie Cooke, and Mitch.*

then you had poor Steve Hunter, every night doing his brilliant guitar work totally straight, as the demons flew light speed around him and he was still able to make sense of it all. He gave it direction. A real country boy.

The recording, having finally been cut to completion, had to now be introduced to the world, and that was where Barry Kramer was at his best. None of the writers at *Creem* owned an idiomatic style, but their intentions were unique. Dave Marsh had evolved into a national reputation and was asked to write the liner notes for the album.

Another character, Lester Bangs, had arrived at *Creem* with great talent as well, and the quality of writing and the magazine itself were now being taken seriously in the marketplace. Lester presented no apologies for his often-acidic reviews of the new wave of artists being promoted by the major labels. Like Dave Marsh, he understood that the music coming out of Detroit was fundamentally unlike the wimped out West Coast pablum, or the cold, calculated, contrived steps of the New York "wunderkind" that were being shipped out to the heartland on a weekly basis.

Barry had acquired the new distribution deal with Curtis Distribution in New York and people like Charlie Auringer brought the layouts and photographs to miraculous heights. The writing, interviews, and critiques were a far cry from the original *Creem*. The magazine now had some power and influence on a national scale, and was steadily increasing circulation. The Curtis deal would prove to be temporary, but necessary.

Barry knew all of this, but instead of stopping to take a bow, he began to apply the magazine's influence toward his goal of resurrecting Mitch Ryder. On the down side, the success of *Creem* and the spotlighting of regional talent it did, served to increase competition to the Mitch Ryder goal.

We had a very good product in the *Detroit* album and with Barry's connections and favors we marched back into the belly of the beast, New York, with a promotion money could not buy. I wasn't overly anxious to return to New York, but felt somewhat protected from the ill-will of my enemies under the protective guidance of Barry.

We released a single called "Rock 'N' Roll" that was written by Lou Reed. Lou had been the first suburban Long Island young white person to admit on a recording that he was using heroin, scoring it in the city, and he referred to black females as colored girls. The homeboy himself came to one of our showcases and publicly declared our version of his song was "the way it was supposed to sound." But before I could ask him to share his drugs, he was gone.

There were press parties, the Rainbow Room, and countless interviews that made it all very exciting, and I felt a flood of old memories from the successful Bob Crewe days wash over me with each round of media attention. I wondered if we might somehow have found our way back to the familiar but distant fame I occasionally had vague recollections of.

Kimberly was mightily impressed, as was I, at the quirky nature of the business I had chosen to give my vulnerable gift to. The album, in spite of almost unanimous great reviews, failed to ignite the imagination of the public and we were left to wonder where we had failed. It was 1970. Many in the industry believed that Paramount, our record label, dropped the ball. I thought they might have, but it wouldn't be on the part of the artist or, for that matter, their public relations department, which was at that time run by Danny Goldberg. Something had gone wrong because even Billy Joel, one of my stablemates, wound up leaving Paramount.

The remainder of my time with Barry was a growing nightmare fueled by a band that was angry at birth and heavy into drugs. There were a few ventures into bonding with Barry that only left me depressed. For example, there was the day he invited Kimberly and me out to his farm where he took me for a ride in his brand new GMC four-wheel drive truck. He drove the truck to destruction, speeding in and out of ravines and ditches, over and through trees, burning out the transmission and ripping apart the outer shell. I didn't think it was funny. Kimberly and I had no money and the waste made me angry, but I kept my mouth shut. It was his money to do with what he wanted.

His wife, Connie, had been chased all the way to Morocco in his bid to propose marriage to her. While we were there, Barry fed their son J.J. raw, bloody beef as the child sat in his high chair. The baby silently sucked away on the blood from the raw meat. Connie would have killed Barry, had she been aware. One time we attended a party where there was only Barry, Connie, me, Kimberly; and their house guests, *Saturday Night Live's* Gilda Radner and her boyfriend (and later husband), G.E. Smith. I don't think Barry ever allowed anyone to really love him. I could relate to that.

The business of the band was the topic of most of my communication with Barry. The earlier players who arrived for the reformation of the Detroit Wheels were more toned down and nowhere near as violent as the band that became Detroit. Boot Hill, the marvelous piano player, became disenchanted early on, citing his need to be near his woman as his reason for leaving.

The same could be said for Ray Goodman, the guitar player who was a proponent of non-violence. (Ray and I continue to work together from time to time). John Sauter, the fretless bass player who had been recommended by Steve Hunter and brought up from the same farm country as Steve, appeared on a couple of tracks that ended up on the *Detroit* album. But, he couldn't handle the metamorphosis into the band called Detroit. Mark Manko became another casualty.

The band had a strange attraction for me as it reminded me of my early teens and the gang I belonged to under the leadership of Danny McCrary. A couple of the players had guns and short fuses, and very much liked the biker image we were living. The music was always powerful and filled with angry emotion, but it was spellbinding, sort of like a scripted snuff film. The public enjoyed it, but they always seemed a bit intimidated, unless we were performing for people of that culture.

The tough guy image had a down side, though. We were performing in Boston at a small club when Ronnie Cooke decided to help himself to a bottle of whisky from behind the bar. At the end of the evening, after the band had gone back to the hotel, Cooke and J.B. went to the office to get paid. When they entered the room, the club owner was standing there with two goons from the club. They had emptied his safe of all the money and laid it out on his desk. Also on top of the desk were bags of cocaine. J.B. knew it was a set-up and started to leave. The goons held J.B. and made him watch as they pistol-whipped the crap out of Cooke, opening his head in several places. Ronnie and J.B. ran for the truck, and while they were making their escape the club owner and his pals put several bullet holes into the cab and trailer. Unfortunately, this was not the only time someone got hurt.

The violence worked in reverse as well. We were playing at a club in Detroit when some of the Renegades arrived to watch our show. A fight broke out between them and the club bouncers, and ended with the club in shambles and two people in the hospital. There was damage at all levels.

One night in Manhattan we were playing at the Mudd Club. The crowd outside was angry because the doors were now more than half an hour late in opening. Inside, the leader of the New York Hell's Angels was sitting at a booth with me, trying to get me high on coke. He kept feeding it to everyone off the edge of his knife. Then he began laughing at me. I wanted to open the doors before my fans got pissed and left. I decided to tell him I was going to open the doors whether he was ready or not, and as I went to wipe the sweat from my face I realized he had cut my nose open and I was so frozen I didn't feel it.

On another occasion Kimberly and I had been set up when we went to a party at a Canadian biker club, except there was no one there except one big biker with an attitude. He beat the shit out of me in front of her because one of our biker friends had done something, somewhere, at sometime. There were too many of these incidents connected to the band Detroit, and promoters were becoming aware of it. Barry had promoted the band as a bunch of street-wise, hard-edged hombres, and the band tried its best to live up to the hype.

Finally, after two years of living out this image, came the predictable reaction on my part to an unforgivable wrong that I was being forced to live with. Poverty. My insecurities took me to the edge of reason as the band continued what was supposed to be a tour, but was really work when we could get it. The strain of almost two years on the road with no money, waiting in dingy broken down motels, unable to check out until the next job came along, the depression and loss everyone felt with the failure of the album, not able to pay our bills, not able to send money home to a wife or girlfriend, the endless driving around the country searching for something to believe in as we watched the changing seasons from the seat of a car far away down some unknown road. It all took a toll and a couple of us, upon returning to Detroit, insisted on a meeting with Barry and an accounting. Until this point no one had complained, but nothing had changed.

Barry was more than a little nervous as we arrived at his farm, but it wasn't because he was unprepared or unable to answer our questions. He was. It was the manner in which we chose to ask. Ronnie Cooke and I had both arrived with loaded firearms, which we laid openly pointing toward him on a table next to the tape recorder we brought along. We had put Barry in a position of no retreat in his own home. It was officially over. Years later I had the good fortune of being offered the opportunity to apologize to Barry for that evening from hell. He graciously accepted, which embarrassed me because there was no excuse for that evening. Just me.

Shortly after I apologized, Barry had an accident in a Birmingham, Michigan hotel room. They found him on a bed with a black trash bag lashed around his neck and a tube of lethal gas running into the bag through the tightly bound opening and leading down to a large canister of gas on the floor next to the bed.

As I stood there at his funeral I wished it was mine, and I thanked him for not letting it be.

◆

a window to my soul

As a man in America today, on the issue of abortion you are allowed an opinion on the matter, but that is all. If you happen to be with a woman you have made pregnant and she respects you, she may allow you to have a bigger role in deciding what to do with the "fetus," formerly know as "the baby." This, of course, was before the baby's validity and definition were reduced to incremental time passages by the cold clinical analysis of empty people who are not in awe at the wonder of creation and life, because it has no meaning for them. Sadly, in way too many cases, men are unwilling to take responsibility for the children they helped to create. I believe men should allowed one mistake, and then, from that point on be castrated. But the women? It is their body. So I will take the feminist mandate of "equality" to one of its many logical conclusions. That is only fair because logic, in all of its emotionally free forms, is the argument that is left at the end of the day—even for feminists.

Out of all the issues I could compare this to I will choose my favorite: the armed services and their ability to make war effectively. War has always been the domain of men, men who defend their wants and are willing to die defending them, and/or men who wanted something that someone else had, and lived with enough conviction to kill for that thing. War is about survival. But not survival for everyone. It is cold, cruel, and just the thing when words will no longer do. And that was the biggest problem—getting women to stop talking long enough to follow orders.

It is a tribute to the feminist cause that women were able to bring themselves down to the level of men with regard to the armed forces. Much easier than rising above, I think. Women today are more than welcome in the armed services, but only to a limited degree in combat. That needs to be changed. Any human, despite its gender, who can slaughter and butcher, or give the okay to slaughter and butcher, somewhere over 53 million babies since Rowe v. Wade (this, according to the Guttmacher Institute) is definitely the kind of person I want on the front lines shooting at our enemies. Talk about a fight to the death. An army capable of killing the innocent surely can vanquish the hordes of guilty enemy who attack our liberties. Just cut out their tongues and tell them to keep their mouths shut.

The figure of 53 million over such a long time pales in comparison to the millions of born babies and children who die every year from disease and starvation all over the world. Their parents did not have abortions. Their parents did what impoverished people the world over do. They made, in the midst of a desperate and futile existence, their claim to the only thing left to them that vaguely smacked of dignity, the continuation of their marvelous genetic qualities. And because, in their uneducated, arrogant, and sorry minds, they saw their children as extensions of their will and struggle to survive. They ignored reality and rolled the dice.

Or maybe it is simpler than that. Maybe the creation of life was the only feel good entertainment they could put their hands on. My point is, we are Americans. We are educated. Am I to believe that all abortions performed in this country were for uneducated women? Women who were too stupid to come up with other choices? An example that readily comes to mind is contraception. Or, were they educated women who found a baby to be "inconvenient" at that particular moment? Or was their will to know right and wrong overpowered by their need to please a man? If their body is their temple, then women need to clean up their disgusting little self-centered house of worship. The irresponsibility on the part of men who think they can create life and simply walk away is cowardly, but ultimately the choice to have unprotected sex, risk getting pregnant and having an abortion, is the choice of women.

Do you hear the screams of self-righteous indignation and anger that soil my ears from liberal modernists? The bigger than life, tuff enuff feminists and their slobbering clique of mommy boy men? Okay. Then let's allow for the women whose lives would have been at risk had they chosen to have the living breathing "fetus" wrapped in a blanket in their loving arms. Not good enough? Okay. How about we allow for the women whose quality of life and careers would have been severely altered had they chosen to take the little "fetuses" to school every day. Still not good enough? Well, what the hell, let's allow for the women who spell the word humanity with the letters "me."

Gosh. Kiss my butt and call me sweetheart but I'm a little confused. Are the tears some of these women cry for the baby they just killed, the man they wish they could kill, or the fact they didn't have the guts to kill themselves?

Oh Mommy, please doesn't hate me. I'll be a good boy. I promise. I promise. Just don't rip my head away from those big, soft, delicious "milk of life" tits. Did I just say that? I am so sorry. I meant to say I could not possibly be a man unless I have a woman to impregnate. No! I didn't mean to say that. Damn. I meant to say penis envy has made this country what it is today. Oh, Mommy. Please forgive baby. Baby is sorry. Kiss the boo-boo. Just hold me, you know, deep, like you always do. Flex your "power pac" Mommy. Is it as good for you as it is for me?

Misogynist? I do not think so. No, a misogynist would say something like: "Women, the only animal that can bleed for five days and still not die" or, another old chestnut, "If it wasn't for that gash between their legs there'd be a bounty on their heads." Or, and I just love the simplicity of this one, "I treats all my womens good." One could go on forever. But why? I love women. I love them to a fault. Am I to blame for this dysfunctional existence we call American culture—the early darkening skies of a growing storm that will flatten, and destroy one of the greatest democracies of modern times? Hell no. I'm not to blame.

Chapter 19

THESE DAYS WERE FILLED WITH INVITATIONS from the children of wealthy Michigan families. Kim Breach, Bruce Alpert, and a host of young, rich, entranced, want-to-be-star musicians now wanted to be near the famous Mitch Ryder for their own special reasons. I didn't like cocaine that much, but it was beginning to be the replacement drug of choice for the masses, so I did coke right along with many of them.

FM radio offered me many friendships as well: Dan Carlyle, a young Howard Stern; Arthur Penthallow; Jerry Lubin; and what was referred to as the "X Crew." That mixture was thrown into the melting pot of my music related "friends" and drug dealers. Now I was starting to do heroin with my good friends Taco and Nancy, who bought the Cinderella Theater with their drug profits, and were trying to legitimize the money in a legal entity. Every other band, now that the major label rush was over, still dreamed of a big contract but the only way left to finance the projects was with the help of local drug dealers. Every facet of the music business in Detroit was in some way or another connected to illegal drug trafficking. Big change was taking foot, though.

Unlike the civil rights movement of the late fifties and early sixties—whose cause was painfully clear, and the message and passion deliberately articulated through powerful leaders—the "counter-culture social revolution" held no treatise, no cohesive strategy and no inflammatory, all-powerful guide. Leadership came from student activists and university intellectuals, problematic gurus, and militant proponents of change whose voices were heard through the burgeoning underground press. The messages, manifestos, and communiqués were sent from places with names like Berkeley and Columbia and even Ann Arbor. Sometimes it was just a letter dropped in a post box.

The SDS (Students for a Democratic Society) began serious recruitment drives in universities, and organized protests became effective enough to warrant a reactionary response by police and the federal government. Borrowing slogans from the civil rights movement, such as "Power to the People" "We Shall Overcome," or "Death to the Pigs," the social revolution was turning to a bloody new page. What had begun as a snub to the values of our parents now had the potential for real change, and everyone was lining up on one side or the other.

Blacks seemed to marvel at the media attention given to outraged white youth, compared to the distorted coverage of their own struggle, and began an attempt to draw attention to their programs. This was no longer the American Civil War. This was, in fact, no longer about the war in Vietnam, or the freedom to smoke pot, or have open sex. This was about anarchy. This was the true beginning of insurrection, and the zeal with which young radicals embraced violent confrontations, determined and unafraid, was beautiful to behold. The peace/love romantic, middle-class generation was now, under demand, being asked to put up or shut up. It was as if someone had eaten a bean burrito and decided to ride in your elevator. To quote Ross Perot, there was a "giant sucking sound," as most everyone fled back to the painfully familiar.

The brutish mind-set of the establishment was not foreign to the city of Detroit. As children, we had heard inspiring stories of conflict as union organizers struggled against the automobile companies. The bloodstained Rouge Overpass in Dearborn at Ford Motor Company, the great labor union hero Walter Reuther, the company goons and flailing nightsticks against the backdrop of police with their heads turned the other way, the sit-in at General Motors in Flint, all of them great legacies of blood and courage by men and women, our mothers and fathers so to speak, who demanded the dignity of a day's pay for a day's work and a safe working environment. If they were going to break their backs for the company, then they wanted to know their odds of survival would be worth the effort. Even if they were just "working class," they still had families and dreams for the future.

Fly into Detroit today at our new airport and go down to get your bags at baggage claim. Up on a huge wall for everyone to see are the images of those people we feel should be honored by the passing parade of world travelers as they pick up their luggage: Rosa Parks, Walter Reuther, and even Jimmy Hoffa—the great teamster organizer and legend who did battle with the descendent of another gangster offspring, Bobby Kennedy. No, it's not a mistake. We do have our priorities in order.

It was with this in mind that I allowed myself to consider the revolution at hand as an opportunity. I certainly hadn't had much luck with the status quo music industry. Kim and I were happy together, but I could tell that she did not hold the same attraction to radical change that I did. I had yet to come to that place where I would destroy myself, rather than play the game by "the man's" rules.

Kimberly had come from the middle-class and her parents, Russ and Dora, had provided her with comfort and material rewards that she believed I would also deliver. After all, I was a recording star and I did still have a contract. From my perspective, the lack of money was nothing new. Other than the short years of success in New York, which had now taken on the looks of an aberration, life without disposable income was the norm. However, it did occur to me that what was trendy—in this case radicalism—might also be commercial.

I approached a man named John Sinclair. John had been a guest of Kim's and mine at our apartment after he had come out of prison. He was considered a radical, but had proven he was willing to work within some of the boundaries of the establishment as manager of the rock group MC5. He also had his own underground publication called *Sun*. While he was in prison I had performed several benefits for his commune, the first at the behest of Barry Kramer.

John was an intellectual and a writer. He was a big, long-haired man with a menacing stare that was betrayed the instant he started to laugh. The trick was to get him to laugh. MC5, which started out on a parallel universe with John as their manager, abandoned his communal philosophy at the first sniff of commercial success. John was quartered near the campus of the University of Michigan-Ann Arbor in an old mansion that sat near the fraternity houses on Hill Street. He had a flair for the obvious and enjoyed things like having his followers dig huge craters in the front lawn of the mansion to protest bombings by American military forces in Vietnam and Cambodia. John was one of our homegrown radicals, and his early radicalism was rewarded with jail sentences and little name recognition beyond the networks of other radicals.

When John Lennon, the good Beatle, performed at a benefit and rally for the release of John Sinclair from prison—ten years for two joints—the entire world heard of him. Lennon had not been made aware of John's priors until afterward. Those were difficult times to decide where your loyalties lay, and I heard that John Lennon suffered post rally reservations about his support. Apparently it was "fabulous" to be associated with someone on the edge, but if you journeyed too far you could risk losing your credibility with the status quo. And this wasn't so much about John Lennon, because his fame was such that few could question his direction. Rather, it was about lesser beings who were struggling with how far to take their beliefs before shooting themselves in the foot because, in spite of their innocence, most radicals I had been exposed to were serious about their convictions and willing to pay the price. Pun Plumundon comes to mind as he attempted to blow up CIA headquarters in Ann Arbor. Rennie Davis of Chicago Eight fame, sitting with me on a quiet, peaceful, sun-filled afternoon and coming on to me was a different radicalism. I had no idea.

John Sinclair was a believer in revolutionary change. I am convinced of that. Today, as he wanders the world having lost Detroit, having lost New Orleans, and now trusting in Amsterdam, he is a scholar. When he knew me and was my manager, he gave me gifts like *The Little Red Book* that contained Mao Tse-tung's six essays on military war. This was an account of the Red Chinese army and the campaigns against the Nationalist Chinese army, and the British and the Japanese in their campaigns through Burma and China. I, without John's knowledge, balanced that against *Stillwell, the American Experience in China*, written by the great American general of the same name in which he described the very same conflict. It was great fun.

John saw in me what I saw in him. Opportunity. Here was a chance for John to legitimize the political, musical arm of the commune with a genuine American rock 'n' roll star. I saw it as a chance to bring credibility to my standing with the "righteous and hip" crowd. It was a monumental blunder. In spite of that, there was an element of danger that was exciting, and everyone I associated with at that time pushed him- or herself toward that danger shielded by their childish and innocent politics.

The band Detroit, though seriously wounded, was still together and we geared up for the road one more time. Our road crew was from Ann Arbor, and where we used to haul our equipment and stacks of *Creem* magazines, we now hauled our equipment and huge black plastic lawn bags filled with marijuana for sale and distribution.

I had evolved to a dream-like state where the first thing I did in the morning, before even getting out of bed, was light up a joint. I can't honestly be certain, but the band Detroit seemed more powerful than ever, and more dangerous. The "What, me worry? " attitude that resulted from the constant pot and heroin use left me inattentive to everything around me. I didn't care how I looked or even if I had clothes to wear. Whenever the occasional gig appeared we all attacked it with an energy that could only have come from men trying desperately to free themselves from unseen restraints. And, the press no longer gave us the national attention we had become accustomed to with Barry Kramer.

John suggested that Kim and I move into the carriage house behind the mansion, but I declined when I discovered I would have to contribute twice as much to the commune as I was paying in rent for our apartment.

John had a great abhorrence of racism and found it difficult to be around certain members of the band Detroit, due to their biased ignorance. John was a self-made, complex man with many conflicting goals, but he was disciplined. I could not tell whether he genuinely liked me or not. It could have simply been my usefulness to his cause. We have in these times today carried on as if we were friends, but in his assessment of his journey and his perception of his reality as a major player in the literary world, he has distanced himself from all references to me.

In the short year and some months that had transpired while with John, America had come to some conclusions about the "social revolution" and decided that, even though it had been a hell of a ride, we wouldn't be repeating it soon. The war in Vietnam was still going strong, but you could now sense the lack of resolve in the public will to continue. The deadly tragedy at Kent State University, in which students were fired upon and killed by the National Guard, brought a sobering new look to the national angst over the war.

Crosby, Stills, Nash and Young were the quickest of the musical stars to exploit the dastardly deed for monetary gain. They claimed it was to raise public awareness and bring about political change. I had been completely schooled about music and politics, and it looked to me that maybe they were going to give the profits from the sale of the song "Ohio" to relatives of the dead and wounded students. Or was I wrong?

The Michigan State Police kept what they called the "Red Files," red being equated to communism. John was in them, and by association, I was too. Surveillance was pretty much wherever we went but it wasn't as intense around my activities as it was for the commune. At first I had the romantic notion that being a communist was heroic. I thought it gave just deserts to my country for allowing private industry, in my case the record companies, to rip me off for the millions of dollars that Bob Crewe and his brother Dan had weaseled away from me. But in the end, communism was a philosophy I couldn't embrace. You are not a star unless you believe you are, and that was hard to believe living in poverty with a famous name. I hadn't given up on my country, but I was almost ready to give up on the music business.

John wasn't able to make it work. The band was broken in spirit but was desperately holding to the belief that some little miracle would appear to save the day. The country wanted to get away from anything that reminded them of counter-culture and revolution, and that included John, and through him, me.

Kim and I had now acquired the initial glue that would hold our relationship together and carry us beyond the realm of sexual attraction. We compared our scars from the battles we had braved together and slowly began to function as a single unit. Neither of us was willing to get married, but we were very much partners and we both needed to now step back and look at our lives. We needed a rest. I said goodbye to John Sinclair and to the band Detroit, and Kim and I returned to our apartment to lick our wounds.

Paramount Records was still owed an album, but I wasn't up for it. I heard that John was able to negotiate a second Detroit album with Paramount, separate from my contract, and my replacement singer would be Rusty Day. Rusty Day was later murdered in front of his twelve-year-old son, and then they killed the son since he was a witness. Drugs.

My life didn't make any sense. I had been too negligent in my responsibilities to my health, my image, my relationship to Kim, and most painfully, to my children. It was no longer about being a star. I had lost my pride and self-respect as a human being.

I had allowed myself to be taken to a place where I couldn't pay my bills. I couldn't pay Susan's alimony, my car had been repossessed, and we were being evicted from our apartment.

The IRS sent me a notice, so I made my way downtown to their offices for my appointment. The agent listened to my story and ended up giving me a silver dollar to keep in my pocket so that I might never be broke. Kim, thank goodness, had kept her old Volkswagen Beetle from college; otherwise we couldn't have gotten around at all. There was nothing to live on and I couldn't think clearly. It, in hindsight, was disgraceful.

The continual sacrifices and increasingly lower standard of living coupled with a reckless lifestyle had torn Kimberly away from her upbringing. How could a beautiful young woman like her still be with me? Had I destroyed so much of her that she couldn't leave the sinking ship, or did she really love me so much that she would tolerate the indignity of the unwarranted poverty I had brought her? Was she as weak as I was? We would find out very soon, because we no longer had money for, or good will enough, to hang with the party crowd.

Kim and I moved in with my relatives, Uncle George and Aunt Erika. George Mc-Daniel was my mother's step-brother, and Erika was born in Germany. She met George while he was stationed there as an MP. George had a gunsmith license and a small machine shop in his garage. I watched with fascination as he started with a block of wood and slowly cut, shaped, and sanded it into a beautiful rifle stock. When my mother and father had taken me as a child to visit Erika's parents on Second Avenue in Detroit, George was living there. He turned me onto the Green Hornet, an action hero on the radio and taught me how to fence with a rapier. He knew me as a boy, and now he was facing me as a man. He didn't care what was going on in my life, he only knew I was in trouble and was willing to shelter us. That was enough.

Uncle George was a self-styled intellectual who could speak for hours about any subject and held an opinion on everything. He spoke fluent German, and he and Erika spoke it around their house when they didn't want anyone to know what they were talking about. Against his advice, I began doing a few gigs with some of the players from that side of town. It was pretty much a bar band and, as I could no longer afford drugs, we began to drink heavily. Although still manageable, it showed the potential for problems. The band was called The Knock Down, Drag Out Party Band, which was later shortened to The Knock Down Party Band.

The group had some excellent players: ex-Detroit members, ex-MC5 players, and a lot of great music that was really gutsy rock 'n' roll. I had no expectations from the gigs, other than the badly needed money. Wayne Kramer had a great take on my condition at that time. Too high.

After a while, I drifted away again and couldn't bring myself to get a straight job. Every time I accepted the reality of my situation, an errant gig would came along and fooled me into thinking I was still a star.

I had stopped doing drugs . . . almost. We had now begun social drinking around my uncle's house with Erika and George. Apparently they saw nothing wrong with drinking. But, I was hiding some real problems because one winter night I went to a bar and got so drunk that my uncle woke me up late the next morning from a deep sleep inside the car. It wasn't the first time I had passed out in such as way. Nor would it be the last.

Chapter 20

KIM TOOK ON A DISTRAUGHT EXPRESSION to her face. She began to withdraw from her usual outgoing and upbeat personality, which we had both come to rely upon during our endless times of crisis. Her lovable adopted confidence of the worldly-wise woman was now replaced by the helpless look of a lost little girl. She became quiet and depressed, and asked me to hold her as she lay her head on my chest and quietly cried, not saying a word. I gently rubbed my fingers slowly back and forth across her brow trying to make the wrinkles of despair fade from her beautiful face.

In four short years the hard and fast life I had been living, the exhausting attempts at touring, the tiring endless miles of highways, the smoke filled clubs and halls, the parties that lasted 'til sun-up, the disappointing attempts at a comeback, the desperation for money and now, without even the privacy of our own home, the truth of our situation overwhelmed us. Kim and I lay huddled together in the makeshift bedroom of my uncle's basement against the insanity of reality.

I needed to admit defeat, turn my back on what was left of my career, clean myself up, and cut my loss. I needed to stop dragging this woman through what had proven to be a demeaning and unforgiving struggle to satisfy the addiction of stardom. I needed to give her something other than my life to live for. If I truly loved her, which I said I did, I should offer her the choice between getting married and starting a new life, or setting her free.

I didn't do either. I didn't do anything. I let her choices be her own. She was more than welcome to stay with me, because I was frightened to be alone and could hardly think for myself. I had nothing to offer other than what she had already seen and the faint distant star I was following. I neither owned, nor claimed, anything else. It was only about me and my selfishness and my fears. I was delusional, and felt that if I didn't somehow keep walking to the footsteps and beat of the music that lay unclaimed in my head, that I would cease to exist.

Our bond was growing—but mostly at the expense of happiness—as Kim blindly threw away her independence to more deeply invest in the future of the star known as Mitch Ryder. I began to see Kim as a different person. A kindred spirit. A soul whose hurt could be easily felt. In my mind she had been my lover and comrade, but now she was becoming my equal, and what she couldn't match in talent and ego, she was forced to match in monumental sacrifice. I would see to that. Even though we weren't married, it was beginning to feel as if we were and her commitment to me had significantly raised the stakes for the two of us.

We took another trip to New York. While there, we discovered that one of our more pleasurable acquaintances, the J. Geils Band, would be performing in Central Park. The band had come to visit us when we still had an apartment in Royal Oak, Michigan. I remember feeling so special at the time, and when I think about it, I wonder if I would have taken precious hours out of a tight schedule to do the same.

Kim and I desperately needed something to lift our spirits, and we were having fun sitting backstage in Central Park watching the band perform. Our emotions were running high as I looked out at the adoring audience and pretended it was my show and they had all come to see me. God, I missed it so much. The stardom. Now, when I could get work, it was for eighty or ninety people in some small dump in Detroit. After the J. Geils show was over we said our goodbyes and prepared ourselves for the trip back to Detroit where nothing at all awaited us.

As we were walking away a man, who said he was a representative for Windfall Music, approached me and gave me a card. He said they would like to talk to me about my future plans and believed they might be able to help me if I wanted to "get back into the business." I put his card into my pocket and told him I would think about it.

I was pissed. Pissed and confused. I knew I hadn't been working that much and I wasn't recording, but I didn't believe I had ever quit the "business." In fact, I thought I was sacrificing a great deal for the business.

Back in Detroit there was no change of scenery, no fresh start, and no work. My uncle was supporting us and we ate his food every night and drank a lot of his alcohol. The idea of going back to New York scared the hell out of me, but I woke up every morning with the same depressing realization that if I didn't at least listen to what they were offering, I would have nothing at all. Kim and I discussed it, then I called New York and arrangements were made to fly me to the initial meeting.

This was 1970. Windfall Music handled the group Mountain, with Felix Pappalardi, Corky Laing, and my old pal Leslie West. Mountain was riding high on their hit "Mississippi Queen" that Felix had produced and broke in America with the group Cream with Eric Clapton. And, they were managed by one of my most ardent enemies, Robert Stigwood. That in itself should have set off all kinds of alarms for me but for some reason, maybe just the gamble that there was no tight connection between Stigwood and Windfall, I chose to believe that an opportunity had arrived in the nick of time.

I was introduced to a man named Gary who took me to an office where we had a short conversation about my recent past. It left him with the knowledge that I was desperate. He was apparently high up in the organization and stated that he was involved with one of their publishing companies, Lucifer Music. I didn't think too much of their choice in names. In fact, if they hadn't been as successful as they appeared to be, I would have thought it a childish choice. After I met with Gary, I waited to meet the man who would one day define the word "hate" for me. If I were to eventually prove to be a truly evil child, then this man would prove to be my mother. Before this experience was over, I would be crippled in the music business for decades.

I was led to another office and introduced to a man named Bud Prager. Mr. Prager was fit and trim and spoke in a calm, deliberate tone. He looked much younger than I'm sure he was, and I took it to be a sign of the attributes and privileges of wealth. He lived in Montauk on Long Island, had a full head of wavy white hair, and carried an air of conceit. He was both big and little at the same time, and while there was a picture of his family on his desk, his ego blushed with infidelity. Even though Mr. Prager didn't say or do any one thing in particular I, nonetheless, became uncomfortable with his condescending language and attitude. "A star like you," or "A star with your reputation," he said. I totally missed the facetiousness of his tone. His patronizing strokes were being telegraphed from the other side of Manhattan, but my desperation chose to see it as something other than what it really was. If you toss a beggar a quarter onto the street as you walk by and otherwise ignore him, he will hate you with all of his being, but he will pick up your quarter and use it.

He asked questions about what needs I wanted to be met in our contract, which made no sense to me at all. And he never asked if I wanted a lawyer. The dance continued. He said, "How much do you want to make a year?" I didn't know what he was talking about so I said, "I'm sorry, what do you mean?" He smiled and said, "You know, we have to put in the contract how much you need to make a year. Then if you don't make it, the contract is, you know, no good. How much do you want to make a year, two hundred thousand?"

I just couldn't imagine that kind of money. The whole conversation didn't seem real, but it was and he kept pressing me for an answer. Finally, I said, "Two hundred thousand, that's a lot of money. . . ." He stopped me and said, "Well then, pick a number." The concept of projecting a future income, especially one so large, was so far removed from my reality. Plus, the idea that anyone would attempt to guarantee such a high figure in penalty of breach of contract completely baffled me, but at his insistence I gave him a figure. It was, after all, only imaginary money. It was a game and I was a fool.

Prager told me they had been discussing my arrival and had big plans for me. He was anxious to get things started and offered me a contract that would pay me twelve hundred dollars a month for the first year of the contract. That was a monetary figure I could somewhat grasp the importance of, and it meant Kim and I could finally have our own place again. The thought of recording again with powerful management behind me, along with the money to pick Kim and me up from the horrible condition we had fallen to, and the fact that someone still thought of me as a star worth promoting . . . it was all too much for me.

After the meeting and in a moment of true thankfulness, joy, and salvation I said, "Thank you, Bud. Thank you very much. I love you." In the only instance he would ever be honest with me again, Prager said, "Don't say that. There will come a time when you won't feel that way."

What should have served as a warning was tossed aside while my trembling hand waited to sign the contracts. The first check arrived and Kim and I immediately set up house in an apartment in Farmington Hills. We thanked Uncle George and Aunt Erika for everything and moved what little we owned.

I began to write songs again; it had been so long. I even looked to the future with hope. I stayed true to my craft and when I spoke to Prager he'd say, "We're trying to get you a recording contract." I was curious about who they might be approaching, as

I still had a contract with Paramount, but I stayed out of the way and asked no questions.

Another check arrived and another month of songwriting and dreaming swept my emotions to happiness. I was feeling very positive and asked Susan to let my children visit. Soon, Dawn and Joel began visiting more frequently than they had in the previous two years. We were actually getting to know each other all over again and were having fun. Joel sometimes became upset and missed the comfort of his mother's love, but we tried to fight those urges. Joel and I had never gotten a chance to become close, since I left him when he was still in a crib. His insecurity was to be expected.

Dawn, on the other hand, had already become her daddy's girl and a veteran traveler by the time Joel was born, and our love for each other didn't need to be proven. We had missed each other much more than I was aware. The children were still young enough to bathe together and we played games and I tape recorded the sounds of my children's laughter as they played in the tub or in their room.

I also began to care for Kim in a way I never had before, and I surprised myself with such a good feeling. I wanted to protect Kim and help her heal. I was actually falling in love. Of course, I was unaware of just how sick I was.

We had, as far as I could tell, both given up drugs and drinking. Spring arrived and it was the first spring I remembered enjoying in such a long time that I wished it would never end. I walked in the evenings with Kim and reassured her about our future. I told her I was going to reward her for her patience, her sacrifice, her love, and her belief in me. The welcome warm winds of renewal blew around us and I could breathe again.

It's funny how money works.

Chapter 21

THE DISTRUST AND LOATHING BETWEEN ARTIST and management that now existed in the form of the contracts I had been offered said volumes about how the business had changed in the years between 1964 and 1973. Lawyers. Even the contracts themselves were referred to as an exhibit, as if there was an anticipation of litigation connected to them. Well, it was inevitable given the fact that my band and I were only one in thousands of artists who had millions and millions of dollars ripped away from them by thieves known as managers and producers. The "business practitioners," on the other hand, had to deal with the sometimes ungrateful and unreasonable egos of talent that, had they not been promoted by the slime-laced and well-connected scam-artist music establishment, could not have gotten arrested with their song and dance.

Prager's contracts went unread by me and I blindly threw my trust into his hands. These were the same hands that liked to sit on beds during interviews and pound his chest while talking about how artists were endeared to his heart through their courage and sacrifice. Apparently his belief centered around the idea that the greatest music came from extreme and carefully thought out, well-placed pain.

What I needed was money.

For the longest time I struggled with what transpired during my time with Prager. I created two different scenarios for what played out during the course of that relationship. The first came about because I was unable to comprehend a human being so cruel and mean-spirited, as I eventually perceived Prager to be, and so I brought myself to believe that I was somehow at fault for the collapse of the relationship. After all, here was a man who managed a successful act known as Mountain, and when he told me I was one of the greatest things to hit the music scene since white bread, didn't I owe it to him to believe him? He was in a position to know. He dealt with the big boys every day. He told me a starving public awaited the return of Mitch Ryder. He had given me everything I asked for and went out of his way to remake me into the star of the stature I deserved.

I told myself I let him down at every turn. I failed him. What was wrong with me that I could allow myself to hurt a believing, hardworking, dedicated, loyal, honest, and truthful manager to the point that I had broken his heart?

Prager's gallant attempts to resurrect me began this way. First, pull the star up from the poverty he was dealing with. Give him some stability and security. Instruct him to begin writing and have him put together a band. My recording contract with Paramount Records was still in force as a result of Bob Crewe's transfer of recording rights to Famous Music years earlier. This became a big topic of conversation between Prager and me. Prager couldn't get Paramount to release me, probably because he wasn't offering them anything of substance to help recoup the tremendous beating they took from Crewe. I liked to think they cared so much about me that they were trying to protect me from the slowly unfolding sinister plot Prager was hatching.

Prager then induced me to write a letter to Famous Music in which I demanded to be released and further stated that I had never been happy with them and had tried on many occasions to remove myself from the contract. It was true that I was not happy with their performance, but the rest was a lie. There were some great talents beyond the artists at Paramount. Paramount finally, under tremendous pressure from Prager and his attorney, Mr. Allen Arrow, relented. I was free. But now, for the first time since I started my recording career, I was without ties to a label and was at the mercy of my recording agreement with Prager.

Prager suggested the time was right to put together a band that I could take into the studio. I held auditions and after a few weeks came up with a very nice group of players: Timmy Schaffe on bass, Fred "Sonic" Smith on guitar, Wayne Kramer on guitar, and K.C. Watkins on drums.

We began rehearsing many of the tunes I had written over the past months, and also began putting together a stage show. Everyone needed to work and I wasn't provided with a budget for the project, unless I chose to totally deplete the advance money I was being provided for the year. We were now approaching the halfway point of the initial one-year term and I was enthusiastic over the prospect of once again recording. It was at this moment that Prager chose to begin applying in earnest his "management skills."

Prager wanted me to join a tour with Leslie West, the great guitar player from Mountain. The show would be called the Wild West Show. I didn't understand. I asked what I was supposed to do with my band, since we had already invested much time and effort, and he stated I would have to let them go, since he felt the tour with Leslie was much more important to my career. It was very disappointing to everyone. In fact, some of the guys were quite pissed off. At our last gathering I said I was going out for some cigarettes and I never returned. I didn't have what it took to debate the injustice I had just dealt them.

The tour was hard for me. I knew something was at work that I couldn't reconcile, and I began to question Prager's motives. I was doing what I was asked to do, and then suddenly that was ripped out from under me for no logical reason. In my mind, the band was more important than the tour.

I felt alone and without friends for the entire tour, not that I had ever felt differently, and I couldn't talk to Leslie because he was always high on cocaine. Near the end of the tour I was putting down a fifth of Jack Daniel's just to get myself on stage. After the tour, I stopped drinking and returned to writing songs with no clear goal in view, amidst ambiguous and infrequent communication with Prager. One day he called and said he wanted me to fly to Philadelphia for a "meeting" with him and Philadelphia International Records.

I arrived only to find it was an audition, which I had not been informed of and was totally unprepared for. I was greatly embarrassed and noticed an attitude of enjoyment on Prager's part at witnessing my failure to perform anything improvised or original. He essentially was saying, "Here you are you great star, exactly what I know you to be. Nothing."

The money soon came to an end. I no longer had a recording contract, which Prager had seen to. My band no longer existed and I was starting to panic. Then I received the following letter from Prager. His fun was about to begin.

Dear Mitch:

Without going into great detail, after working together for one year it looks like this. We've advanced you $11,649.69. In addition, we spent time and money, including legal fees, in obtaining your record release from Paramount, something that none of your previous managers and attorneys could accomplish. We put you on the Wild West Show, from which you earned $3,517.50 without paying commission or offering to reimburse us in any way.

After that you decided to form your own band. Thus far you've failed to keep any band together long enough for me to bring people to hear it. This, even though I had one company that would have put up $100,000 if they could hear and like you and your band.

During the past year I have tried to make a record deal for you. But it is not easy. Almost every company that knows you or knows of you does not want to be involved with you. The people who previously dealt with you for some reason or other want no further involvement with you. We've had turndowns from Columbia, Atlantic, MCA, Capital, Mercury, and

Island. GRT was interested if they can see you live. The one company that was really interested, Philadelphia International, you blew by being totally unprepared for the audition.

Now when I put it together with Denny Cordell and Shelter, your lack of cooperation and inability to oblige is absolutely shocking. It almost appears that you have no interest in a recording career.

We've certainly tried and we've certainly paid. Whenever you're ready to do your part let me know. I'm sure you can find some record companies that want you, so be sure to keep us posted. Meantime we'll keep looking.

Sincerely,
E.S. Prager.

I couldn't understand or find any logic as to why Prager was trying to frustrate me at every turn, lie to me, and then try to turn everything around in an effort to blame me for following what were clearly his directions. As far as my previous "managers and attorneys" were concerned, I never asked Barry Kramer or John Sinclair to get me released from Paramount. And, the idea that I owed Prager commissions from the Wild West Show puzzled me. They had control of the money and, I assumed by reading the contract, that they were to take out their commissions before they paid me. That was, and is, the common practice.

The assertion that I couldn't keep a band together long enough for Prager to have an interested party view it was a bold faced lie. Prager himself told me to disband the group I had assembled. As far as a company being willing to put up a hundred thousand dollars, I had never been informed of such a situation.

Why Prager felt it necessary to inform me of the many great record companies that had rejected me because they didn't want to be involved with me finally opened my eyes. This man and this letter were meant to hurt and demean me. Now it was clear why he hadn't told me the truth about the meeting in Philadelphia. But his philosophy was taking root at some level, because I now realized I was standing next to an enemy.

I was now operating at such a heightened state of insecurity that when the offer to be involved with British producer Denny Cordell appeared, if there was in fact such an offer, I did not feel trusting enough to pursue it. I remembered when Barry Kramer was my manager we had a meeting in the state of Washington with Denny and Leon Russell. They were looking for a singer to be a part of a project they later called "Mad Dogs and Englishmen." I didn't fear Denny, and if he was indeed trying to contact me, I apologize. I did fear Prager. The only part of Prager's letter that was true was the statement that I no longer had an interest in a recording career, at least not with him.

Here was a powerful, successful man who was obviously trying to harm me and I struggled with the distasteful question of why? What had I done to him that would cause this behavior toward me? When he first sought me out it was obvious to everyone that I was foundering and about to go under. I hadn't approached him making claims to be a super star or the chance to be back on top. That notion was decades away. I hadn't approached him at all. To the contrary, I was so close to finally getting out of the business, so bruised and beaten, that the only roadblock to that end would be the one final crushing blow that I was most certainly now receiving.

Prager called himself a genius of sorts: a guy at the top with good connections. So, it made sense to me that he was experienced enough to know what my value in the market place was worth. If the long list of rejections by various recording companies was true, it should have come as no surprise to him. But he wasn't finished with me yet.

Prager continued to deride and bait me with his sarcasm and said if I sent him some new music he would make one final attempt at getting me a deal. The money had been shut off, but Kim had been saving a little behind my back and she hesitantly offered it to me for the studio I had booked.

I only had enough to cover one hour at a nearby studio that was being run by a legendary Detroit engineer named Danny Dallas. I walked into the studio completely at a loss where to begin, and sat down at the beautiful baby grand in the middle of the otherwise empty floor. Danny asked how I wanted to approach the session and I told him I had no idea, but to go ahead and start rolling the tape.

I sat there for a long time with my head bowed staring at the keys and then I lifted my hands to the keyboard and began to play. I established the left hand bass line on a three-note pattern and added the minor key chords with my right hand in 4/4 time. I opened my mouth and began to sing and didn't stop until the song was finished. When it was over, I just sat there and everyone was silent. I had never before in my life touched a keyboard. I also couldn't remember the words or the melody I had just performed. It had all just appeared from nowhere.

The song would gloriously outlive my experience with Prager and become one of my most cherished writings. I called it "Freezin' in Hell." There wasn't anything extremely innovative about the lyrics, they were just a blues-type message with classical root notes underneath, but it was the way it came to life through the power of something beyond comprehension that made it special.

I sent a copy to Prager, hoping that whatever offense I had brought to His Majesty, he was now ready to forgive and begin treating me nicely again. I wanted to hear back from him. He didn't respond, so I called and finally got him on the phone. He said it was good but he wanted to hear more. Much more. He also said he was disgusted with my behavior, my attitude, and my inability to produce. He said with no hidden sarcasm to keep in touch and let him know how I was doing. My heart sank and I went to Kim, broken and defeated.

While all this was going on Prager had been promoting me as an important artist or actually, more cynically, as an artist who thought he was important. He sent this message and promoted this image to whatever segment of the industry that was willing to listen. There were a lot of humorous characterizations of my behavior and the dilemma I found myself in being played out and circulated within the industry. I became a joke. Some of my friends in Detroit were aware of what was going on and asked me why I had done this to myself. I had no answer.

I was hurting emotionally, spiritually, and financially. Nameless people began calling my phone and threatening my life. The fear of my suspicions over Prager's intentions and actions had driven me to get a prescription from a doctor for Valium to quiet my nerves, and I had also begun taking a powerful, halucinogenic street drug that was derived from THC, an animal tranquilizer.

I forgot about my music and began writing a series of rambling discourses that covered my protestations and unhappiness with the world in general. These culminated in a proposed amendment to the Constitution of the United States titled "White Male Liberation." It declared that all of the ill will, hate, war, and rage that mankind was presently experiencing was the result of white male control of society, and that white males needed to change their course if peace and happiness were ever to be secured for all the world. In my drugged state and through my tears, it appeared to be the answer.

In an extremely emotional fit I fired it off to Prager, who received it with great rage and anger. The document was circulated through whatever means he had devised and the resounding laughter and disgust from inside and outside of the industry tore right through my soul.

Chapter 22

THE SECOND SCENARIO I CREATED FROM my relationship with Prager was that I received powerful paybacks from the industry I had alienated. Felix Pappalardi, the original bass player for Mountain had produced the first American hit album for the band Cream with Eric Clapton. Prager, being working partners with Robert Stigwood, put himself in as henchman for my former managers, Robert Fitzpatrick and good old Robert Stigwood. They had conspired to mentally and financially stretch me to the breaking point, embarrass me, and even tempt me to suicide.

A few years later, Robert Stigwood, finding that I had not succeeded in killing myself, launched his premier and failing label, RSO Records. He allowed his company four major releases with a group called The Rockets. The group consisted of two main players, both original Detroit Wheels: Jimmy McCarty and Johnny Badanjek. Much to Stigwood's dismay, the group never was able to rival the success of Mitch Ryder and the Detroit Wheels. Poor Stigwood. I had auditioned for the group and was turned down by Jimmy and Johnny—just for you folks who keep asking "Why don't you guys get back together?"

Anyway, back to the damage done by Prager. I remember it as a quiet, cold but sunny afternoon. Kim was in the living room reading and I was lying down in our bedroom. I didn't know how to share my depression and fear with Kimberly and I realized it was a terrible burden to her, but in spite of that, she made attempts to comfort me. When I explained the conspiracy theory to her it sounded crazy, and hard for anyone to believe, but it was what had happened. That afternoon she came into the room to check on me and said she wanted to get away from the apartment for a while; did I want to join her? I said I wasn't up to it, but to go ahead without me and I would be just fine. As the door closed behind her bringing back the silence, I thought how much we had been through together and how little happiness we had enjoyed in the course of our struggle. I doubted her love, so how could I ask her to go through another day of this madness? I thought about that time so far distant when I had first walked up to a microphone and discovered the magic of God's gift to me, and how uncomplicated His love had been presented. I would never know that in such an innocent way again.

I lay there and played back my accomplishments and disappointments in my big "star" career. I felt the shame, embarrassment, and ridicule I was bringing to my family, friends, and my city. I thought about my high school friends and wished it were possible to go back with Tommy Theut, Tom and Jerry Moore, Jim Moscow and Joey Kubert. To be safe. To be able to laugh again. I thought about my children and what their future would be with a famous and now infamous father who couldn't manage to support himself.

I had taken a job at a nearby gas station pumping gas in the winter, but the money was nothing and I kept getting sick. People recognized me, and some were mean and others just laughed. Kim and I were facing another eviction and I thought about Prager, who had brought me to this point. I was in an unbreakable bind. I took his contract to the musician's union headquarters to see if they could help, and all they did was shake their heads in sympathy.

I decided I wasn't going to go through it all again. I was tired and beaten. There are so many more persuasive and compelling arguments for a person to consider taking their own life, but at the same time suicide is an extremely subjective personal deliberation and each individual can be the only judge of how much they can handle. I was weak from the beginning, and my chances of finding the courage, strength, and faith to go on was being drawn from an empty moral reservoir.

In some instances it takes more courage to end your life than to continue on in a situation where the end result is a foregone conclusion. It was the fact that I had sacrificed everything and everybody for self and ego that I now stood alone with nowhere to turn. People who could have cared were afraid, because I had put so much space between us, always making sure to never let anyone get too close.

I had never been instilled with enough fear of God to keep me from making my choice, so I went to the kitchen, took out a quart of beer and swallowed it down. I then went to the bathroom and took out of the medicine cabinet two prescription bottles. One was a brand new prescription for thirty ten-milligram Halcion, and the other was filled with twenty-five twenty-milligram muscle relaxers. I threw them down and washed them through with some vodka. Then I went back to the bedroom, pulled out a quarter gram of THC, and snorted it down.

Going back to the bed I stopped to get a pen and paper so I could tell Kim I was sorry and tell my children I loved them. Isn't that about the sickest thing you've ever heard? It is for me, and I was the one who did it. When I felt the lethal combination start to take hold I began my letter to Kim. I was sad, but relieved that there would now be some peace. At least for me. As I continued to write my letter, I felt myself slipping away. I couldn't write anymore and I lay my head down on the pillow and said goodbye to the world.

As if Woody Allen had written the script, Kim returned unexpectedly early and dragged my limp, unconscious body to the car and rushed me to Botsford Hospital. When I first awoke I saw the hoses used to pump my stomach and the I.V. dripping life-saving fluid into my veins. Then I turned my head sideways and saw two uniformed state police officers. They asked me over and over where I had gotten the heroin. I didn't have any heroin and hadn't had any for well over a year. Finally they left.

Kim came into the room and stroked my hair as I lay there realizing I had failed. I began to cry and she said not to think about anything or to worry, that she would take care of everything. Uncle George and Aunt Erika had again offered their home as sanctuary and we drove back there in silence. Some days later we all drove back to the apartment and moved out all of our belongings.

Prager tried to exploit the incident for laughs, but to his disappointment not everyone was willing to share anymore. The hospital was kind enough to list the occurrence as an accidental overdose and would eventually lose the records altogether.

The hardest part of the aftermath was the lingering perception by many, as advanced by Prager, that I didn't have the talent or the courage it took to become a huge star. According to him, the suicide attempt was unfortunate, but only served to underscore my weakness under his demanding management. The idea was that I couldn't handle the pressure. Yes, I could, and had under Bob Crewe. I did, however, have difficulty handling the targeted and hateful pressure directed at me for the sole purpose of destroying me. The idea of not being able to handle the pressure was Prager's representation to his cadre of hyenas as he pled his innocence of culpability in the matter. I reject that and call him what he is. A coward. I know, because I was cut from the same cloth. The premise that you must attempt to destroy someone to get them to produce your desired result is evil by concept and nature. So, dear Bud, alas. You were evil. I am not at all sorry to report that he died in 2008.

This is about paybacks in a business that lacks morals and ethics, and I don't mean politics. If he was anything at all, Prager was persistent and the punishment continued.

The easiest part of the aftermath for me was my willingness to commit to the notion that I no longer wanted to chase success. That was probably because I was too stupid to realize I had already achieved it. Some months prior to the suicide attempt, Kim and I had taken a train trip to Denver, Colorado to see my older sister, Nina. This was at the height of Prager's efforts to shine the spotlight on me. As we walked through the station and approached the platform, I was so paranoid that I actually carried with me an unsheathed and loaded rifle that I held close to my side. As we continued on we were flanked by two photographers who were flashing away. I reasoned they were either from the press or the government. Then, while sitting in our seats for the Chicago leg of the trip, a Catholic priest took a seat across from me and began praying aloud.

Now we were making that trip again, only this time I had such an overwhelming feeling of relief at having gotten out of the music business alive that I hardly had a care in the world. When we arrived in Denver I went into a long convalescence hidden away in the back of an aging mansion my sister Nina had acquired to do her spiritual work in. I was exactly the image of Humpty-Dumpty, cracked head and all. My body's systems were taxed to the point that I could have died under any more pressure.

The day we arrived I had to throw up and instead of the usual barf, something resembling a long dehydrated turd came slowly up from my throat. Months passed before I felt strong enough or safe enough to venture outside. Nina's husband, Willy Trobaugh, and I began to go on fishing outings and on one occasion were followed and observed by a young man with a camera and a quick little car who ended up getting a blurb somewhere in *National Lampoon*.

Other than that, two things happened of great importance. Under the awesome power and beauty of the Rocky Mountains, life became more tolerable and my fear slowly melted away. Now there was peace and time, and the opportunity for privacy and reflection. I never heard from or saw Prager again.

The second important thing to occur was the empty slot in Detroit that could now be filled by the next talented local boy or girl. The whole Mitch Ryder ordeal distracted away from the natural creative process for which my city is world renowned.

Chapter 23

MY SISTER WILLINA, WHO PREFERRED THE NAME Nina, had quite an interesting life going for herself. She had established a church for lost and searching souls, and was in the process of creating a ranch near the foothills of the Rockies where she and her considerable following could go to be away from the madness of modern society. I, naturally, found their motivation all too familiar and was intrigued by the fact that other humans could share in my desire to rid their lives of an age and time that found itself wrought with cynicism and hurtful behavior.

It was the time of Watergate, and the media took on a new importance and level of power they wouldn't have dreamed they could hold just a few scant years earlier. Richard Nixon had just been driven from the presidency by the media. No one else. The country plunged into a deep period of introspection and self-whippings that could be the envy of any radical fundamentalist Islamic religious student.

I sat in my sister's library for hours and read volumes of religious and spiritual writings by her, and others, and always walked away feeling a great desire to learn more about this philosophy of love for mankind. It was in direct conflict with the prevailing attitude of society at that point. It was also ironic that I would be reunited with my best friend Nina after all these years. When we were small children, it was my big sister Nina who watched over me and protected me from everything dangerous—real or imagined. Such a long passage of time for two different worlds to finally come together as one.

I had spiritually evolved to a place I would never have dreamed possible in light of my past, but it was unlike any death bed conversion I had heard or read about. It wasn't about finding God after man had brought me down. It was, instead, a cautious examination of self, guarded by a distrust for any human influence, and depended mostly on a communion with nature and the simple beauty of life in it's most uncomplicated forms. It was about the re-awakening of all living things under a warm, spring sun after a hard, cruel winter. It was the birth of a child before the parents had an opportunity to imprint their mistakes and ignorance. It was about renewal without conditions, and help without a price. But mostly, it was about learning to love myself along with the world that exists outside of "civilization." The quiet world. It was about love for more than one.

Nina was my teacher and she shared, by word and example, all that she had learned on her journey to enlightenment. As time passed, and within the first year as her guest, I felt strong enough to face the world, and Kimberly, through her gift of patience, was still willing to face it with me.

Nina wanted me to go more deeply into her world but I felt, with some misgivings, that the communal experience, which had been badly tainted by John Sinclair's vision, was not to my liking. And so, Kimberly and I set about finding employment in the "outside world." Having been involved in music from the age of sixteen, and not feeling safe enough to go back to it, I chose the only work my past had prepared me for. I became a common laborer.

My first job was hanging gutters for one of the church members who had a business doing seamless gutters. That's where I met Forrest and Doll. They were great people from down Louisiana somewhere, but the job didn't last very long once my fear of heights was exposed.

My second job was the only other work I did while in Colorado. I became a warehouse worker for a chemical and scientific supply company called Sargent-Welch. I made friends, but the inevitable question always worked its way to the top. What are you doing here?

Kimberly had gotten a job working for one of the Coors boys and together we now had enough money to get our own place. I don't know how to fully explain how good that made us feel. We no longer had to live on the edge wondering where our next meal was coming from. As long as we remained healthy we could depend on a paycheck every week. We could make commitments and keep them. We could have some order in our lives. This probably sounds crazy to anyone who hates their job and the boring regimen of an eight-hour day, day after day, year after year, but you have to understand that we had never known the security of any constant in our lives. We had been stuck in that "glamorous" world of show business and our little jobs, as petty and unimportant as they might seem to anyone else, were a big deal to us.

Denver, Colorado, as compared to New York City, was pretty laid back, but it had a subterranean cosmopolitan air that stopped short of the gates of Hell, which made nightlife for the adventurous something to do. We didn't hang out that much because we were pretty wiped out after work each day. We usually ended up at the pool or a barbecue, took in a movie or, more often than not, headed to the mountains.

Kimberly and I decided that we were going to get married. A retired judge performed the ceremony, and Nina and Willy stood up for us. The reception was held at Nina's mansion and Kimberly and I both felt relieved after it was all over. I was actually afraid she might have said no, given all that she knew about me—especially the suicide thing. She certainly could have done a hell of a lot better than me. So we happily faced the future with the promise of peace and contentment before us, blindly overlooking the shit trail whose path reached all the way to our assholes.

This, I think, would have been the perfect place to end this story, but that is what is so fucked up about my life. And that is what most people don't understand about music.

◆

I admit to the unbreakable addiction of adoration and fame, but beyond that is the reward of the creative process itself, which, without the above-mentioned by-products is enough to sustain the drive and motivation of the artist. Music was my first love, but I also enjoyed writing, poetry, sketching, and oil painting, and after work each day and as a continuation of the therapy I had begun at Nina's, I began to use those mediums to express the visions and feelings I had kept bottled up all day at work.

My oil paintings were a source of great satisfaction and I would, years later, adopt them as album covers on the music and lyrics I wrote while in Colorado. I also wrote poems, some of which also found their way onto future recordings. But for the moment, it was enough to experience the fulfillment of creation, and I threw myself into the process using every available amount of time at my disposal. During my four and one half year stay in Colorado, I finished seven oil paintings, twelve watercolor and charcoal/pencil/pen and ink sketch books, two books of poetry, twenty-seven songs with music and lyrics, and a complete novel of fiction.

I was not completely removed from live performances either. Obviously, I had not been allowed to keep any of my royalties and therefore I couldn't sit back to take a breather from music. It pissed me off when music industry people said I had left the music scene. Artists who had control of their money and the luxury of taking years off between projects were not being labeled as having left. I found musicians, we made demos, performed for prisons and homes for mentally challenged individuals, and did charity fund raisers. What the hell, in many cases they were more worthy of my efforts than a paying audience would have been.

It was during this time that Bob Seger broke through nationally with the Silver Bullet Band. In truth, he deserved to be on top long before this. And so it was with joy and anticipation that I listened to a live broadcast Bob was doing that was affiliated with the local rock radio station and broadcast all over Denver. I did stop to scratch my head when he gleefully tore into an original song called "Gang Bang," which pretty much was about the title. Kind of a "Lock and Load" that slipped under the radar. My mind was content to know that the empty slot had been filled upon my vacating the territory. Music was on my mind every day.

Dawn and Joel came out to visit, which lifted my spirits immensely. Dawn, more than Joel, had missed me terribly and cried when she had to say goodbye and go back home. She wanted to stay with me, but I promised she would come back again soon, and she did. Kimberly and I also took a trip to Tennessee to visit my mother's folks. Dawn made the journey with us and we flew Joel down to join us.

I caused a scene at the airport because I had gotten a reservation number for a car and a price, and I came prepared with the money and the confirmation number, then the agent refused to give me a car because I had no credit card. Our whole trip, the time off from work, the meeting of the family . . . all lay at risk. I became outraged to the point that people were pulling their children away from the rental car area. The manager took pity on my poverty, lack of certifiable societal affiliation and gave me a car that was barely running, but we made the trip.

I missed my children a great deal, but Kimberly was different. She was nice to them because at that time she was a nice person, and she also wanted me to be happy. But she was afraid to love Dawn and Joel. After several years I became increasingly restless and did not want to continue to see my children grow up in front of me with only two short visits a year. I knew I had no life with Susan, but I wanted a life with my children while they were still young.

Kimberly and I talked about how we could accomplish that. The most agonizing issue revolved around whether or not I would re-enter live performing. I still did not want to return to the stage but the reality, especially from the financial point of view, left little room for compromise. Our combined income per week was something less than three hundred dollars, and we knew that would not be enough to make it in Detroit. Still, I refused to go back on stage. So, we agreed on a compromise because we were both anxious, for reasons of our own, to return home. Given my great mistrust of the music industry my compromise was demanding and I was hard pressed to find a way to make it happen. But as I said, most people don't know what goes on in the world of music. Kimberly would have to get a job that would support the two of us until my plan could be realized. It was almost as if she was supporting me while I made my way through my particular education of higher learning.

Chapter 24

ON THE LONG DRIVE BACK TO Detroit, as the Rockies grew smaller in the rear view mirror and finally disappeared altogether, Kimberly and I talked in quiet tones about fond memories we had taken to our hearts and wondered if we would ever see our friends from Colorado again. I certainly knew that I could not have survived without the love and care of my sister Nina when we first arrived. Beyond the friends and loved ones, though, was Colorado itself and the magnificent beauty of the mountain lakes and streams, the clear open spaces, and the number of days in the year during which the sun shined.

In Detroit we would return to a climate in which the sun would generally disappear from the end of October until the beginning of May. And then there was the intuitive sense that as we geographically came closer to Detroit the negative energy became more pronounced, something we both agreed did, in fact, exist. The journey did not end without sadness, however, because we had brought along a cat we had taken in as a stray. She had been with us for more than two years in Colorado. As we pulled up to Kimberly's parent's house and opened the car door, however, the cat bolted out and we never saw her again. We must have stopped ten or eleven times on the trip back, sometimes in the open desert at night and that cat always returned to us—and the car. Not this time.

Everything else aside, we were re-united with our families. Kimberly and I settled in with Russ and Dora, Kim's parents, and Kim began looking for a job. I applied for and received thirteen weeks of unemployment insurance and everyday, after half-hearted attempts at finding work, wrote lyrics and composed music. Kimberly landed a very good job with the Xerox Corporation and we started looking for a place to live. Near the end of our stay at her parents' house I was outside trimming a shrub when a car pulled up to the house and out stepped a young man who would open the next chapter of my musical life. His name was Billy Csernits.

I had been laying low and was surprised that anyone was able to find me, but apparently Kim's father, Russ, had mentioned to one of his co-workers at Ford Motor Company that his son-in-law, Mitch Ryder, was back in Detroit and living at his home.

Billy explained that the co-worker was his father and that when his father mentioned my presence he was compelled to seek me out because I was one of his heroes. We talked for a while about what he was doing in music and what I had been doing. I was guarded at first, but Billy had a calming effect on me. Plus, I trusted Kimberly's father a great deal and didn't believe he would expose me to a situation that would bring me harm. Actually, I think he just wanted me out of his place.

The conversation with Billy didn't last all that long but I found myself enjoying his company enough to agree to get together again. Neither of us knew it at the time, but Billy would become my most trusted friend and confidant in the years to come. Billy would help me understand and serve as my window to the new generation of music and musicians that had evolved in the years of my absence from live performances. He would also become my new spiritual guide.

I had spent a great deal of time thinking about how I would re-enter the music business and had developed a plan that, at first glance, almost guaranteed failure because of the inherent exclusionary foundation from outsiders. I wasn't in a very trusting mood. I had been maligned, ripped-off, conspired against, and treated badly, and I was fond of quoting an acquaintance who often said, "Just because everyone's out to get you doesn't mean you're not paranoid."

I was going to make another recording and I was going to control every inch of it. There was no reason to believe anyone still cared whether or not there was a new Mitch Ryder recording. What mattered to me was my quest—which goes on even today—to provide an account of my growth and progression as an artist in the world of music. People have hit records and some will go on for a while and others will fade away. Even though I was not in the consciousness of the buying public, I wanted to continue to fulfill my destiny and pay gratitude for the gift I had been blessed with. All the other stuff, the material belongings, the women, the drugs, the perversities, the ego trips, the money, the self-serving pleasures . . . a waste of time. For some reason, we define success in this country in monetary terms. That is true even with our public servants. But I've never had any money to speak of. What has messed with me every waking hour of my existence is fame.

I decided that on my next recording I would write all of the music and lyrics. When I say write all of the music, that meant the musicians, for the most part, would play the chord patterns and beats to my requirements. I would own all of the publishing, I would create the cover and liner notes and credits. I would produce the recording, own the label, and direct distribution of the product. Naïve would be a workable word for such an ambitious plan, but I would settle for nothing less because it was in all of these areas and more that I had been taken advantage of.

It was in this frame of mind that Billy introduced me to an acquaintance of his named Tom Conner. Our first meeting took place at a huge warehouse out of which Billy and Tom were supposedly doing interior van customizing. When I arrived at the site I walked through the front door into what was supposed to be the lobby office. There was an empty desk, a lone chair, a small space heater, and a telephone on the floor that, in light of the exposed multi-colored wires that had been spliced together, had obviously been illegally hooked up. There was no one there so I walked through a door that led to the warehouse. There was a Lotus sports car and way over on the other side of the cavernous building was a small chest of tools. Great, I said to myself, a drug dealer. Just what I need. A fucking warehouse front for a drug dealer.

I turned to leave through the lobby and bumped into Tom Connor. The last thing on earth that Tom looked like was a drug dealer. He looked like Mr. McFeely, the friendly postman from *Mister Rogers' Neighborhood*. He had the kind of friendly smile that could stop a small child from crying or put a small animal at ease. Tom had dabbled in music, among other things, and had at one time been assigned to the first nuclear powered Merchant Marine ship. He was an impassioned opportunistic entrepreneur whose light hearted view of the world came to serve us very well, considering what I was going to be asking of him.

We didn't speak long but agreed to meet at a restaurant for a strategy session that included young Billy. I was nervous about the meeting and hadn't yet gotten to know Billy and Tom very well, so I ended up drinking way more than I should have. That probably would have killed any deal I might have made had it not been for the fascinating and convincing plan I laid out before them.

I had been drug and alcohol free for almost five years and had only started drinking again while we stayed at Kim's parent's home. Her father loved to drink rum and coke, and that quickly became my drink of choice. In the past, sometimes months—and several times in my life, years—went by without drugs or alcohol.

Kimberly's father actually became something of a surrogate father to me. He was ex-military, decisive, and seemingly in control, and I gravitated to that in a big way. Compared to my father, Russ was powerful. Even with his advice in hand, I approached the recording task in front of me with a great deal of caution.

The first recording I made with Billy and Tom was nothing more than a vocal over-dub on an already existing track called "Long Hard Road." The lyrics had been written by someone else. This was the nature of my relationship with Tom for some time, as we struggled to understand each other better and worked toward feeling comfortable enough to start a partnership. A little project here and there to test the waters, measuring and testing each facet of our individual strengths.

Eventually we came to the point where, even though my demands seemed excessive, Tom was willing to work within the framework I had insisted on because he believed in my talent. Now feeling comfortable with Tom, and Tom with me, we agreed that there would have to be new product and we formed a record company together called Seeds and Stems.

Tom had set up shop in his farmhouse out in the country and had been nurturing an idea for an album even before he met me. He wanted to do an album called *Michigan Rocks* and wanted to market it by mail order only. He set about acquiring the licenses and rights for a variety of songs by Michigan artists and our first release became a reality. Although it had been greeted with small success, we were inspired enough to begin discussing my first album. We were dealing with seven different independent distributors, and they all had to be organized in a manner that allowed for coordinated promotion, a recording budget, and a synchronized method of payment to preserve a tolerable cash flow.

As far as the band was concerned, Billy and I, with Tom's help, assembled a group that was made up of Billy on keyboards, Wilson Owens on drums, Mark Gougeon on bass, and Joe Gutc on guitar. Next to the Detroit Wheels this configuration, with a few interchangeable years between Wayne Gabriel and Rick Schein on guitar, proved to be the most powerful and talented group of musicians I had the pleasure of recording and performing with to this point. In some instances they excelled beyond the Wheels because of their versatility and openness to experiment. I also had Billy Lee.

Billy Lee, as a member of the Peps and the Detroit Wheels, lasted three and a half years. The big band, Spirit Feel, never realized full potential and lasted roughly two years, The band Detroit, a powerful but destructive entity, also lasted around two years. Now there was the group I would come to call the Thrashing Brothers. The Thrashing Brothers lasted longer than any of the others for many reasons, one being Tom Connor's reliable stint at the helm.

There were other musicians, some for a day, some for a month, some even for a year, but these above-mentioned groups were, basically, the groups I recorded with. I'm sorry that Spirit Feel never had a chance for the public to hear their interactions with me in the studio, but I do have a completed album of just such a thing, and at some time in the future I will place it in the natural sequence of events.

As usual, there wasn't enough money to lay back and record at will, so we were forced to perform live. This made me unhappy because I wanted to focus on making the best recording of my career. I wanted to prove to the world that the New York music industry was being punitive and vengeful, and by creating a work whose artistry could not be denied, I would restore my rightful place in the history of rock and roll.

Oh, I forgot one important thing. Why would radio play this record if they hated me? I wasn't in the mood to deal with simple truths at this point, so we began to tour with one small concession to my delicate psyche. We would not tour in the United States. I can see where that appears selfish and mean-spirited if you are one of my American fans, but I held so much contempt for the American music industry that I was only willing to work within boundaries that I absolutely had to. So, for more than a year and a half, we toured every inch of Canada.

The most important change for everyone, but especially for me, was how I now perceived myself. I had found fame and lost my fortune as a star but now I considered myself an artist, and I began taking myself very seriously. To take myself seriously I had to go back and examine my entire career. Then, once committed to and under-standing the revelations, I adopted those lessons in the form of a daily routine of self-criticism and dedication to my art form. Then I had to back off and lighten up a little, or run the risk of taking myself even more seriously. It was a delicate balance in view of the fact that I was, in the beginning, the only person to see myself in such a way.

What made the proposition even more difficult was my resistance to re-examining my life outside of my career. My personal life. Consequently, I was short-changing the entire truth of my experience. Having recognized the problem, I began to tap into my feelings much more deeply than I thought possible, which was an uplifting accomplish-ment. Still, although my art could now be filled with passion and truth, I refused to take the painful extra step forward that could lead me to the only real reward in the lives we live, and that was to change myself, my behavior, and the bad habits I so de-pended on for my validation as a human being. For a long time it seemed I could not summon the courage to bring about such change. My ability to find happiness was put on hold as I continued to revel in the role of the victim.

Suffering makes for compelling drama and from an artistic view there is nothing more cheaply purchased and yet so gratifying as cheap drama. It is the place where artists go to show they are still alive, but haven't begun to live. My story was going to be honestly told, so I didn't want to complicate the process with the time consuming effort to better myself as a person. I felt that if I took that path I might somehow per-vert or destroy the reality I depended on to create. As a result, many of my efforts for years to come, however important, were created through the honest but clouded view of substance abuse and alcohol addiction.

I'm well aware of the arguments that could be made to challenge my claim to the legitimacy of my work through those times, but such arguments are lies from people who never had the courage to undress in public. I was creating. And it was beautiful to experience, drunk or sober. I began work on the album *How I Spent My Vacation*. It was to be an auto-biographical concept album that showed a side of me that had never been acknowledged or made public, and it was also going to be as honest as the day is long.

The "Vacation" album took a year and a half to complete, due to budgetary concerns, and it stands as one of my better achievements to date. The magnificent contributions and professionalism of Wayne Gabriel on guitar demonstrates the unveiling of the musical intensity and interpretations that permeated the entire album, infected all the players, and challenged them to rise ever higher in their individual contributions. Wayne had a reputation to protect, having been a player and studio musician for John Lennon, and he didn't want to see it shattered by Mitch Ryder.

Lyrically, I was able to tell my abbreviated story with unusual clarity and my vocals accomplished everything I had reached for. A few of the tunes were written on the spot, but most of them were from the "vacation" in Colorado. Some of the impromptu lyrical performances continue to fascinate me even to this day.

As far as the writing credits were concerned I listed on most of the copyrights Kimberly's name as well as mine, because I reasoned that even though I might be stupid enough to get ripped off again, she would never allow that to happen to her, even though she hadn't written a word or a note. That is how deep the New York musical machine had worked its way up my ass.

Reviews of the album were more positive than I ever imagined possible because, even though the album was an extraordinary effort, it was not written or produced with a commercial market in mind. I suddenly found myself doing interviews with *Rolling Stone* magazine and even the *New York Times*, where the writer constantly referred to me as "Mister" Ryder.

I got an invitation to sit with Seymour Stein, who had now become a major player in the music industry. I sent a representative, Peter Derby, who is very important with the S.E.C. By the way, Peter married a genuine Russian princess and now has a wonderful family. He began his music industry work with me as a road manager, and we used to marvel at how he managed to herd our wild collection of personalities through some of the dirtiest gigs and cheapest motels, and still manage to bring along his smoking jacket with the velvet and silk lapels.

Nothing came of the meeting with Seymour, because I refused to meet directly with him. And nothing came from the album, other than fine reviews. It's an old story. If you can't get it to the marketplace, you can't sell it. There was still some of the old bitterness and hate from the list of my still-active enemies. But, I took the unexpected attention to be an acknowledgement of me as a true artist and came to another important decision. Up until the album had been released we were working and performing exclusively in Canada. We were in Vancouver and Tom tried to talk me into jumping across the border for one brief performance in San Francisco and then returning to the Canadian tour.

San Francisco represented many things to me. In the sixties it was one of the first cities in the United States to go top ten with my first hit. It was also the place that I came to another realization a few years later. My music at that time was about to run its course in terms of popular taste and was falling out of fashion. In much the same way I realized that truth back in New York City when I headlined the show over Cream and The Who. So for me, this date in San Francisco was a test of my new music and a chance to see if I was able to come back as a legitimate artist, as opposed to a rock 'n' roll star from the sixties. In addition, San Francisco loved art for art's sake.

I can't recall another time where my anxiety held so much fear and love at the same time. We walked into The Old Waldorf and performed a set that included my early hits, but was easily dominated by my new material. I now view the concession of including the old hits as a major mistake, but the reviews were tremendous and the audience was gracious and thankful. Tom had brought me back to my native country. The next gig we did in America was strange, as I watched from the stage while an audience member doused my jacket that I had set on the edge of the stage with lighter fluid and then set it ablaze as we played.

The Vacation album and its subsequent reviews afforded me the confidence to begin a stronger working relationship with the band, and I began putting together the second Mitch Ryder album for Seeds and Stems Records. This album was called *Naked But Not Dead*. The cover was the second of my oil paintings to find a way onto my albums, the first being the Vacation album. This painting had actually been exhibited in an art gallery in Detroit, and featured in the Detroit newspapers. The photograph on the back of the album cover now included Richard Schein on guitar, who had replaced Wayne Gabriel.

The truth was that Wayne had been disappointed in my inability to parley the album into a success, and it was too expensive to fly him from New York to anywhere America for each little gig we did, so I had to rely on Detroit talent.

The night we took the band photo at one of our gigs, our opening band was from Indiana and its front man was a young singer who called himself John Cougar Mellencamp. Fate would eventually lead me to a future encounter with John under much different circumstances. With the release of the "Naked" album we again received good reviews and even got local airplay on a station called WRIF with a song called "War," but all of the ground-breaking artistry still remained the domain of the Vacation album.

Bob Seger, however, liked the second album enough to insist we open a week-long appearance for him at Cobo Hall in Detroit. I heard his manager, Punch Andrews, got really pissed because the original openers had shipped thousands of units of their own product into the market in anticipation of their appearance.

We were also experiencing problems with our seven independent distributors. We couldn't get them to agree on timely, coordinated placement of product, or their payments to our record company, and so everything from securing promotional budgets to development of new product began to suffer under the uneven cash flow.

Tom found an agent out of Cleveland to carry our product to France for the music industry's annual MIDEM (*Marché International du Disque et de l'Edition Musicale*) convention, an event where product was licensed or picked up by foreign record companies for distribution in their territories. We were desperately hoping for a foreign release while we tried to re-arrange our American strategy.

Chapter 25

IT WAS NOW 1978 AND I was starting to feel more like a workhorse than an artist as we toured America with no hope of a breakthrough into the world of successful comebacks. Given the size of our nation, you wouldn't think one could ever become tired of touring here, but I had now been at it for the better part of thirteen years and, at times, it seemed the only real change was the model of the cars we were renting and driving.

Kimberly and I had been living in an upper flat in the Lonyo McGraw area of Detroit's west side, about a mile from the Dearborn border. Even though we hadn't been able to secure a house of our own, Tom's creative understanding of financial institutions was able to secure us both new cars and the first valid credit card I had held since 1968, when I had filed bankruptcy. We were slowly working toward outward respectability, and clinging proudly to each little upward movement as if it was the only way we could measure our self-worth.

We had become close friends to our landlords, Connie and Charlie Navarro, who lived downstairs. Although I liked them, I didn't like the fact that when I came home in the winter I had to fight with the neighbors for a parking space on the street. Some people even placed chairs in their spaces. No one had a garage. Once, one of the neighbor's children shot a bullet into our front window trying to kill our cat, and the Navarro's son was shot in the leg. Kimberly helped clean and dress the wound, since nobody wanted the cops involved.

Personally, Kim and I were drifting apart. She had found a new group of friends and I was always out touring. No longer were the days of traveling without her unbearable, and it didn't bother me that I had taken to alcohol as a brain-numbing shield against the truth of our existence. Our marriage was tentative. There were too many selfish expectations on both our parts, and too many unrealistic goals, given the reality of our situation and absolute denial about either of us having addictive personalities.

While I have not mentioned it, Kim had not been a saint during our relationship and marriage either. With me around, how could she have been? But that is her story to tell. Two problems between us were that my dysfunction focused on other women, and I was okay living in an upper flat. Kim expected me to somehow manufacture money to raise us up and didn't understand I was incapable. I believed in my music, but the issue was that I didn't care if anyone else did or not.

As far as family functions and traditions, we spent more time with Kim's clan than mine. It was fun—mostly—because everybody got drunk and melancholy and there was little violence. From the outside, I'm sure they all looked like a typical American family who enjoyed the holidays. And I think they actually might have. Colorful lights, a beautiful tree, story tellings, memories, singing, and an abundance of alcohol.

My family's Christmas, Thanksgiving and assorted other gatherings were subdued by comparison, mostly because the majority of my family did not drink that much. We had more fun with Kim's folks, and we never even thought about counseling. The fights came and went; they were that much a part of our lives.

It was this particular winter that Tom told me I was about to receive visitors from Germany. I had traveled to a few foreign locations, but Germany was a mystery to me. I knew from the un-ending American media representations that it was a conquered nation full of Nazis. That was a mainstay on American TV. Sadly, it still is.

◆

a window to my soul

Privileged American world travelers and business people, who easily fool themselves by putting themselves into the position of being able to say, "Some of my best friends are Germans," don't understand how easily this stereotype can spread into hate. Nor do military personal who have family and wives and children in Germany.

I'm getting a little old to be talking about a hateful representation of a people still being spoon fed to American audiences. And yes, I'm resentful of German school children who are made to take "field trips" to Holocaust museums. Lest we forget. That war killed millions of military combatants, and millions of innocent non-combatant women and children—and most of those people weren't Jewish. If I wanted to understand why "my" people were so easily hated and destroyed I wouldn't separate myself from mankind and demand they keep looking at the evil that was done only to them.

In the example of the Jews I consider myself as, and insist upon being, an equal to all mankind so not one person could say I was different. And instead of creating museums in Germany that showed six million Jews being destroyed and tortured, and put in camps, I'd create a museum that showed all ten million human beings who were destroyed and tortured, and put in camps by the Nazis.

But that wouldn't make me special would it? It was a need to be special that drove the Nazis into their philosophy of superiority. In their minds they were the chosen ones, except they didn't need "their" Bible to confirm it. Their Messiah was Adolf Hitler.

◆

In any case, three German gentlemen arrived at our flat. One, a very tall music journalist; another, Richard Wagner, one of the producers of the TV show they had come to negotiate and; the owner of the new German label that had leased Vacation for the album's maiden release in Germany.

Uwe Tessnow was the owner of Line Records out of Hamburg, and held the title of "the golden boy wonder" at his previous corporate job. Uwe loved music. All kinds of music. I never did ask him why he chose my album at MIDEM. He was sort of like an un-knowing angel.

The concert they wanted me to do was called "Rock Palast," which was a multi-act concert broadcast once a year on a special night not only in Germany, but through-out Europe. The estimated viewing audience would be well over one hundred million people. I was being invited to be part of the show, which consisted of me, South Side Johnny and the Asbury Dukes, and Nils Lofgren. It was to be the perfect kickoff for Uwe's new label and a tremendous opportunity for me to enter a marketplace I had never been in before.

In the early days with the Wheels we had cracked the British top ten a couple of times, but we had never been entrenched in Europe because my management focused on English speaking countries. I do have to laugh because I own a copy of "Sock it to Me, Baby" on a Japanese label on which they totally screwed up the translations for the lyrics. If anyone owns a copy of "Devil With a Blue Dress On" sung in Spanish by Los Lobos, you'll understand what I mean.

At this time, the persuasive, addictive powers of rock 'n' roll were spreading like the Wall Street panic and Europe was coming of age. The site of the concert was a large indoor auditorium in the city of Essen, and even though the site would be filled with people, mostly young Germans, the entertainment would also come to the millions of people watching on TV, and they could benefit from the many different camera angles, close-ups, controlled sound, and pre-show interviews with the artists.

Kimberly and I were thrilled to be asked to join the celebration and became very anxious while putting together our travel plans and preparing for our journey. Kimberly's parents, Russ and Dora, saw us, along with my band, off at the international terminal in Romulus, Michigan, a place I hadn't seen in many years, and the excitement was barely controllable. Russ and Dora were happy for us, because they could see the happiness in Kimberly's face and they knew exactly how hard it had been for us since my return to music.

I must admit it was a big boost to my self-esteem and I settled into my seat on the plane and entered into the land of make-believe. As the plane approached Germany, all I could do was stare out the window and watch the landscape and houses as they became larger and closer. There was nothing to say, because no one in the band had slept. Instead, we all spent the entire night talking and dreaming of the coming adventure.

As we left the plane and cleared our luggage we were greeted by Uwe, Jorgun the journalist, and Peter Bruning, who was on Uwe's staff in promotion and public relations. It was strange to compare what I was actually witnessing with the American thought of stereotyped, goose-stepping Nazis hiding behind every wall and around every corner. One thing that was true was the presence of police armed with fully automatic weapons patrolling the airport. Terrorism was already a mainstay in Europe, although it would be decades before our country would come to that.

This was the beginning of an education that left me bewildered and angry at the great bias that existed in my country toward a Germany that had nothing in common with what we Americans had been taught. It also opened up the forbidden question of who was responsible for such a great misrepresentation of the facts.

Kimberly and I spent our first day in Hamburg before we headed down to Essen. Unfortunately, our curiosity led us to explore when we should have been resting, and our spirit of adventure carried well into the night until sheer exhaustion forced us to sleep.

Upon arriving in the Koln/Essen area, we were taken to our rooms and we unpacked. It was always an adventure, sharing a hotel room with Kimberly, because I had to wait to see just how much space was left for my belongings and me. In that way I think Kim was a typical woman traveler. I also think younger people don't concern themselves with so many necessary personal items. I absolutely know that most European women use much less cosmetic junk than American women; and as a result they have a more natural beauty about them. I wonder if it has to do with having so much less after the war.

Next we were off to meet the press and the *burgermeister* (mayor) and be officially welcomed to Essen. For a fall afternoon it was unseasonably warm, and we ate an afternoon lunch in a charming outdoor café. Uncle George had mentioned many times the brilliance behind the making of German beers. Most cities and many towns in Germany have their own special breweries and their own local beer. At least that was the case in 1978.

German beers go back centuries, and are brewed much the same way they were in the beginning, with all natural ingredients, no preservatives and, as with most liquid refreshment at that time, served at room temperature. One of our hosts told us that many Germans believed cold drinks were an unnecessary shock to the human body's system. We sat down and enjoyed some of the best beer we had ever tasted in our lives. McDonald's, the burger champ, had just launched two or three restaurants in Germany. One was in a rebuilt, bombed out, church. They served beer on the menu and you didn't have to be a certain age to buy it.

My uncle had also told me that Germans believed if you let the young experience alcohol at an early age they would not crave it as a forbidden fruit. There were many cultural things that would, year-by-year, as America's corporate hold on Germany strengthened, disappear and then quickly reappear as American. Free enterprise. That is what had brought me here.

Having started the afternoon with an incredible buzz we went on to the venue for our sound check and some promotional events with the other artists. The mood of the band was good, and things went quickly. We then went to a scheduling meeting where I was informed that I was closing the show. I was pumped to think that I was headlining, but that soon took on a different color when I discovered I wouldn't be going on stage until two a.m.

We were now faced with the prospect of spending the next eight hours hanging out. Under normal circumstances that might have been hard, but tolerable. The thing about this band, the Thrashing Brothers, was the fact that everyone except Richard Shine didn't handle alcohol very well. We were led to our dressing rooms and began to make up ways to busy ourselves. Unfortunately, there was plenty of food and a wide variety of alcohol.

Tom and Uwe were walking around somewhere and a plot for the conquest of Europe was being painstakingly formulated. They were both nervous and had popped in on Kim and me several times as they made their way back and forth through the hall. Night approached and the show was about to begin when I ran into the two of them again in a hallway. Uwe was in tears. Apparently he had entered one of the dressing rooms to bolster the spirits of the band members only to discover two of the boys destroying the room in the heat of a fistfight.

This band was different from the Detroit band in that physical violence was directed inward toward each other, as opposed to an outside entity. Over the years to come there would be many fights, but most of them included Wilson Owens, our drummer. I managed to convince Uwe I had things under control and not to worry. Then I made a half-hearted lecture to the band about self-conduct. Now we gathered around some of the backstage monitors to watch the other acts.

Something from my past has always forced me to view other artists on the same show as competition. Only then could I allow myself to be entertained and appreciative. The hours rolled by and I noticed that after each of my co-star's shows were finished, they were led to a backstage area where they were interviewed and asked to sign a portable guest wall that contained autographs of the great artists who came before them. When my chance finally came I defaced the wall by writing my name over the names of as many of the other artists as possible.

We had worked hard to obtain the optimum buzz for the show, which we had already approached and lost several times, when the unthinkable occurred. For one reason or another some genius had decided to place our interview *before* our performance. Why? Why didn't we get the same treatment as the other acts? I became angry and indignant. Did someone need to clean up early and get the hell out? Was it a union problem? Were the other acts so boring that they had lost all meaningful numbers in terms of viewers? I was pissed, and I was about to become legendary.

When I approached the area where the interview was to be held everyone was smiling, but you could easily sense the nervous nature of their friendly status. After all, they knew very little about me, compared to my co-stars who were still connected to the industry in America. They had come to Germany to pick up some extra cash and be seen by a large number of viewers who might then be tempted to buy their successful American product. I had come to start a career. I was no longer connected to the industry in America. My product had been rejected by anyone who could have seriously helped.

I didn't see Europe as a market. Tom did. And Uwe did. I saw Europe as a wide-open, fresh piece of canvas. I saw it as a place where I could be allowed the respect of an artist, which was the very thing that had been called into question, ridiculed, and denied in the United States. But first I would have to try to destroy that opportunity with the pre-show interview. I was fueled by a blood alcohol level that would have killed a horse.

The man chosen to do the interview was young and English, and had a reasonable grasp of the German language. Like so many of the interviews I did in Germany, he asked me a question and then translated the question and answer in German. I wondered how it had come to be that he had been chosen for this job, because it seemed to me that he would have been better suited for some important role with the BBC. His name was Alan Bangs, and as much as I tried to fluster and irritate him, he remained focused and steady.

He asked me the usual questions, but then would pull something out of the blue worth answering, and I was starting to enjoy him. Since enjoying him was against my mission, I walked over to a sidewall where his girlfriend Elizabeth was standing, pinned her up against the wall with my body and began speaking closely into her ear. I looked back and he still wasn't rattled. Was this the famous British composure that I had vowed to prove a lie?

I went back to the interview area more determined than ever to take control of the situation, and then the break I had been waiting for appeared. He asked me a question about my host country, Germany. Included in my thoughtful answer came blurting out a drunken attack upon the conservative nature of the government I had thus far been exposed to. If my state controlled television company and crew were now recoiling in horror, the young viewing audience, the few million still awake, turned their heads and lifted their ears. There were a few more questions, but the main image put out to the audience was one of rebellion, the backbone of pure rock 'n' roll.

In spite of the fact that the band and I were totally messed up, we gave a performance that was light-years removed from the entertaining, but predictable, shows of our co-stars. The performance became known as "The Legendary Full Moon Concert." I interacted with the audience directly, jumped into the crowd, sat with them on the floor, and sang to them. It was like the early days of Billy Lee and the Rivieras. I let them know that I was one of them, and then I went back to that place they either didn't have the courage or ability to reach. The stage. The show took on a special beauty and only stopped when the band exhausted itself and had given everything.

After the performance the band knew, as I did, that we had pulled off something special. Unfortunatcly, Tom and Uwe held a different opinion. Their input from the producers had been very negative, and Tom took me aside and began a sermon. Uwe was crushed, and Tom held me directly responsible for destroying the career of the only man in Europe who was willing to gamble on me. We made the long ride back to Hamburg in complete silence, except for the noise of the wind as it whipped through the back of the car while I held my penis out to piss on the Autobahn.

Two days later, as I sat in my hotel room waiting for my plane ticket to become useful, I was summoned to a meeting with Tom and Uwe. To my surprise they were very friendly and wanted bygones to be bygones. As if by magic they received wonderful feedback about the show from the young audience, and lots of orders were coming in for my recordings. All of a sudden I was a good guy again. The news of our breakthrough provided a building block for my new career in Europe, and more specifically in Germany, because during the show it was a young German boy I had chosen to teach me to say, "Was ist das?"

Using Uwe's connections and guidance, my future European career would be split into two homes and spheres of influence. For years I operated out of Hamburg, and then out of Berlin. Uwe gave me the best he could give, and hooked me up with one of the bigger booking agents in Germany, Karsten Janke. Unfortunately, I think they usually booked shows for more cultured and civilized artists then they did for someone like me.

At one point Uwe was a friend. He is a big part of my life today for something he did many years ago, but he is also bitter and feels betrayed. He need not feel that way. In the end, my story with Line Records is very close to the relationship I have with BuschFunk out of Berlin. These are not major labels in Germany, and if we get a hit it will be because the song I create will be so strong that humanity itself cannot deny the rightful place it has in music.

The long flight home and the hassle at customs, where they marveled at the odd collection of drinking glasses, posters, ashtrays, etcetera, did nothing to dampen our spirits, and for the next few weeks, at all of our little haunts and bars in Detroit, the story of our triumph and the magic of Germany was repeated over and over again to whomever would listen.

Chapter 26

THE BAND NOW HAD SOMETHING TANGIBLE to hold onto. We were something new and quite different for the Germans, and we also welcomed the change. The days and nights in Hamburg allowed everyone to meet and make new friends, which was important because we would come back many times, due to our success. Most of my time was meant for meetings and interviews and the usual formula, but the band was cultivating lasting and meaningful friendships and relationships with club owners, bartenders, and street people, some of them known as fans.

Now Tom was excited and he saw a real chance to make something happen. And since it had nothing to do with the sixties, I was happier than I had been in a long time. But, in all honesty, the thrill of seeing and learning about Germany played more in my mind than the success of our appearance.

We returned to do an extended tour in the winter. Because of our triumph, we were getting a lot of record company and booking agent support, and our transportation was what one could consider normal. We actually had a bus with a driver, instead of tiny rented vans. We had tour jackets with thick lining and our individual names sewn on the front. But most importantly, we were doing kick-ass shows, getting blasted, and having a ball. Because drugs were not as easily available as they were, and still are, in America, we drank a lot. It seemed to enhance our performances and we were using the audience reaction as the barometer. I had to remember that the boys were now becoming stars in their own right, and were not the next parade of the Detroit Wheels, which is more or less what they were seen as back home, in spite of the lack of a band name.

We had gotten a good reputation after our first tour, and the sales of Vacation and *Naked But Not Dead* were close to, but not quite, the kind of sales expected from a group that was getting much positive feedback from the street and concerts. I was very happy to hear that Tom and Uwe agreed to make another recording in Germany. It had to come, for financial reasons, at the conclusion of the next tour, and it occured in the little village of Wilster.

I was concerned because my voice would more than likely be torn up pretty good after any tour. Our tours were almost always long strings of one-nighters, with no nights off. I had written about six tunes before I knew we were coming back to record, and I trusted myself to come up with the other songs during the tour. That training, or position of chance, became important to me. I very much like writing under pressure. I think if you have all the time in the world to create, you end up with enough time to second guess yourself. My difficulty was making sure I was always going to be in a studio, and if you don't make hits, that is a hard goal to achieve.

By the time we hit the studio we were beat and under the effect of a full winter storm. We each had a room of our own at the studio, and everyday there were big meals served by an on-sight cook, a woman, which was a headache since we were out in the country and some of the guys liked sex more than they liked music.

Where the Vacation and Naked albums were crafted over many months, we enjoyed no such luxury with this project. We only had two weeks to complete it, and Christmas was just two and a half weeks away. Everyone wanted to be home for Christmas. During the recording process, I was up all night writing, and then spent the days in the studio. While the band waited for the next tune, they got drunk (sometimes) and their frustrations came boiling to the surface.

One night I received a long-distance call from Kimberly, who had stayed behind. The media in Detroit wanted a quote from me regarding the assassination of John Lennon. I was stunned and speechless. I couldn't believe what I was hearing. It was the only contact we made with the outside world while we were recording, and it had to be that. I don't remember what I told Kim to say on my behalf, but after the call was over I went to my room and cried.

I remembered how that beautiful man had made room in his busy life to save me from psychological ruin and destruction those many years earlier in the London countryside. He was the most human and accessible of all the members of his band. It was a great loss. "Mr. Lennon, Mr. Lennon," and bang! Gone forever. I wanted to say something about guns and the mentality of some of their users, but I also wanted to address the issue of war, which was equally as stupid as an individual murder, but a concept still embraced by the world. So I wrote the song "Bang Bang."

As the album neared completion it became harder and harder to keep the band focused. I didn't have the time I needed to deal with the band's emotional needs and still keep things on track. The band had too much idle time. It was in this pressure cooker when Wilson Owens, our gifted and talented drummer, forced to the surface an issue I had long thought resolved in my life. Racism.

Wilson was our black drummer of wonderful musical expression, but he also carried a ton of personal baggage into that arena. In the past I had gone to court in Ann Arbor to plead for his freedom on charges of possession of heroin, and promised the judge that he was essentially a good man who now had an opportunity to turn his life around by working professionally with me. I gave the judge my word that I would be his mentor. My name had once again become useful.

But, Wilson was also a man with whom I had gotten into two different fist fights. In one of them he tried to kill me and we both bear scars on our faces from these encounters. He also attacked Billy Csernits while we were recording "Live Talkies" in Hamburg, knocking poor Billy to the ground and beating him as Billy tried to stand up with a full leg cast on, the result of a hip displacement from a show we had done days before in Paris at the Palace.

Wilson also attacked Lance, one of our roadies, and cut him with a small knife. Violence aside, the man could play drums like very few others. But now, back in the studio, Wilson was quite often getting too drunk to perform his duties and a new confrontation seemed inevitable. I wasn't going to allow Wilson to sabotage the album because of his mental problems. Everyone had put too much into this effort and we all wanted to hear the finished product. I was angry, but Wilson refused to hear any arguments against his behavior, choosing instead to cite racism as the reason for me singling him out.

None of us were angels—and most definitely not I—but when it came to the studio I didn't waste my energy getting too high or drunk to perform. That was hard enough without complicating it further. But all of us paled in comparison to Wilson. When he had a good buzz on he was a complex individual, and you wanted to understand him because he was gifted and talented. But once he started getting high it was easy to resent, and even hate, his behavior. He stole and lied and generally fucked you over until you could no longer tolerate the ordeal. So, at this critical time near the end of the album where he was single-handedly delaying the completion of the project with his behavior, we butted heads again.

This resulted in another fight during which, for the first time in our long relationship, I called him a stupid nigger. He was not as surprised as I was. It was as if he expected that from me, even though he had to wait through many years of provocation. It only served to validate his sick view of whites. In hindsight, bad and even repugnant behavior is not the exclusive domain of a person's skin color. To this day I am sorry for having said it. I regret what I called him, but I am grateful as well because it showed me the condition of my humanity and its weaknesses.

Uwe was there and witnessed it. I don't know what was going through his mind, since it wasn't too many weeks prior to this that he had to pry Wilson off his wife as Wilson molested her in front of his eyes. It also showed me how far I had fallen, and how hateful a person I had become as life did its business of breaking us all down. I thought back to my days at the Village and with the Peps, when skin color meant absolutely nothing to my conscious mind.

The project got finished and the band went into Hamburg for a few days before our departure, while I stayed at the studio to complete mixing and other details. We took the album cover photos at our then favorite pub, Onkel Po's, and *Got Change For a Million?* was born.

The songs on the new album were good, but the production quality suffered since I was maxed out for time and wore too many hats. The album did increase the size of our following, though, and guaranteed us a return visit. An unexpected bonus was to be nominated for the German equivalent of the Grammy Awards as best new artist of the year. We didn't win, but it was fun. I was very pleased, and my belief in my artistry was complimented in another way as well. A couple of German artists did cover versions of several of the songs I had written. The song that got covered the most was "Ain't Nobody White Can Sing the Blues."

On a subsequent tour I was watching a popular German soap opera and a male character sat down at a very critical emotional moment in the story and began to play one of my songs on his stereo. It was "Freezin' in Hell" from the Vacation album. I was not in the mainstream yet but I was jackin' around the outer edges. It felt good. Here I was in the beginning of the 1980s doing original contemporary material, finding success, being well reviewed, capturing new fans and what did I have back in America? The love affair with the German people was heating up and we made plans to return within months to enter into the studio again.

Chapter 27

IN THE EARLY DAYS OF MY existence in Germany everything was magical. Even though I had first come dragging all of the bitterness and anger from my experience in America and wouldn't have been surprised if that were to become the same in Germany, I was happily disappointed. It was as if someone had opened the gates to an enchanted castle and the band and I had free roam of the place. The friendships we were cultivating and the people we were running with, some of them with serious problems, were very open and wanted more than anything to please us. And in return, they wanted only for us to be their friends.

I remember a combination pub and restaurant called the Pic N Pac putting out an entire Thanksgiving spread for us, even though they knew nothing of the significance of the holiday. How amused they were to watch us eat corn on the cob, which at that time was generally reserved for livestock feed in Germany. We listened intently and carefully as they spoke of their experiences growing up in a conquered nation sadly divided by the spoils of war. That division was important, because many of them had relatives and loved ones in the communist controlled East.

Our record company promotion man took us over there one night while we were in Berlin. We went through the American controlled sector called Checkpoint Charlie to a bar seven blocks in. Images of old American spy movies danced through my head as the dank and sparse and quiet of the East became more present with each passing street. The walls of the buildings were cold and gray, and in need of repair and cleaning. The streets were empty and the cobblestones were difficult to walk on. But oddly enough, there was no litter. Anywhere. We had been told that East German economy was the strongest in the entire communist controlled satellite countries. But here— seven blocks removed from West Berlin and the wall, the neon lights and the streets filled with people, shop windows filled with things to buy and the sounds of music drifting through the air from apartments or clubs, and the wonderful smell of tantalizing foods drifting out into the streets from the restaurants—East Germany looked weak and impotent.

We were also told that, although things in the East were inexpensive compared to the West, whatever change we received from our West Gernam marks would be in the form of Eastern marks, which we would not be allowed to take back with us. Therefore, spend wisely. I was told the reason we couldn't take the Eastern currency back was because the government was embarrassed by the relatively low value of their money compared to the West.

We thought we had gotten lost because we could not find the bar we were looking for. There were no signs outside. As we stood on the street one of the guys heard what he thought might be music. We headed toward the direction of the faint noise, reached the building it was coming from, and opened the only door available.

It was as if we had gone to a speakeasy during prohibition in America. Once we opened the door the laughter and music drowned out our ability to talk and we had to yell to each other to be heard. The place was full of life and we drank a lot, and I think some of us ordered food. When it came time to leave I tipped our waitress fifty Western marks, which was around twenty-five dollars, and she cried and hugged me.

The experience made me think about how difficult it must be for those generations who are removed from their fathers' errors to be demonized, as the citizens of Germany have been since the Second World War. Then, to have the double whammy of one half of themselves painted as even more evil when they had no control over their circumstances. But, I'm getting ahead of myself, since my early years in Germany were spent in the relative wealthy confines of the West.

Our home base in Germany was Hamburg. The stories of our drunken exploits around Hamburg in those early years were almost always true and factual, but I can dismiss them with no regrets because whatever the emotions and the feelings of the band were, our tours were mostly thirty one-nighter dates in a row with no days off. Some of the guys missed home and family, the group was totally comprised of drug users or alcoholics, and we sometimes hated each other.

None of that meant anything, though, when you asked someone who had been to our concerts what they thought of the band, because it was that energy and frustration and drive to do our best and succeed that they cared about. In Berlin we opened for The Dave Mathews Band and The Police. Tom Connor has a tape of that concert. We weren't to be taken lightly.

The band I fronted with Mark Gougeon, Billy Csernits, Wilson Owens, Rick Schein, and Joe Gutc would never be as famous as the Detroit Wheels, but they inspired me and drove me to heights as an artist that the Wheels were incapable of doing. And it wasn't the Wheels fault. It was Bob Crewe who killed all possibilities with that band.

Unfortunately, the Thrashing Brothers and I had a lot of personal problems that we either buried, hid, or refused to deal with. Our life on the road, particularly in America, was dangerous, at best. It was proven that if we stayed on the road for more than three to four weeks without a break all hell would break loose. There were many fights and other destructive behavior, and the lack of privacy, since we all had to share rooms, had a great deal to do with that. There simply was no place to get away when any of us needed to be alone with our thoughts or to clear our minds.

Whether it was demolishing a rental car outside a club in Germany, or starting a riot by refusing to take the stage, something always came up. Of course that wasn't as bad as whipping our road manager with a metal chain across his face as he drove our limo. Those actions were the domain of the band Detroit. But we had a few members in this group who carried guns.

One night we were all held at bay while our road manager poured lighter fluid on the club owner's bar and lit it on fire, threatening to shoot anyone who called for help. My particular penchant for thrill came from urinating on stage. One night in Texas we performed at a club called Fitzgeralds. Doug English, a former Detroit Lions football player, had come as a guest of my wife Kimberly and me. Doug knew nothing about my dark side, and so it was with amazement that he proclaimed to my wife, "Kim, I believe your husband is pissing in that man's hat!"

Doug had brought me down to appear in a celebrity golf outing for one of the many charities he was involved in. I loved to perform charity work. I loved football. I used to go to parties at the home of Pro Football Hall of Famer and former Detroit Lions tight end Charlie Sanders on Outer Drive where he and I and a bunch of other guys stood on his front porch and sang. Same thing with baseball players Kirk Gibson and Dave Rosema. We partied together and one time when the Tigers were playing the Yankees in New York they brought down some of the guys for our show.

But they never saw the *really* bad side of me. Even wonderful Ernie Harwell, the voice of the Detroit Tigers, used to announce the arrival of my wife Kimberly and me as we entered the park for a game. Ernie and I even collaborated on a couple of songs together. He used to say it was the biggest no-hitter he had ever seen. Celebrity carries responsibility and expectations and standards of conduct. Since my activities of vile and disgusting behavior were subterranean and below the radar of the standard press, these honorable men had no reason to doubt the full value of my stardom.

Once and for all, just for the record, let me say that my antics regarding women, infidelity, drugs, lies, and a variety of minor crimes, like my time in the Los Angeles County Jail, were shameful, embarrassing, and without redemption. Sometimes I think that is what this "Jerry Springer" generation wants to hear and read about, the more disgusting the better. Well, I did it all. For this I am sincerely sorry and apologize to those I have hurt. The list is too long to detail. It was a part of my life—a major part of my life—and it wasn't going to become any better until I could purge the resentment and poison that had been spoon fed me in New York. The notion that I could succeed as an artist in Europe would slowly wash away the shit I had been handed in the "great" city of New York by the criminals that exist there in the form of the entertainment industry. Finding a good moral compass; that would be the only way to save me.

Back in Germany I relied on friends. My wife was a different matter altogether. She was ignored by me and allowed herself to find solace and good feeling by entering into a world in which we didn't communicate. At all. Billy Csernits became the closest thing to a friend I had known since the early days when Joey Kubert and I were teenagers. Billy and I shared a great deal of our personal lives with each other, and I trusted Billy's instincts and critiques where my music was concerned. Billy once gave me the Sex Pistols first album *Never Mind the Bullocks* as a Christmas present. A few years ago a friend called from Minneapolis to tell me he had just heard an interview with their lead singer, Johnny Rotten, in which he named me as one of his influences. How cool is that?

Billy was a tall young man with huge hands. When he played the keyboards his hands sometimes got in the way but the music was always perfect, and more importantly, always from his heart. Our best times together were in the two-year period before Germany and the three years after our arrival there. He was the ice-breaker, whether it was in a room full of strangers or simply getting to know our different German crews, Billy was the one with no inhibitions and a friendly smile. I can't count how many times I found myself doubting my resolve or courage to take the next step forward, only to find Billy standing firmly behind me pushing me on. It was his caring and respect for me as an artist that was essential in enabling me to create the wonderful songs for the first four Line Records releases.

Joe Gutc is innocent, in spite of his protestations to the contrary. He is a child locked in a man's body. Joe is also a truly original slide guitar player. His tone, however, was very hard to record because had fallen in love with a cheap guitar and refused to abandon it. To me, it sounded like a fishing rod casting reel unwinding too fast as you threw out the line. But Joe's mind and the musical notes that he created for his solos stand alone in the world of original music. Joe was our jester and a serious practical joker. I could never talk with Joey the way I talked with Billy, and so I could never uncover what it was that caused him such deep sadness. I believe the reason he carried such sadness was the fact that he was always joking about something. He always kept us laughing, but he feared the night and sleep the way many of us fear death. There was no audience then, and he had to be alone. Joe is not a disciplined musician, but his music is beyond compare.

Mark Gougeon was the brooder in the group. He was also, compared to everyone else, a professional. He was serious more often than not and he was in a serious and loving relationship with his wife. Mark was ambitious, productive, and not afraid of hard work, and he was usually the first one to crack if we were away from home for any length of time. He brought to the stage a great look, a professional attitude, and he was active and pleasant to watch. His down side was that when he did occasionally drink, he became a violent ugly drunk.

Rick Schein came from a well-to-do family and was a partner in his family business. He owns three of my original oil paintings, two of which appeared on album covers. Rick chose to balance his family business with the opportunity to be in a real rock 'n' roll band. I first met Richard when we were doing the track for "Tough Kid" on the Vacation album. I don't recall who brought him into the studio, but I asked him to play a short lead solo for the track. It was the most alive, energetic, and awesome solo, and it fit perfectly. He got the job.

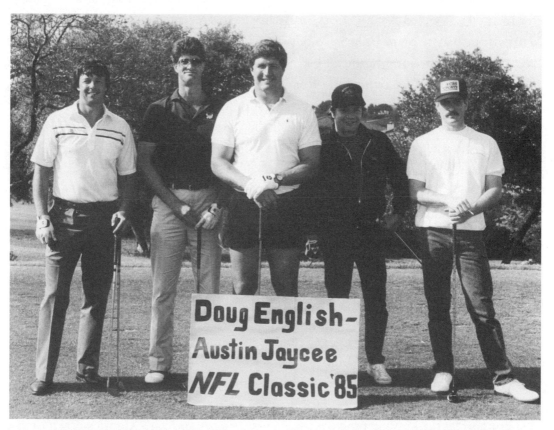

Former Detroit Lions defensive tackle Doug English (center) and Mitch (second from right) at a charity golf tournament in 1985.

We've already spoken about Wilson Owens. And so I had the Thrashing Brothers. The antics and history of the original Thrashing Brothers would become folklore, but I was starting to blaze a trail separate and apart from the group.

At home this manifested itself in an area of Detroit we called the Cass Avenue Corridor. I had played the Corridor quite a few times with the band Detroit and with the Thrashing Brothers, mostly at a club called the New Miami. It was a small club with a small stage and I remember it today for two reasons: I held the record for the most beers sold for a performance, and it was the place where Bobby Rodrigus, the drummer for the Edgar Winter Band, was beaten to death by three of Detroit's finest killers.

The punks were giving the effeminate keyboard player a hard time over his sexuality and Bobby tried to get them to back off. As the three men delivered each deadly blow, Bobby's will to survive made it very hard for them to end his life, but their numbers finally prevailed. What glory those cowardly men who still run free and un-convicted must feel when they repeat their brave heroics to their children and grandchildren. Bobby was a beautiful person whose life was taken by scum.

But there was also an artistic enclave in existence in the Corridor and the place I frequented was called Alvin's, short for Alvin's Finer Delicatessen. Mostly it served students from Wayne State University, but at night, the old brick walls and rickety chairs and tables and the long beautiful bar became the place to witness some of the best music and art that Detroit had to offer. There was also a similar scene in Hamtramck, my birthplace but, for my taste, I spent most of my free time at Alvin's. All of these clubs were very close to where I had originally started over at the Village.

It was in the Corridor that I fell in love with the group Shadowfax. They were the kind of band that other musicians came to see because their music was so perfect. I came to be friends with George Konig, the bass player. George ended up flying all the way to Europe just to bring me a song he thought I should include on one of my albums.

Another talented and gifted player I liked was Bobby McDonald, a local keyboard player. It was heavenly listening to Bobby sing and play the piano. Bobby was afraid to leave the Corridor and afraid of success. He didn't think he was good. The truth is, he was brilliant. I proposed to him that he allow me to record a set of songs, but he wasn't thrilled about the idea. Bobby never ate. He just drank and played when I knew him. He eventually died from the drink.

It seems that many of the artists, save Tommy Ford, never made it out alive. Bill Hodson, one of the guitar players for Shadowfax, took his own life in New York City. I spent a great deal of my time over the late seventies and early eighties down on the Corridor. It was special. Dave Chambers still lives, God bless him.

Chapter 28

SO THERE WE WERE, HAVING TO drag our bodies once again all over America in every little club and bar that Tom could find for us. And just like Sinclair and Kramer before him, we got to some of the gigs broke, only to find the club owner couldn't pay us. This was the exact bottom end of the professional star days when the powerful booking agent made sure you had at least fifty percent of your money before you even went to the gig.

It was something I observed many times watching older pioneers like Chuck Berry and Jerry Lee Lewis. They had to go through that same thing until they got fed up with it. People used to think they were strange and arrogant for demanding every little penny that was due them. But I understand completely. Bar owners take a chance on the door to be able to pay the artist. And then when you don't get paid, you're stuck and out of money. We were very disgusted with our lack of progress in the States when the call came to go back to Germany for our fourth tour. Naturally we were happy to oblige, but it was going to be another long tour before we could get into the studio. This time was different though, and the reason was a man named Jurgen Osterloh.

At this point sometimes I was taking Kimberly with me overseas and sometimes I wasn't. This time I was, and after the tour we had a couple of days to rest, so we made plans to run down to Paris for a few days. The last time I had been in Paris for pleasure was in 1968 with Susan. At that time we had flown over from England and did the typical *touristo* deal. We had no friends there and no business connections, so the trip was confined to restaurants, hotels, and photographs at famous landmarks. The only memorable moment came while we were walking down the long approach to the Eiffel Tower and had somehow been overlooked by the security forces surrounding the North Vietnam peace contingent that had come to Paris for peace talks with Henry

Kissinger. As we walked toward the approaching assembly of diplomats we were quickly surrounded, questioned, searched, and then released. This time with Kimberly would be much different.

The Paris trip began in the German offices of Karsten Janke, our booking agent in Germany, as I was speaking with one of our agents, Neil Thompson. Neil eventually became my road manager but today he was helping me find a guide and a translator. He had a friend who knew a man, and after looking in his directory he handed me a piece of paper with the name, address and telephone number for a Jurgen Osterloh.

We arrived in Paris and took a small (really small) hotel room near the airport. We unpacked and were discussing what to do next, because we were so removed from everything except airplanes. I decided to call Jurgen and ask him what was near us that we might enjoy—restaurants, etcetera. As soon as he spoke I could hear excitement in his voice and he was very happy over my arrival. Jurgen was a German national who had been living in Paris for some time. He was aware of my rising popularity in Germany through his many friends there, and insisted we throw our belongings back into our suitcases and spend our holiday with him.

When the taxi arrived at *Du bis Vitale* we realized we were in a very expensive part of Paris called *Trocadéro*, about five blocks from the Eiffel Tower. Jurgen's home had four levels and was done up nicely, and the neighborhood was a scene from *Irma La Douce*. At the end of the block was a bakery and a grocery, and directly across was a bistro filled with characters from an Edgar Allen Poe novel. We spent our entire holiday with Jurgen going to clubs and restaurants, parties, and racing about Paris in his big Mercedes sedan touring the architectural wonders. It was magnificent. I promised, at his insistence, to stay in touch.

When we arrived home I rang up Tom and told him Jurgen had offered his assistance in getting me hooked up in France and was willing to entertain a meeting upon our return to Europe. To be honest, I had reservations about Jurgen's ability to pull that off. My first impression of him was of a wealthy playboy with hip connections and a constant flow of beautiful young women who were all, ironically, models, when asked what they did for a living.

Jurgen was also an extremely handsome man with an excellent command of the French language, which became obvious when he and his French maid carried on with their bickering and fighting as if they were an old married couple. Jurgen's face was much like a young Clint Eastwood, and he was tall and elegant and yet very masculine in the way he carried himself. He had spent time in prison in Germany for the crime that had given him his wealth but, in fact, it was no crime at all. It was a legitimate con of European corporations who, when faced with the fact that they had been taken by this brilliant young man, could do nothing to hide their embarrassment other than insist he do some time. If Jurgen cooperated he would be allowed to keep his fortune—provided he leave Germany.

We were about to return for another tour and to record the album that was supposed to have been done on our last trip, but the technology wasn't ready. So we held the meeting with Jurgen in Paris and he introduced us to his French partner and friend, the very likable Bernard Ossude. Bernard's grandfather was an artist who had some of his works displayed in the *Louvre*. A deal was made and Bernard arranged for us to license some of our masters with Underdog Records in Paris. I was thrilled. I felt as if I was slowly but surely going to conquer Europe, and I also could someday force my way back onto the American charts. Things were looking up and it was settled that we would perform at the Palace in Paris, with national television as well.

I did have a moment of doubt as I wondered how all of this would sit with Uwe, because really, it was Uwe who had made all of this possible. I had become very fond of Uwe in spite of our initial bad start, and held so many loving memories from my few years in Germany that I didn't ever want to do anything to lose that or to harm it. I soon discovered that the Germans really weren't concerned with the French and the French didn't give a damn about the Germans, so everything was going to be fine. With that in place we began to move forward.

We began the tour in France with the TV appearance and the show was brilliant, but Billy Csernits had thrown out his hip while gyrating for the cameras and was in pain. To "help," someone gave him some heroin. I had done heroin in the past and had gotten over it, but this was an introduction that Billy might still be having trouble getting over. It would all come down to how strong his will was, because what I've learned about recovery and recovery programs is that there is no accountability—you can slip a million times and still have welcoming arms awaiting you. That is bullshit. You either have the will to stop or you don't.

Narcotics Anonymous and Alcoholics Anonymous are the only two disease-related groups that trumpet and celebrate the growth of their membership. If I was dealing with terrible disease I wouldn't be happy about growth. I would be alarmed and start looking for a cure instead of a fellowship.

To celebrate our Paris success, Jurgen threw a lavish party. Prior to the event we ate at a restaurant called *Ban Douche*, and were hosted by the two brothers who owned the place. There, I was offered heroin. It had been at least ten years since I had any and I wouldn't be shooting, I would be snorting, so I wasn't that concerned with the cut. I should have been. As we ate I began to sweat, and I didn't notice until I looked at my clothes and felt my hair. My entire body was dripping with sweat. Then I felt weak and faint. One of the brothers grabbed me and we began to walk. The next thing I remember is lying on a cold, empty tile shower floor and hearing the voices of two frantic men talking about where to put the body. When they realized I wasn't going to die, they cleaned me up and we returned to the meal. Then it was on to the party at Jurgen's. Eight balls, hash, and magnificent vintage French wine was being circulated.

While we were there, Billy made an interesting friend who was an associate of the William F. Burroughs gang. Wilson was in the basement having sex with one of the female guests next to the furnace on the floor. Richard moved about as if he were the American Ambassador to France, and Mark and Joey hung with the road crew and laughed all night. Kimberly and I met everyone at least twice and then the sun, as it usually does, brought everything to an end.

The tour was a great success if we remind ourselves we are talking about a cult status, and not an arena success. Then came the studio and our first digital recording. It was 1981. This was also the place where the infamous Owens on Csernits attack took place. Uwe was dumbstruck, because after a few minutes to rest following the fight, the band was back in place and recording. In the end we came out with the product called *Live Talkies*, which would turn out to be our biggest seller yet. Tom estimates that Uwe sold around eighty thousand copies of *Live Talkies*. In Germany that is a lot of sales. Whatever was going on in America I now became oblivious to, because I had finally found a way to achieve my dream—outside my homeland.

We had to go home sometimes and when we did we toured in an RV Tom acquired for us called a Palm Beach. It was a GMC vehicle that we took all over the country. It was in this vehicle over thousands of miles and months that every human drama possible was played out. We had taken a friend of ours, Jerry Lubin, who was an ex-DJ for WABX during the high-flying hippie days, as our road manager/driver. But Jerry didn't appreciate our sense of humor.

One day we took off and he noticed debris trailing the RV as we drove down the road. He stopped and went to the back of the vehicle only to find his suitcase strapped to the back bumper. He was furious, but because he didn't want to go to jail for killing someone all he could manage was a quick, almost foreign sounding growl that seemed to say, "Wall to wall assholes."

Tom was no longer on the road with us. I think what did it for him was planting the child porno magazines in his luggage without his knowledge, and then delighting in his attempt to explain it to customs on a trip back from Amsterdam. He now worked hard at building the European market since our label, Seeds and Stems, was defunct. In America there was no breakthrough, and I realized I had been with this band for six years, in the business for nineteen and with Kimberly for fourteen.

In 1982 Kimberly and I finally moved into our own house. True, it was a rental, but I don't think I can tell you how happy that little accomplishment made me feel. I hadn't had my own house since 1967 when I was with Susan. Just to be able to live in a house with your own yard to care for and a garage brought me immeasurable amounts of joy. I thrilled at the notion of having a simple laundry chute in the bathroom wall in which to drop my clothes into the basement. True, we were still in Detroit, and there was still more crime here then elsewhere, but at least we had our own place. The house was in a section known as Warrendale. As I sat in the quiet of the house, the tranquility allowed me a moment to reflect on my life thus far and take another accounting.

Over the years my relationship with Kimberly had gone through some subtle but disturbing evolutions. It was a difficult concept for me to take on because it was like a man capable of stealing a watch calling someone capable of stealing a wallet a thief. When Kimberly worked for Xerox, she had become accustomed to meeting with her co-workers after work for drinks. It was my belief that she and I were both now alcoholics. The difference was, and it really is no difference in the end, is that I believe she also required other stimulants as a part of her pleasure. As far as the alcohol, I held it better and had a higher tolerance for it than she did. We were now a very long way from the clarity and sobriety of those years in Colorado. Whatever meaningful conversations we attempted were now being cloaked and the truth concealed by substance abuse.

But Kim and I were also spending more and more time together. We often went to neighborhood bars together and danced and enjoyed evenings of blind abandon. To the bar crowd we were a happy couple, and delightful to be around.

But at home, in our new-found privacy, our communication often became combative and hostile, and we used our verbal skills and knowledge of each others faults and transgressions to hit hot buttons and torture each other with our words. Colorado had been a brief respite, and as they say in the "program"—and they have a million sayings—you pick up from where you left off.

It seemed like a cop out to take counseling, because we were married to each other for better or worse for the rest of our lives. I had sworn that I would never get another divorce because I was haunted by the tragic mistake I made when I left Susan and my children. Plus, Kimberly and I had sacrificed so much to stay together. It was as if, in the face of those sacrifices and the absence of material wealth, I could make up for it all by staying with Kimberly. Sadly, we went on. Our current dysfunctional behavior was only a glimpse of the future.

As always, I escaped into touring with the band, and putting in more miles as we crisscrossed the country over the same roads we had been doing forever. I was jealous of Tom because he had the comfort of remaining stationary. He also was able to enjoy a degree of family life that I couldn't, even if I had the time. My life was a mess. Even though things were crazy between Kim and me, I still considered the house my home and when I was there I flourished in daily tasks that one did around a house: building

things, repairs, and especially working outdoors in the yard. It gave me peace and soli-
tude, and time to think.

Career wise I came to the conclusion that Tom was unable to take me to the next
level. Yes, we had a good thing going in Germany but we had to live in America and I
remembered that Tom and I had already failed with our own record label. Ultimately,
I felt he was incapable of securing an American deal for my beautiful music. Tom and
I desolved our partnership, but continued to work together in Europe. The next project
he worked on with me was a compilation of materials culled from the Line Record catalog called *The Beautiful Toulang Sunset*. It contained two or three new originals, and the
rest was a "best of" from previous releases.

Here in the States the band was still thrilling people, but we weren't doing many
of the European releases because I became aware that our audience really only wanted
to hear the hits from the sixties. That holds true even to this day, in spite of the excellent
creations I have recorded in Europe.

I became very pissed off one night when Chrissie Hynde of the Pretenders came
to one of my gigs in Dallas and asked that we talk privately for a few minutes. I found
a table and had every intention of asking her to give me a few weeks to divorce my
wife and marry her, because I was certain that our two talents together would produce
the most acclaimed artistic children known to mankind. But the band had different
ideas and would not leave us alone. She became frustrated and begged leave. I don't
know. Maybe *she* was going to ask *me* to marry her. She's still very hot.

It was time to prepare another album for Europe. I had a case in which I kept
hand-held tape recordings of melodies and lyrics. It also held paper after paper of
thoughts and ideas and titles and poems. I opened up the case and began the writing
process once again. I did not want our European fans to be separated from us for any
length of time that would allow them to forget us. I cherish them and always find a
way to get product, even though it is hard to find, into their hands. My European success is also a good record of my growth and progress as an artist, and is essential to
whatever final judgment is made about my struggle and ability.

I contacted Uwe about funding the record, which would be the first Line Record
not recorded in Germany—and the first without Tom Connor. He eventually agreed
and I began work on my fifth Line Record release, *Smart Ass*. The band would have a
slightly different line-up because I had to let Wilson Owens go for stabbing one of
our road crew in a fight. The new drummer was named Al Wotton.

Although I didn't know it at the time, Wilson Owens would return after the recording due to the untimely death of our new drummer. The songs were brilliant but again,
because Uwe was so stingy with the funding, I was under a lot of pressure to do everything quickly and cheaply.

The result exposed that the mixing was left to the ears of an engineer who was a drummer, and in the end that was the predominant sound. All the other parts worked well but were buried in the mix, and the vocal leads I performed were nothing more than pilot vocals. I needed a little more money to correct things, but Uwe was unwilling to give more and so I went with what I had. Uwe decided he didn't like the album and therefore didn't market it with the conviction he had for previous releases. *Smart Ass* later became an album that John Mellencamp plucked three songs from.

Visiting the studio during that session was a woman named Mary Gail, whom I had met at Alvin's. She was a singer who had recently been through a divorce from a doctor and she had a young daughter. Her father had run a successful booking agency in Detroit, and her brother was a star in Hollywood on a popular sitcom. Mary was driven to be successful, now that she was on her own. She was independent and I liked that. We began an on again off again sexual relationship that lasted several years. Mary moved to Berlin, and one time I ran into her she was very angry to find my entire catalog in all of the record shops. She wanted that for herself, but for the moment, she settled for me.

Kimberly no longer had time to worry about where I was or what I was doing. She was caught up in a world that had her own friends and places. We still went places together, but the days of home-cooked meals were a thing of the past as we drifted further and further apart.

I had gone back to Europe and Kim was going to attend a party at a friend's house in Ann Arbor, a sixty-mile drive from our home. A week before I left to deliver the *Smart Ass* tapes to Uwe I bought a new car from my friend Wally Schwartz. A Riviera. While I was gone, I called Kim every day to ask how my car was. She always replied, "It's in the garage." I thought wow, when I get back I can't wait to drive it.

What she didn't tell me was that it was in a repair garage. Apparently on her way to the party she ran into a divider on an entrance ramp and drifted into a twelve-wheeler truck. The entire front shell had been completely torn off. There were no fenders or hood. What remained was an engine, four wheels, and a windshield. Kim somehow proceeded to drive to the party, and a friend has a video of her pulling up to his house. There was no police report since the truck suffered no damage.

Much of this was my fault for enabling Kim with money and time. Once Kim left Xerox she didn't have to work again until years later when we finally divorced. But for now, and for the next ten years, she rose and fell with my fortunes. For the first time I was able to put a portfolio together with savings and stocks and metals. Sure, it was small, but it was a beginning. I paid my taxes on time and had some disposable income. The problem was, my guilt over not taking Kim to Europe made me decide to give her money.

I still had to be careful because my career had never been consistent enough to make commitments to anyone. Not the church. Not the installment plan. Not anything that required regularity and consistency. And so you end up telling little lies and pray that something will come up while you frantically seek employment in your career as an "artist." It was a terrifying balancing act trying to figure out how to save enough from an unknown amount of income to spread evenly through times when you already knew you would have no income at all.

Chapter 29

IN THE LATE SUMMER OF 1982 an interesting development was in the making, and Jerry Lubin was responsible. Jerry had gotten his fill of being road manager for our band and had returned to the radio. One day John Cougar Mellencamp came through the studio on a promotion blitz. At this point in time he was a young, rising triple-platinum star, and he noticed one of my posters hanging behind Jerry on the wall. He asked how I was doing and Jerry told him. Mellencamp then did the unthinkable. He proclaimed that he would like to talk to me about working together on a project. He said I was one of his early heroes and was eager to speak to me. Jerry, aware that Mellencamp was not privy to his relationship with me, supplied John with the telephone number. All of this took place for the public to hear. I imagine it surprised the hell out of John, who must have forgotten that he had opened for me just a few years earlier in Canton, Michigan.

John and I had an initial conversation that covered what I was doing with my career and life, and what my future plans were. The second conversation we had he made a proposal to produce my next album. He said it was his way of giving back to someone who had greatly influenced him. He also took the time and trouble to tell me he had picked me from a list of artists that included Donovan and Eric Burdon. I was fortunate to have won that lottery. He wanted to hear something I had recently done—I assume to determine if I still had a voice—so I gave him a copy of *Born to Laugh at Tornados* by Was (Not Was), which I had been a guest artist on the "Bow Wow Wow Wow," cut. It was less than a year old. I also gave him a copy of *Smart Ass*.

Convinced that I still had my chops, things began to move quickly and he announced to the media that he was producing my next American album. From that moment on, things all around me began to change. It was first noticeable at the neighborhood bars Kim and I frequented. When I first started hanging out in them I was so low key that many people didn't even know I was Mitch Ryder, and for a long time I didn't tell them. I just wanted to be one of the regulars. After a while though, they found out. I guess the thing that puzzled them was the fact that I didn't live in the expensive suburbs, but was indeed their neighbor. In any case, over the couple of years that we first lived on Winthrop, I became friends with a lot of the regulars.

When I wasn't at Alvin's I preferred to hang out at a place on Warren and Greenfield called Dunleavy's. I became friends with Tommy Dunleavy and his brother Kevin, who split their time at the bar. I went there for the Euchre tournaments. I knew a lot of the detectives and off-duty cops from the local precinct who shot pool there and, like most of us, anxiously awaited St. Patrick's Day, the high water mark on the drinking calender, and the busiest night of the year for an Irish bar. I also went down the street to Ozzies a lot. That's where Kim and I danced.

Eventually I met a man named Phil Stemelo who played Rugby, was an ex-Marine, a member of a bike gang, and the owner of a place called Rutgers. Phil was involved in two of my musical projects, one being "Good Golly Ask Ollie," a spoof of Oliver North and the Iran Contra affair. Phil and I actually found a pool hall in Manhattan while we were working on the deal. He also made sure my dress for the cover of the Oliver North send-up was militarily correct. We shot pool together on the Busch League, and enjoyed each other's company.

Phil also, almost single-handedly, put together the album cover for my CD *Monkey Island*, which would come a few years down the road. He wrote the liner notes and was a true believer in me. He owns a share of that recording and has yet to see any return for his investment.

When the news that Mellencamp was going to produce me hit, all of my friends greeted this with well wishes and were happy over my good fortune. Before we ever set foot in the studio, the press response was greater than any I had seen in years and a flurry of activity greeted each day like a flood.

John Mellencamp wanted to see my band perform, so he arranged and paid for a rehearsal hall in Troy. It was actually a church. I assembled the band as it was at that time and there was no Wilson Owens. Instead, we had a temporary drummer, a friend of Richard Schein's.

Through the years I have had people ask if I remember so and so, because he used to work with me. I've come to understand the meaning of that to apply to someone who was on the same bill, someone who sat in at a rehearsal, someone who worked with me a week or two on a temporary basis, or some other transitory position. That's why, in the beginning, I don't give credit to a few of the musicians who, although very good, such as Mike McClellan, never served any real time with me in the trenches. Ray

Goodman is another story like that but not the same example. Ray is a very good guitar player and served as one of the revamped Detroit Wheels under Barry Kramer.

In another situation, Ray put a band together and we toured out West. We even did duets from time to time. In fact, I recently played with Ray in Ypsilanti. Musicians sometimes find better gigs and move on; things change and they come back. Basically though, since I stopped doing solo gigs forty some odd years ago, I've really only had the Wheels, the Thrashing Brothers, what I call the George Brothers, and Engerling, my German band.

So John, in spite of my belief that I only cared about the quality of the music, began to watch as the group performed, and he was watching with an eye on appearance. He wanted young, skinny, good-looking, and talented. I protested and he lay down the ultimatum; his way or no way. I imagine because of his success he had his own notions about what was marketable from an image point of view, and even though he respected me, he felt I was out of touch on this issue. So, more than half my band was gone immediately. He did not want to fail. I think that would have bothered him.

From my point of view beauty only mattered as to how it applied to the music coming off the stage. Everyone I turned to for advice told me to do what John said, because he was offering me an opportunity that I had been unable to create for myself, and it might never come again.

After the recording was finished, John hand picked the musicians who were the nucleus of my touring band. He did allow Mark Gougeon to stay, and at the time of the rehearsal we were experimenting with two keyboard players: the fading Billy Csernits, and Harry Phillips, whom I had last worked with in the band Detroit. That was in 1970. This was 1983. But Harry somehow appealed to John and he seemed to have mellowed. Harry was a good friend of a man named "Chooch," who has since passed away. Chooch was a friend and satellite figure to the Rolling Stones entourage and Harry supplied him with some of the best pot known to man. Harry also possessed the rock 'n' roll look John was seeking. The rest of the group came from John's backyard in Indiana.

Having cleared that hurdle, John wanted to start picking out songs for the album. He chose two of the songs from the *Smart Ass* album, wrote or co-wrote some, and took songs from outside writers. He also had a great idea in pairing me with Marianne Faithful, who had also been trying to establish herself overseas. There were other guest artists as well. Gina Schock (drummer for the Go-Go's) played drums on one of the songs. John used every trick in the book and in the end, the album sounded great.

John insisted that I appear on the American Music Awards with him and got his way. The press coverage was excellent, crossing from the *New York Times* to *Time* magazine. Looking in from the outside one would have to say that John Mellencamp did

Mitch a favor that Mitch should be eternally grateful for. Polygram pushed the product well, but a local Detroit television station, WDIV, pushed the project better than anyone in New York. They did a week-long daily segment on the making of a recording and followed the process every step of the way. The single from the album, a Prince composition called "When You Were Mine" from his *Dirty Minds* LP did very well in some segments of the country, but poorly in others. Polygram dropped the option, and under normal circumstances, that would have been the end of the story. But there is another side that is much more compelling, especially in light of the fact that the album sold nearly eighty thousand units.

In the beginning, when I was told I would be making the album, I started to put together a local crew to shoot the video for the single. MTV was relatively new, but old enough to have become an established part of the model for releasing records in 1983. I quickly found that was out of my hands. In fact, the entire process would be out of my control and I had to accept it on blind faith. How shitty could it get? John knew what it was like to grow up in the Midwest and what it felt like to confront the establishment in New York and L.A., and I believed he still carried that connection in his bones. My conflict was being able to let go of putting my own album together and trusting someone else to make decisions in my best interest.

Behind the scenes in all of this lay the involvement of a man I consider to be a good friend. As you know, that is a very rare occurrence in my life. His name is Geoffrey Fieger, and he is an attorney. A year prior to these events now swirling madly about me, I decided to stop renting the house on Winthrop and made an offer to buy it from the owner. I was given a telephone number for an attorney who was familiar with real estate named Bernard Fieger, who was Geoffrey's father. It was through Bernard that I was introduced to Geoffrey, whose brother, Doug Fieger, became famous with the group The Knack. You might recall a hit single of theirs, "My Sharrona." Geoffrey had also gone to school with noted record producer Don Was, whom I already knew and had worked with. The two of them had gone to Oak Park High School, as had my first wife, Susan. When I went to Geoffrey's house, a small bungalow in Oak Park, I was introduced to an extremely beautiful woman named Keeni. Keeni was from Garden City and eventually married Geoffrey.

When the Mellencamp opportunity presented itself, Geoffrey served as my attorney for the contract negotiations, which really weren't going to be negotiated that much because everyone knew I was not in a position to make many demands. It was more about Geoffrey taking care that I was treated with respect. Geoffrey also arranged a marketing deal for me and brought in an outside song, "The Thrill of it All."

I did however make one demand, and I stood fast on it. Everyone thought I was crazy. I demanded that Uwe Tessnow and Line Records be allowed to license the recording in Germany. I don't think Uwe realized what that took to do and what it meant in terms of my affection for him.

Uwe kept me on Line Records for a long time, but it had its foolishness and strings. For example, Uwe would, every three years or so, license his catalog to different distributors for advances. When I handed him *Smart Ass* and wondered why it wasn't doing so well, he hadn't bothered to tell me that the distributor dealt mostly with country music. And he still had the nerve to tell me the recording was not very good.

Having signed the contracts, I appeared on John's label, Riva Records, distributed by Polygram. Polygram did a good promotion but Riva could care less about the new album, *Never Kick a Sleeping Dog*. What I didn't know, but was later told, was that John was re-negotiating his contract with Riva and could not, or would not, record a new album for them until the negotiations were complete. Riva desperately wanted to keep John, especially in light of his triple platinum success. Apparently there was a clause in the existing contract that, even though John could choose not to record, he was allowed to produce an outside artist. Hence Mitch Ryder, hence a budget, and finally continuous cash flow.

John has publicly stated that he thought I believed his production and effort was going to be the last chance I would ever have at reaching comeback success in my career. Nothing could be further from the truth. I saw it as a great opportunity, but whether it was John in 1983 or someone else in another year, I believed in my soul, and do to this day, that I am capable of reaching the mass American public again. So if John's efforts failed, it certainly wasn't going to crush me.

Besides, nothing could equal the beating I took from Stigwood and Prager. From that day to this I have never had another manager. I don't know what opportunities or deals might have come my way if I'd had a big New York manager, probably quite a few, but the foul taste of Prager has kept me from ever drinking from that well again. That is why you have, in America, a very subterranean Mitch Ryder. As of this publication I have recorded twenty-five CDs. Can you name more than three?

The budget from Polygram and John's cash flow. Ah, yes. There was a shell of a house under construction in the woods near Seymour, Indiana that belonged to one of John's relatives. John decided to build a studio inside of the house. After the recording was over the house was finished off as a real home, and occupied by one of his clan. John's first wife owned the rooms that Mark, Harry, and I occupied for the months we spent there, and she was paid lodging, expenses, and catering. The cost of bringing in other artists, Marianne Faithful from Paris, for example, was all part of the budget. John's brother did quite well as road manager, driver, etcetera.

The video for MTV was over budget, like everything else, because John wanted to work with László Kováks, an Hungarian cinematographer who had worked on the film

Easy Rider. John had plans of one day making his own movie and he needed to make connections in Hollywood. The original screenplay for the video consisted of me lying on a bed in high-heels and a blue dress while two midgets leaped up and down on either side of me in umpire's uniforms. And they say Hollywood has lost its imagination.

In a strange way John's nepotism was expected. John actually reminded me of myself, a young Mitch Ryder, when success first leaped into my life. But with John there was no Bob Crewe pulling the strings. It was clear that John was in control. What we both held in common, I believe, was a rebellious attitude that we had both come by honestly, through our experiences at the hands of our industry molesters. In a more innocent moment, John shared his joy over receiving a writer's royalty check for some hundreds of thousands of dollars. He didn't show it to me to make me feel bad, or unimportant, or jealous. He showed it to me because he wanted to share his excitement and joy.

As always, there is more than one side to a man's character. We did some recording in Miami. One of the things John asked me to do was keep an eye on Marianne, since we were in the same hotel on the same floor. I agreed. When we first brought her luggage to her room, which was just one large duffle bag, she began searching the seams of the bag. While she did that I stared at her, and two things were going through my mind. So that's the famous "almost Mrs. Mick Jagger," and *Broken English*. An excellent recording.

The first morning I came to get her to go to the studio she called me in, and as I looked down the long vanity mirror I noticed a pattern emerging. As she groomed herself, putting on some last minute make-up, she systematically went down a line arranged in front of her. First the line of cocaine, then the Courvasia, and then the quaalude. This arrangement repeated itself snaking halfway down the length the counter in front of her. When she had completed the ritual, only then could we leave for the studio.

One night, after we had done "Thrill's a Thrill" together, we were sitting on her balcony twelve floors up overlooking the Atlantic ocean, quietly enjoying the crashing sounds of the waves below and the warm Miami breeze that was only appreciated by people used to cold climates. She leaned over the edge of the railing and I was concerned, because she had a buzz on.

As I watched, I saw her feet start to leave the cement floor of the balcony. Time suddenly took on a strange characteristic. I leaped toward her, placing my left arm in front of her body to counter act the direction of her leaning, which had actually turned into a fall, and brought my right arm down against the back of her legs, which flipped her safely back onto the balcony but landed her on her butt. She brought herself to a standing position and slapped me hard across my face telling me to never touch her again. I went to John the next day and said, "She's all yours."

Back in Seymour, I visited John's house and was introduced to his second wife, but I never hung out and that suited the both of us very well. John liked his privacy, because he gave so much of his time to the demands of the industry. When I was a young star, when John was at his peak, and even today, there is a truth. The industry is full of powerful, perverted ego maniacs who enjoy watching the egos of the artists leveled to their standards. Their jealousy and hatred of artists is very clear. That's why you have someone like John Mellencamp proclaiming he is "an artist and would never make a commercial" and a few years later he's pushing Chevy trucks. It's always about the money when it comes to artistic credentials in America.

Even though my album with Polygram sold between sixty and eighty thousand units, a number given me by a Polygram staffer, they did not pick up the option. Any new group that had sold that many units would have likely had a second release. Their A&R man said, "We expected your legions of fans to come out." The truth was that John had gone way over budget to the point they could not recoup with another promotion, and John had signed his new contract so they didn't need me anymore.

There were two incidents that disturbed me during this process. One was watching John hit drummer Kenny Aronoff in the back of the head on the way to the American Music Awards for wearing a jacket of his own choice, and the other was the reaction to piano player Harry Phillips firing his handgun in the direction of the control room at the studio in Seymour. Several nights later Harry and I and a friend of John's were at a nearby bar and a group of Seymour's gun carrying mafia would have killed Harry on the spot if I had not gotten him out of there.

John and I have not spoken since. I had to forge my own relationship with the Indiana boys John picked out for the band. That band lasted for maybe a year. It included taking them to Europe and having a Thanksgiving Day party at the American consulate. It also included the introduction into my life of rock guitarist and songwriter Robert Gillespie.

Years later I went to one of John's concerts at the Fox Theater in Detroit, but I spent my time talking to some of my old Indiana band mates, who were now with John. I waited for the customary invitation to see him, but it never came, and I was reminded of the rebellious and vindictive nature we both had.

Since then, John has moved from Riva to Mercury to Columbia, a label noted for having only the best artists. When I think of Columbia I always get a kick out of thinking about the time they dropped Bob Dylan because he was no longer selling enough records. I can't think of a better way to illustrate how out of touch the self-important heads of the major companies are with the true character of art. They couldn't create a piece of shit if their bodies didn't override their minds.

Chapter 30

I HAD BECOME SO ADDICTED TO Germany that I went over a couple of times by myself just to keep it fresh in my mind. I always feared losing the bond that existed between my fans and me. I meant to keep it fresh forever. I also took side-excursions to Paris to be with my friend Jurgen. One time I went over to promote a dance single of a Bob Dylan tune called "Like a Rolling Stone," produced by Don Was. It was released in Germany on RCA records, and the promotion man was an actual German prince.

Kimberly no longer tagged along because I had asked for a divorce in 1983. As I remember, she and I attended an all-nighter at a place called Harpo's (where one night we were shot at by a sniper as we stood outside the stage door). On the drive home in our rag-top Jeep I remember yet another argument that began. It reached its zenith when she kicked me in the face with her cowgirl boots. So there we were, sixty-five miles an hour in the middle of heavy traffic, my prescription glasses broken and twisted on my face, blood flowing over my right eye, me trying to keep control of the vehicle with one hand and keep her from leaping out of the Jeep with the other as she screamed, "I'm going to kill myself if you divorce me."

I didn't divorce her. I didn't want her blood on my hands.

The next morning I flew to New York City to appear on the *CBS Morning Show* to promote the Mellencamp produced album and all I could focus on was the newly forming scab and black and blue around my eye as I hid behind a pair of dark glasses.

During this time, or any other in Germany, I rarely picked up women. That's unusual when I think about it, but when I did, it was always different and exceptional. I liked to hang out at transvestite clubs in all the major cities. In Hamburg, it was the Pulverfast. In Berlin, Romey Haig. In London it was London Lee's. One night I was hanging out with Hans Reibe, a former road manager from the Tom Connor days when

I was signed to Karsten Janke. Hans now enjoyed a very profitable relationship with a German clown named Otto.

This particular evening we joined two women at a table. The woman I was with, a teacher, spoke little English but was happy to be leaving with a real man. The next morning the German schoolteacher awoke in a panic to discover where she was and what she had done. She flew from the room without bothering to take all of her clothes.

There was another odd woman I met at the famous club, Onkel Po's Carnegie Hall in Hamburg. She approached me because she knew I was American and she was having a very hard time connecting with anyone else. Turns out she was an Israeli Jew. She took me to her room near the airport where we had sex until she had to leave the following day. I wrote a song about our encounter called "I Fucked a Jew in Germany" but Uwe refused to put it out.

But the most important woman met in Germany was Geisela. When I stop to think about the women in my life who have made any difference about how I view life and love you can count them on one hand. Geisela was one. Her parents owned a bakery, but you couldn't tell it from looking at her. She was beautiful and energetic and challenging. She wanted the world and, because I wanted her, I pretended to have it.

In jumped my contradiction. I went to Paris to hang out with Jurgen, as our relationship had become special and our fondness for each other had grown. On one evening we went to visit Elton John at his beautiful home off the River Seine. What I remember most about that visit was the fleeting figure of a young oriental servant running from some unseen danger as he dashed for his life from room to room.

Later that evening, as Jurgen and I sat at a table in a quiet little café, we realized we wanted our relationship to be something that would last, and so we committed ourselves to that end. While we were in the café, we fell to the floor in an embrace and as we were kissing each other, the other patrons became upset and left. I left Paris profoundly changed in whatever notions and doubts I held for my sexuality. but still nonetheless confused.

Because the Mellencamp-produced album and single were starting to appear on the charts in America, we were also enjoying airplay on the Armed Forces Network (AFN). The music was so blatantly commercial American and so far removed from what my German fans had come to expect, that they were having trouble coming to grips with the new direction. From my point of view, that was not the only problem. Now, for the first time, our performances were starting to draw Americans as we played near some of the bases. So, what I held as a special covenant between my German fans me and was now being altered by the presence of Americans in the crowd.

I did the *Never Kick a Sleeping Dog* album songs and the American service people cheered, because they had heard them on the Armed Forces Network. But then I went into my German material, which the Americans had never heard, and the Germans cheered. I did songs like "Bang Bang," which was clearly an anti-military song or "Er Ist Nicht Mein Prasident," which was a criticism about President Ronald Reagan, but also a warning about letting George Bush the First become president, because he had been head of the CIA. The Americans were deeply concerned, but it made me understand that my German material was so far under the radar that no one in America was even aware of my German recordings. For that matter, very few Germans were as well. I left that tour seriously concerned over my future in Germany.

Nearly two years passed before I returned. It was the only time I ever allowed that to happen. I had become nearly hysterical over my absence from Germany, and the Indiana band from the Mellencamp days had pretty much run its course. They were just too pretty, too professional, and too predictable. I began to yearn for the dysfunctional aspects of the old band.

Then fate reared is ugly head once again. The hardest lesson for me to learn is that I am not in control here—or anywhere. Someone, probably Gary Lazar, manager of the ill-fated Rockets, came up with the idea of a Mitch Ryder and The Detroit Wheels reunion concert at Pine-Knob to be recorded and filmed by a huge crew. Capital Records would own the tapes.

This was 1984. We did the concert. I had managed to secure another tour in Europe but I had to take the reunion band. I didn't enjoy it much because I had agreed to sing covers of "Rocket" hits, whatever that was. The music, however, was exceptional with Johnny Badanjek on drums, Jimmy McCarty on guitar and Jim Noel on keyboards. Then boom. It was over and I got my old band back. Wilson Owens on drums, Billy Csernits on keys, Mark Gougeon on bass, Robert Gillespie and Joe Gutc on guitar. We did the usual tour then recorded, coming out with the album *In the China Shop*. "China Shop" contained some exceptional songs, but it also carried with it some of the more important production techniques and shortcuts I had witnessed while recording with Mellencamp. I was not only trying to improve as a singer and a writer, but as a producer as well. That was 1985.

Back home, things with Kim kept swirling about from good to bad. There was a lot of mistrust on both sides, but we occasionally reached a quiet truce that sometimes lasted up to a week. We were living separate lives now and not sharing too much of anything in the way of conversation or information.

I came to realize that my drinking on the road had become un-appealing, but I hadn't brought myself to that place where I would stop. Our contract rider contained only three requests: five bottles of vodka, five quarts of orange juice, and a carton of Kool cigarettes. These were all consumed prior to the show, and the rest of the time we stayed straight. It was a buyer's dream, at least in terms of expenditures.

But when I was home, I spent every free moment at my favorite bar. I eventually started taking my work there and wrote songs and lyrics and whatever came into my mind under the cloud of alcohol.

When I came home from the road, the house was sometimes full of strangers, soiled clothes, unclean dishes with food all over them scattered about the entire house, people passed out in one room or another, and our pets running to me to get fed. I had seen a paper that suggested Kimberly might be suffering from manic depression, what they now call bi-polarism. That information helped me understand what had driven her behavior for many years, but it wouldn't make the next six years any easier. She continued to mask her pain, but mostly she sank deeper and deeper.

I was also in deep pain, and I had two ways to momentarily deny it. I either found a woman to spend a night with or, more likely, drank myself into oblivion. One night after an unforgiving verbal assault between Kim and me, I wanted to kill myself. I could not find the courage to leave and I couldn't stand another minute of this existence. I took my loaded assault rifle and sat behind the garage in my beloved backyard and fired off a few rounds. I knew it would bring the cops. Maybe they would be kind enough to do the job for me if I refused to surrender my weapon.

What I didn't count on was the fact that I knew most of the police from drinking together at Dunleavy's, and their only response was to tell me to sober up and put away the rifle. Then they left.

After the China Shop recording Johnny Badanjek re-entered the line-up on drums, replacing Wilson Owens. Wilson had tried to seduce my fourteen-year-old niece at a gig, so he had to go. George Konig, the bass player from Shadowfax, was back in my life, too. We often went golfing together and sat for hours recalling what we considered the good old days.

One time, when Neil Thompson was our road manager, George and I were walking down the street in Amsterdam. We were following Neil and someone else from the band as we cruised the streets looking for the next exciting place for empty lives to get a refill. Along the way I found a hundred dollar bill on the sidewalk. We were excited, but decided not to say anything to the other two, since they had obviously missed it before we found it. Maybe twenty seconds later we found another one. This time we decided we should share our good fortune with them, and as we approached Neil and as he turned to greet us, we saw that he had taken the night's receipts and stuffed them into his partially opened shirt. He was losing our own money as he walked.

We all wandered on, breaking empty beer bottles against walls, and eventually the police arrived. They were going to arrest Neil. Neil didn't want to be separated or alone, and the police refused to take any of us along. George decided he would stay with Neil, so he walked over to one of the officers and punched him in the face. Off they went.

George was a genuine rarity. He was an excellent bass player, and even though he was not a wealthy man, he knew how to appreciate all that existed that was worth keeping. He loved the excitement of being a social creature, yet he made time to nurture those one-on-one relationships that made someone in his presence feel special. He loved fine clothes when he was out and about, but he was equally comfortable in jeans, boots and t-shirts. He smoked expensive cigars, had a taste for Courvasier and cocaine, and valued and respected women.

After all was said and done, George was one of those Cass Corridor artists who, unfortunately, would burn out or die without ever having given the world what we in Detroit had come to cherish as a part of our rich musical heritage. I loved the way George treated me as an equal, even though deep in my heart I was jealous of his purity as an artist.

Karsten Scholermann was a young German entrepreneur who had been introduced to me by Uwe Tessnow. He liked me very much and was a fan. He had a little dance club in Hamburg and was also involved in a steak house restaurant in the business district. He had done the '86 tour (we called it the "In Search of Heidi" tour) and now invited us back. My daughter had been kind enough to accept my invitation to accompany us in 1986, but this time there wasn't enough money, and besides, if anyone came it should have been Joel.

My relationship with my children was unusual. If ever there was a young woman who wanted desperately to know her father, it was Dawn. Through all those years, from the time I left her and her brother to be raised by their mother, we had to deal with separation and a quiet distance that I had failed to remove from their lives.

In prior years, Kimberly and I had them for holidays—Christmas, Thanksgiving and Easter—and they celebrated with Kimberly's family as well as mine. Sometimes we took them up north to Kimberly's parent's cottage for snowmobiling and things like that, but it was never like the early days when we were home where they came every other weekend or so.

I remember when Joel was younger and it was more important for me to get him on the empty stage before one of our gigs, turn on the spotlights, kill the houselights and let him get a sense of the power that awaited him, instead of allowing him to remain by my side where he wanted to be. Dawn had gone through a painful and turbulent period in her teens, and Joel had taken up guitar in what I believe was an effort to please me.

All the neglect and harmful lack of love that I showed those beautiful children was finally and angrily taking a toll on the only things in the world that I created that was of any real value. Even though I didn't understand the depth of the hurt I had given them, I did understand and acknowledge my selfishness. You can tell someone all day long that you love them, but unless you are willing to sacrifice to prove it, you are a liar.

A couple of years ago I had the fortune of attending one of Joel's poetry readings at Wayne State University in Detroit. Joel, by the way, teaches in the English department there. He has won several awards, including the John Clare Award for poetry, the Tudor Scholarship for creative writing, and the Phillip Lawson Hatch, Jr. Memorial Writing Competition.

At the reading, Joel's confidence surprised me, and the passion he brought to the reading was real. So real, in fact, that the entire audience sensed the fuel feeding his fire, as his booklet for the program printed out his rage and hatred for me. He won an award that day, and I was proud of him.

The band and I responded to Karsten's invitation and went over in the winter of 1988. I remember two things about the tour. One was that John Badanjek, as talented as he was, could not master the free flowing style on drums that Wilson Owens had created. It was particularly obvious on some of our more popular songs such as "War" or "Er Ist Nicht Mein Prasident." John had a vicious attack that was unparalled if you were doing straight ahead rock songs, but he lacked the sensitivity and lightness of touch that made Wilson's dynamics so vital.

When faced with his shortcomings, John decided that the best way to counter my insistence to equal the necessary beats was to chide me into believing that my German fans wouldn't want to hear those songs if they were instead offered some straight ahead rock 'n' roll. John's inclusion into the band also ushered in an era of frequent complaining and criticism over the way I ran my business affairs in Germany.

This criticism would eventually come back to, and include, my dealings in America. But, for the moment, I chose to look the other way because when we were back home, his style of drumming was perfectly suited to the American market, and where we would do any of the German material?

When John Badanjek wasn't complaining, he was joking. He had his hands full with Joe Gutc, because Joe was the master of fun. But complaining and joking are the only two sides of that man I have ever known, even to this day. I deluded myself into thinking that John was grateful to have a gig and would eventually accept my direction.

John didn't make too much trouble in Germany, but when we returned to America he began separating himself from the band and often gave speeches to the band about how he, being a former Detroit Wheel, considered himself different from the other band members. The insinuation was that he considered himself better than the rest of the band.

That was a problem. First, most of the guys had been with me almost three times the amount of years John had. Then he would tell me how lousy he thought Joe Gutc and Billy Csernits were. He liked Robert Gillespie, because Robert shared his view of what rock 'n' roll was supposed to be, look, and sound like. He also welcomed Mark Gougeon because of his professionalism, and because he had survived the Mellencamp cut. My problem with John's belief was the very real truth that my German material was not about rock 'n' roll or sounding like what was on the radio, but was instead based on my sensibilities as an artist.

The year prior, 1987, had taken us to Japan for a five-city tour. It should have been a welcoming indicator for my career, but I managed to derail the opportunity by sabotaging the shows with my alcoholic intake. We didn't have a deal there and I treated it as if it was a vacation, instead of an opportunity. I was also irritated because of the constant friction in the band, and also because Kimberly decided she had to come because her father had been stationed there during the war.

I was miserable. I was so miserable that I made plans to leave the band and Kim and head to Bangkok. The problem was that I told someone in the band, and the next thing I knew was when it time came for the band and Kim to head back to America, that's exactly what they did. In the process, someone had taken my passport and my wallet. So there I was with just a few dollars in my pocket, sobering up to the fact that I was stranded in Tokyo.

I couldn't find my booking agent. Not that it mattered. This gig had fallen into his lap. Since I'd left New York I hadn't been with a decent or powerful agent. I had been with some of the better ones in Detroit, like D.M.A., which was run by Dave Leone, but I had also allowed Ron Baltrus to get me gigs for over a year, when his specialty was putting titty dancers into bars.

I was always scratching and sniffing around for money, wherever I could find it. That's how Richard Schein came to own several of my original oil paintings. That's why I took gigs in clubs where you only had a fifty-fifty chance of getting paid. Some star I was. But you know what? I still had my art. Yeah, the kids had been cut loose. The first wife had been abandoned and the second one was on her way out. I fucked other women. I drank too much and I didn't respect much of anything that couldn't immediately hurt me. I sure as hell didn't know what love felt like. I knew what it looked like by watching other people. But I had my art. On my terms. I wasn't selling shit, but I was continually growing as a writer and a singer and as sick as I was spiritually and mentally I continued to document my life through my music.

Eventually I found my way back to Detroit.

Chapter 31

ONE OF THE TWISTS FOR MY new German promoter, Karsten Scholermann, was the introduction of our band to the dreaded communist East Germans. Karsten had opened a relationship with my German manager, Gert Leiser, and several promoters and party officials who were trying to quell the uneasiness with the youth of East Germany in their struggle to adopt Western culture, especially rock 'n' roll. I don't know how or why my band and I were picked, but along with a lot of cooperation between the communist controlled East German government, Gert Leiser and his friends, together with the efforts of Uwe Tessnow, Karsten Scholermann, and the West Germans, we were invited by the state to perform in a soccer stadium with a huge East German general's tent for a dressing room.

Even better was the television presentation the East Germans put together. It was an opportunity to calm the anxieties of the youth, show off the best of their technologies with regard to lights and sound, and a chance to be seen in person and throughout parts of the communist world. In addition, they agreed to allow Uwe Tessnow to secure the recording rights to the performance. It became the CD called *Red Blood, White Mink*. It was the last recording I made with Johnny Badanjek, and the last with the Thrashing Brothers. It was recorded at the Palast of the Republik.

In these times the only constant and non-confusing aspect of my life was seeking out the means to record as much and as often as I could. I didn't understand why, to be honest. I talk about wanting to keep a journal of my progression as an artist, but there are moments when it rings hollow. But my journey as an artist was, and still is, the only blind trust I get any reward from. Relationships, on the other hand, are just too complicated. Humans demand attention. Music demands invention. You tell me which you would rather struggle with.

I had seen Jurgen Osterloh for the last time in Paris well over three years prior. He had since moved to a more creative and vibrant part of Paris and wanted to be an actor. When he showed me the new home he had acquired it was, as I expected, quite beautiful, but it needed a lot of work. We talked about how to arrange the rooms and colors and such, and we walked and spoke of living together and made plans—plans I knew I couldn't keep the instant I made them.

I believed I loved Jurgen very much. He was the only man I loved that way, but circumstances rule and we never realize what our lives would or could have become. On May 31, 1985, Jurgen died from an overdose of heroin. Bernard Ossude, who also was in love with Jurgen, blamed me for his death. He didn't say it that way, but because my relationship with Jurgen was more about dreams, as compared to his very real and close ties as a friend, Bernard took it out on me—and every other character that had come in and out of Jurgen's life.

One time, a year or two before Jurgen's death, I was on my way to the airport. I knew I could not take any drugs with me, so I left a small packet of heroin behind for Jurgen from the party the prior evening, along with a note telling him I loved him. That is what angered Bernard so very much. It wasn't that particular packet of drugs that killed Jurgen, but it was drugs, and Bernard has not spoken to me since.

Back in Detroit things were taking on a new beat as well. Kim was now a total stranger. I never knew where she was or what she was doing, but I continued to enable her by providing a car and money. While I had asked Kim for a divorce some time earlier, we had not yet dissolved our marriage, mainly because I did not want to go through a second divorce. The pain from the first was great enough to make me try to find some other answer, but nothing worked.

I decided, with the help of my friend Geoffrey Fieger, to go into rehab. I checked out the insurance, made all of the arrangements, packed my bags and got dropped off at the front of the building.

I returned home after a month and a half, began touring, and lived in a house of strangers and users for two years. The band was disappointed for some reason, even though I didn't insist they not use. I should have. It was difficult, but I worked an honest and hard program and after a while, maybe a year, I no longer thought about alcohol. And, my self-confidence on stage was very good, as were my performances. This, like previous separations from drugs, but mostly alcohol, would outdistance the Colorado four and a half years, and last seven and a half. I believe these frequent vacations away from physical and mental chemical alterations are what allow me to have limited health problems at this stage of my life. It's the damned cigarettes that mess with me.

I also began a new arrangement with a booking agent whom I work with to this day, Randy Erwin. Randy was with a small agency called G.M.A., but was leaving to form his own company. I asked him to take me on, and he did. I had burned a lot of bridges due to my behavior under the influence of alcohol and still had a long way to go in learning about myself. I knew I had been handed a raw deal many times in my life, and finally realized there might be some way to deal with all of that other than shooting myself in the foot. So in addition to A.A. meetings and getting a sponsor, I began seeing a psychologist.

Randy, over the years, became one of only a few men I could trust to be honest with me. He helped me repair a lot of the damage I had done. He helped me see life as something not to be wasted, but more than anything, he helped me get over the bitterness I used to justify my rage and self-destruction as a result of the music industry. When that happened, a great change came to my music as well. Not that it had ever been boiling over with rage or bitterness. No. My music now became more precious and demanding; kind of like a growing child. I was changing for the better in body and soul. Not a lot at first, but definitely in a direction I hadn't seen in decades.

In my mind, it appeared that Kimberly wasn't about to change, and in spite of my re-dedication to my art, I still held on to parts of my original mold that was my parent's gift to me as a child. I continued looking for that thing called love, even though I still did not know the meaning of the word. Maybe what I was really looking for was companionship, because I knew for certain what it felt like to love music, but humans . . . that was another question. So, I began seeing other women in increased volume.

Things on the road were making a dramatic change, too. For the first time Randy was approached by two promoters who wanted me to become a part of a package show. I was unfamiliar with package shows and how they worked, unless you wanted to go all the way back to the sixties with the Dick Clark Caravan of Stars, but all of those acts appeared with their own bands. The promoters, Donnie Brooks and Ron Kurtz, wanted me to appear as a solo artist backed by a common band for the entire show. I initially refused, but Randy convinced them to let me bring my band.

In the future, as I became more confident with the situation, I did a good number of performances that way. In addition, the new advent to occur in music was the hiring of artists for work at the ever-growing number of casinos that were springing up all over. We had done Vegas and Atlantic City, but in coming years, thanks to the foresight of white men seeking justice for the Native Americans, hundreds of new casinos would open on tribal reservations. If there were only two descendants of any particular native tribe, it was probably enough for selfless white men and women to help them extract revenge on the scurrilous descendants of whites who, centuries earlier, had stolen their land and their dignity. It was as if white people thought ignorant Native Americans needed white guides to help them navigate the deceiving intentions of fork-tongued businessmen. Hell, I could use that myself.

So that became the routine. Casinos, package shows, and solo appearances with my band. Fortunately, that was only in America. Don't get me wrong. Work is work and I was grateful, but what I had in Europe was so much more special and dignified.

My interest and attention was now fully focused on almost yearly releases of new material, a regular steady band, and legitimate tours of Europe which, when held in contrast to my condition the States, was quite good for my ego. Most American artists don't even consider Europe as a market worth exploiting. It is, for many, somewhere to make quick money when they need it. I viewed Europe as a place to freely practice my art, and in light of the fact that the industry in America no longer considered me relevant, I also viewed Europe as my salvation and a means to remain sane.

One of my favorite stories is about Bob Seger, who to my knowledge has made only one or two trips to Europe in his entire career. His publisher was talking to me and said that he had been holding onto royalty checks for Bob for well over a year and a half that were worth several hundred thousand dollars, and that the Seger management didn't feel it necessary to collect. Ah, the good life.

◆

a window to my soul

Comparing East to West in Germany was to contrast poverty against wealth. Germans who lived under the communist government all had jobs (mostly ones they may not have liked), housing, health care, and education, but not much more. After the Russians took control of the East in 1945, the short story was simply about holding onto their conquered territories and bleeding them dry. Their factories were damaged or old, and ecologically damaging. Their rivers were foaming with deadly toxic materials, the sewers and water systems were badly in need of repair, as were their electrical and gas supplies. Their roads and highway systems were horrible enough to shake the teeth from your head.

Of the pre-war buildings left standing after the Russian's vicious, criminal, and punitive military assault, those that remained—along with the street lights, traffic signals, tunnels, sidewalks and bridges—were falling apart with broken and shattered brick and mortar lying about everywhere. The bending and rusting of faded and twisted tired steel and metal was as if we had been transported back to the First World War and no one had done any repair.

It was the same in the West in 1945, but the Allied Forces, along with the Marshall Plan, went right to work making the infrastructure new and safe. The Russians didn't have the resources, and had suddenly, but not unexpectedly, become our enemies. The war had practically destroyed them.

If it hadn't been for the Americans, the allied countries would have been in the same condition. Britain was especially hurting. Unless you knew the address of the building you were looking for, there was no way to find it. And many times you couldn't find an address. There were shortages of everything in the East including good housing, which was a laughing and shameful matter. The police, under the directive of Stalin, spied on everybody, and neighbor spied on neighbor. Alcohol became the soothing balm. I could relate to all of it.

◆

Many of the fans I culled from this situation were not so angry with the Russians, because many of them were children and grandchildren of mixed marriages between German woman and the occupying Russian soldiers. Most of the German males had found their end fighting for the German army, but those who remained together with their wives after the war gave birth to what became the elite of East Germany. Pure Germans. Pure survivors. Information was at a premium in the East, and that explained the beautiful image as I stood for the first time looking over East Berlin and saw the color gray like a giant forest. Except there were no trees.

There were, however, television antennas reaching for the sky everywhere you looked, all searching for a view of the West. The East Germans had the highest GNP for all of the communist block countries, but that was more a tribute to the character of the German people than anything else. To contrast that against the excesses of the democratized bold swagger and decadence of the quickly adjusted behavior and post war inheritance of the West was to create a vision clouded by tears.

My original fans were in the West and even though they felt the pressure of gross American capitalism, they were culturally distinct from American kids. It was not their abhorrence of materialism or the language barrier that set them apart as much as it was the result of the British, French, and American occupation.

This provided three different views on instilling democracy and each is very distinct. In a nutshell, the British occupied the North, which included such cities as Hanover and Hamburg, while the French occupied the part of Germany that ran next to it's Eastern border around cities such as Saarbrucken. This left the Southern half of Western Germany pretty much to the Americans around Bavaria and cities like Frankfurt. Berlin, the half that was given to the Allies, was shared by all three, and sat in the middle of the Russian sector completely surrounded by the Russians.

Naturally, because the Americans were the only one of the allies in a strong economic condition after the war, the cities to first rise up from the ashes and devastation were those in the American controlled zone. Even though all three allies had a say in the fate of Berlin, it was the Americans who helped West Berlin survive the Russian attempt to blockade and starve the West Berliners into submission, demonstrating courage, commitment, and compassion. This was the better side of my homeland. When the attempt failed, the Russians, with their East German puppet government, built a steel and concrete wall that spanned and separated the entire city into two halves. They could no longer tolerate the free flow of their brightest and most industrious escaping to the West.

Children born in the West at this time developed a hybrid philosophy of French liberalism, with a hint of socialism, British conservatism, paranoia, and American conquering hero democratic strut. The second language for most city dwelling Western Germans is English, because they—as I would in the same circumstance—follow the smell of success. In East Germany the second language offered was Russian, but more people learned English on the sly than all who took Russian in school.

Materially, the West eventually became the second strongest economy in the free world and the first participant of the war, including all of the Allies, to pay off it's war debt. You gotta admire that kind of shit. Beyond their desire to succeed is the question of national identity and pride, and that is a question that runs deep. I'm sure the first thought, once they had reached a competitive economic level against America, was to sit back and say, "I think we can beat them at their own game." But the danger in a coup against American culture is the decadent and violent nature of the beast. Economic considerations aside, one of the fuels that drives the American machine is its ability to adapt to all its divergent cultural differences, and turn them into commercial entities. What I keep hoping for is a Germany that will cherry pick the best parts of the American experience and leave the crap alone.

◆

Sadly, Kimberly's mother had been killed on February 26th, the same date as my birthday. I credit my previous drug use for my inability to recall the year. All I know is that every year after that when my birthday came, there were no Billy birthday celebrations from Kim, only the missing of her mother, the loneliness and pain. Things had become very grim around the house. But none of that could tear me away from the woman who had given her life to me, except for one thing.

One night I was awakened by a terrible headache and a pulsating pressure on the right side of my forehead. As I became conscious, I turned my eyes to the right and discovered Kimberly holding a loaded handgun to my head with her finger on the trigger. Her speech was slurred and her movement dangerously chaotic as I tried my best to talk her out of her intentions.

My twenty-one year marriage with Kim finally hit rock bottom and I went to see an attorney about a divorce. It was the hardest thing I had ever done. Kim retained one of the best divorce lawyers in the state and I couldn't reconcile my guilt over a twenty-one year relationship with so many shared scars and triumphs.

What I have stated here is so mild compared to the real nature of my divorce and marriage to Kim. My attorney said that in his thirty some odd years of divorce law that he never had a judge seal the contents of the allegations and proceedings—until now.

I promised the court way more than I could afford. My attorney knew it, and I knew it. But so great was my guilt and shame that I gave Kim practically everything. It broke me. It took two years from the time I filed until the divorce was final. Kim eventually married a man some nineteen years younger than she was and after a few years they, too, divorced. I don't ever want to re-open that chapter of my life again.

Chapter 32

MY MUSICAL TRANSFORMATION TOOK A SIDE-step to accommodate the exit of John Badanjek, because he had found a better opportunity somewhere else. And that's how it was with him. John came and went from my groups several times over the years, as dictated by outside opportunities. His exit was quickly followed by the departure of Robert Gillespie, who believed that Badanjek's thinking concerning the futility of the band's future warranted such an action.

This was all a knee jerk reaction to the departure of Mark Gougeon, the bass player, who at the very last moment, after the tickets had been purchased, refused to go to Germany unless I gave him a raise. Tony Suhey, who had performed bass on "Nice N' Easy" from the Vacation CD jumped on board. Ray Goodman replaced Gillespie and Danny McAleer, a drum tech who was introduced to me by Dave Lewis, the road manager who had replaced Marty Augosta, became the drummer. Joe Gutc remained on guitar. It was a short and semi-professional tour, but it became the nucleus of the next band, which included Joe Gutc and Ray Goodman on guitar, Danny McAleer on drums, Billy Cernits on keys, and Tony Suhey was replaced on bass by a recommendation from Dave Lewis named Barry George. Barry helped bring a guitar player named Bart Grimm into the band for a very short time. Billy Cernits left and was replaced by Leonard Moon on keys. It was this group of musicians that was the line-up for the next tour and the next CD, *La Gash*.

At this point it is necessary to stress how much sacrifice, professional hard work, tireless effort, and sheer belief in my future Marty Augosta had given to my cause for so many years. As road managers go, he was quality. The guy was made for the job, but personal matters, as they often do in music, compelled him to move away. But Marty never lost faith in the belief that I would someday rise again.

I saw Marty a few years ago and he, like all of us, showed the unforgiving signs of life's toll as we stumble through our variety of dreams in hopes of ending it all on a good note. I sometimes wonder, had we all been privileged and able to afford to avoid the pressures of bill collectors, street life, hustlers, con artists, ill-willed characters, police, drugs, overwhelming medical needs, search for decent shelter, and safety from the masses that tear each other apart like cannibals in order to eat enough to survive, would we still show the tell-tale signs of a life spent and wasted?

I am blessed to have escaped some of this. There is no secret. It is just conceptually beyond proven truth for most of my fellow common folk. Love what you do in this life. In my life, that has sustained me, but I also had to take the ugliness and digest it into a form that, when put on display, looks charming and acceptable. Call it artistic illusion. Call it denial. But however I care to bury the distastefulness of life, I have not let it consume me. Some may laugh and say if that were true you wouldn't be writing an autobiography. I'll deal with that issue in my summation.

On the musical side of life I wanted to make higher quality albums for my future works, but Uwe Tessnow was unwilling to put up the money necessary unless he was given a bigger piece of the pie. Because the growth of the music itself was so important to me, I gave him control of the masters and *La Gash* became another upward step in terms of my writing, production, and artistic growth.

The weakest part of the album was Danny's drums. Although he had come a long way in a short time, he was not a drummer of vast knowledge regarding the different musical styles I presented to him. Nonetheless, *La Gash* gave me more confidence and demonstrated to Uwe that I was capable of creating better and better music. The first single was called "Do You Feel All Right?" It is sometimes still included in my European show because of its mood and quality.

This group would last a good while in America. One reason I believe is because most of the musicians wanted to continue to come back to Europe with me. We were wild on the road, but not the dangerous wild of former groups. It was an innocent, almost immature, kind of wild that made us do things like cover the door handles of rented cars with peanut butter, so when one of the guys went to open the car door they ended up with peanut-butter all over their hands. The ringleader title of these childish pranks was split between Danny McAleer and Joe Gutc.

My personal life was transforming as well. I had never made a link between having a good personal human relationship and making good music, so I tended to separate the two. It was like being married to two different women, I suppose. After the divorce from Kimberly, indeed, while I was waiting for it to become final, I began a relationship with a woman named Megan, to whom I am still married. But it did not come without a price. The price she asked, to be in a relationship with her, was communication, truth, fidelity, sobriety, protection, shelter, ambition, praise, no abuse, and unconditional love. It makes me wonder as I write this if all of the above mentioned were unconditional.

Unlike every other relationship with women that I had been in, my relationship with Megan did not start out sexual. We first met at a Kmart store. I was trying to figure out what I needed to plant roses, and while walking to the garden section fell behind a woman pushing three pre-school children in a cart. As she walked with her hair all wet, obviously having just come out of a shower, her sun-dress moved in the rhythm and fashion of a free, happy spirit who enjoyed life to the fullest with a basket filled with mischief-making children.

We both arrived at the garden area at the same time. Then she turned, and our eyes met. Well, not quite. I had on a pair of very black sunglasses. But even through the sunglasses there was much to ponder and think about. Her confidence. Her beauty. The deep blue color of her eyes. The wet hair. The peaceful stance of her body language. She was one of those dammed mother earth women so connected to the universe, able to walk unafraid in the here and now.

She didn't waste any stares on me but I continued to watch her until I had a need to hear her voice. I can tell a world of things about a person if I can hear their voice, and so I asked if she knew anything about roses. It turned out she was looking for small white fencing to put around a little garden she was making. She said no and that was it. She moved on and I stood there thinking, my God I can't let her get away. But that's exactly what happened until, having gotten what I needed, I happened to end up behind her at the checkout counter. She placed her items on the rolling rubber and I placed mine behind hers.

The cashier rang up her things and then continued to add mine to the collection. Megan indicated to the cashier that we were separate and I, for whatever reason, said I would pay for it all. Megan looked angry, as if I had assumed she needed monetary help. Or maybe she thought it was one of the worst pick-up lines she had ever heard. In any case, Megan began to walk away and I was trying to get the cashier to hurry up with my things, because I didn't want to lose sight of her. I had no idea what I was going to say to Megan if I did catch her, but I had to come up with something.

I come from an age where people were judged on what kind of vibe they projected. Megan's vibe was positive, alive and hopeful, and there I was hurting and in pain over having ended my long relationship with Kimberly. I just wanted to be in the kind of company that had what Megan had. I wanted her inner peace.

Again, unlike any relationship with a woman I ever had I did something quite remarkable that I have never done before or since. First, I managed to talk Megan out of her phone number. She must have wanted me to have it or she wouldn't have given it to me. My initial guess was that she recognized me, but I was wrong. She is thirteen years younger than I am, and "Jenny Take a Ride" was not a currency she could relate to. Now, after twenty years with her, I realize she simply saw me hurting and reached out to a fellow human who was obviously in pain.

I said, "Take a couple of days and think about whether you've done the right thing or not. I'll call. Then if you regret having given me your phone number tell me and you'll never hear from me again. I swear." One half hour after we had spoken I arrived home and dialed the number. God, I was embarrassed, but I needed to know if it was a real number or not. Instead of an answering machine where I would have the chance to hang up, she answered.

Our courtship lasted well over a year. It was a year in which I was with several strikingly beautiful women. I was lonesome and I didn't see my leaving Kim as an opportunity to find out about myself, which it was. One of my buddies suggested I might want to seek professional help. Find a way to deal with the loneliness and sadness without becoming entangled in a rebound situation. I followed his advice, but continued looking for female companionship. One of the questions my psychologist insisted I face was my awareness of my sexuality. It was a fair question, given my sparse and extremely infrequent encounters with men, but mostly always at a conscious level.

There is a gay author who wrote a book called *Rock on the Wild Side*. His name is Wayne Studer. Mr. Studer refers to one of my musical compositions as the "most eye-openingly 'gay' album I've ever heard by a sixties star of Ryder's stature." He goes on to state, pointing to one of my songs, "For all its tastelessness, it sounds happy, honest, and unpretentious; sexy, fun, and as gay as can be."

I have pondered this deeply, but rather than

making a dishonest proclamation about "At last I'm free and I'm coming out," I think it is more honest to say that if I were to find a person in which love, true love, was the essence of a relationship for them, their sex would not matter to me. That is what I was on the verge of finding with Jurgen, the man, and that is what I have found with Megan, the woman.

Megan and I talked on the telephone, wrote letters to each other from Europe, or even just from Michigan, went out on occasional dates, lunches, drives, and came to explore each other's personalities. It was the way it is supposed to be done. We also both attended twelve step programs. This was exceedingly important to Megan. She also had no right to question my relationships with other women because she was removing herself from her ex-husband and another boyfriend.

She had, on the day I met her in Kmart, two sons from two different fathers, but the boys in the basket were not her children. Turns out she was babysitting. Well, two of the three were not hers. The little child with the blond hair, the chicklet teeth and deep blue eyes was her son, Ian Edward Beals. Her older son with the same deep blue eyes, Thomas Emmanuel Beals, was not there that day. Tom was old enough to be in school. Her boys were three and seven when we first met and I would end up raising them. Eventually.

Back on the band front, Barry George went on to control a band that would do a long run with me, but this band never had, in spite of some remarkably good performances, an opportunity to record together. The exception was Barry, who appeared on *La Gash*. Eventually Barry brought in his brother Bobby on guitar, a new keyboard player, "Rico," and after Badanjek came and went again he was replaced by Tommy Clufetos. Tommy left for a better gig with Ted Nugent, was stolen from Ted by Alice Cooper, and finally ended up with Rob Zombie. Barry then, on a temporary basis, brought in his brother David, who remained our drummer for some years. But the man who ended up, on and off, serving the most time with me was Robert Gillespie.

When I realized I could not tour Europe any longer and meet the demands of the band's asking price, I began looking for a German band of quality, and I hit the jackpot. I did, however, for a number of years, take either Robert Gillespie, Joe Gutc, or Steve Hunter along as my American guitar player because I believed, on guitar anyway, that you couldn't beat an American guitarist, especially when it came to the rock 'n' roll songs we included. Robert was special in many ways, but I swear to you the thing I respect most about Robert is that the man has never told me a lie. That's hard to say about a relationship of over twenty years.

Engerling is a funny sounding name for a band but it was the name of the band I was now beginning a very long relationship with. All East Germans. All could read and write music. That in itself was different from most of the American musicians. More than anything, was Engerling's gratefulness at being given the chance to perform with me. Our exploratory rehearsal was unforgettable. Gert Leiser, who managed Engerling, gambled that his boys would be good enough to do a tour with. I walked into an old, small youth center in the still undeveloped East Germany, and came face to face with all of the players. I think everyone was a little afraid. I didn't want to do a tour with a band that sucked, and they didn't want to fall short of their innate abilities, which were, I discovered over the years, quite remarkable. I knew I had to make this work, because we had already accepted the tour and I was relying on Gert's assessment of his boys' talent. By the end of the first rehearsal I had come to two conclusions. One, they were indeed talented, and two, I wouldn't want to have been a paying customer as this young group of strangers began trying to figure out their destiny.

"My boss is talking, but I don't speak English so I just keep smiling." That became one of Engerling and my long-standing jokes about their first drummer, a guy named Peter who lasred just two days. Band leader Bodi Bodag (keyboards and harmonica) and guitarist Heiner Witter were the only two remaining members of the original group. Bassist Manne Pokrant, now my co-producer on all of my European recordings, finished off the quartet. Additionally, Bodi's son Hannas and Vincent Brisach have also both played brums for the band.

There are two lasting impressions about Engerling that I love. They are so worthy of any effort I make to help you understand the intensity and caring I hold so deeply in my heart for them, and for the German public I have served for so many years.

The first impression comes from a story about the next recording I made. It was an artistic breakthrough for me as a writer and producer, and the album was called *Rite of Passage*. Engerling, Joe Gutc, and I all settled into the recording studio to create the CD. On one of the tracks someone made a mistake. In America it would be a quick shout from the control room: "Okay, someone fucked up. Let's run it again." Not so with my new German friends. Immediately, every one put down their instruments, pulled briefcases and chairs into a circle, broke out the score sheets, got some coffee, and began a serious conversation about exactly what had occurred. I was blown away. The attention to every detail was of supreme importance to them.

After ten minutes everyone indicated they were ready to resume and we did the take without error. In fact, they were so immersed in each song that there were very few mistakes. It must be a German thing and made me think back to the 180-degree kind of recordings I did with the Thrashing Brothers where drinking, exhaustion, fighting, and mistakes consumed a lot of studio time.

Engerling had an inherent discipline that I had not seen since the days of professional studio players back in New York City. It was their pride and professionalism that made me know from that point on I would be surrounded by men of music who, although they were one step removed from the American heartbeat of rock and R&B, were men I could teach. To top it off, they were eager to listen and learn.

The second impression is much wider in scope and a bit political in nature. Experience tells me that people who come from countries unfamiliar with freedom, liberty, and consumer driven economies, as expressed in American terms, are lost when first introduced to this new reality. It is without question the under-privileged, poverty stricken, and lower classes from any society that work harder and create more effectively to reach their dreams than established upper classes with their built-in connections and protections. Ruling classes, especially in the business world, have bought and paid for a law of the land that is specifically tailored to help keep their domination in tact.

The most visible demonstration of the lower classes access to a better life comes through sports, music, other forms of entertainment, and serving. Entertainment and serving the public is what the higher classes control, but don't or can't actively involve themselves in, given the fact that for most it requires too much physical energy. I always laugh when I hear politicians comment on how long or how hard they have worked to serve the public. I'm not saying the upper classes don't work hard or like to get dirty. It's just that their mandate tells them the reason they must work hard, think, and play dirty is to maintain control. In my mind, that's way different than working hard and getting dirty to raise yourself up from poverty and make enough to help your family survive. That is an honest and righteous pursuit.

I like sports and boxing, as I have stated previously. Since the fall and re-shaping of the old communist controlled countries, we are beginning to see not just boxing, but all sports showing a tendency to become dominated by people from the old communist Eastern bloc countries. It is no different in music, which brings me to my point.

Musicians from East Germany are hungrier and more focused on their goals as musicians than most other musicians I've been exposed to. Engerling is a good example. In Germany, this fact along with many other political decisions about what to do with German tax dollars has brought deep resentment between the two different Germanys that have now become one. Likely it will take another generation or two for the two sides to embrace their fellow countrymen.

In one of the first performances I did with Engerling, I introduced them to my Western fans and the band was booed, but now, after years of touring with them in East and West Germany, they are welcomed, expected, and accepted by all of my fans.

Attending the recording of the CD *Rite of Passage,* as she had done for *La Gash,* was Megan. As our worlds became more and more visible to each other, her price for a relationship was being tested by me way more than it should have. I was only just beginning to understand how fucked up I was as a partner, and also as a human being. Alas, I was no longer alone.

From Megan

9/23/04

Well it's After 2:00 Am And I'm still Awake feeling so many things that you could NEVER EVEN comprehend. I know It's ~~sad~~ I've been REDUCED to Kim's letter writing — but if you'll indulge ME this once. — After 17 years of All that I have lived through with you — And it doesn't matter what I can prove on paper or with concrete ~~material~~ material things — I know that you know what I'm talking About — So After 17 years I cant even be trusted to go have tea + noodles with my Girlfriend. How incredibly hypocritical — AND

UNFAIR — you who CAN'T STAND
to be QUESTIONED on ANY LEVEL — even
After EARNING the distrust 2,000
fold. Like I'VE TRIED to tell you
before — this is A NO WIN situati
for me. You do the BAD behavior
but don't want ANY CONSEQUENCES —
I GET out of preporti consequeces
for nothing — it's INTOLERABLE.
I told you that I would SEE
you through your SURGERY hoping that
when it WAS OVER you would GET
off the DRUGS — ~~_____~~
~~_____~~ AND MY life would
be WONDERFUL — WELL I GUESS

the time comes in every persons
life when they have to face reality.
Here's more - you will never
be the person I need - someone
who loves - cherishes - respects and
values me. And from the
start I was never supposed
to win - just be the person
next in line to take all they
could until you moved on.
   Well - I don't have to go
crazy or hide in drugs or
turn gay or destroy myself.
I have had enough - you
   And I don't care if ~~you~~
and all the losers you surround

yourself with think that
not being in your life means
I loose —

I know that surviving
this situation — ~~doubt~~ with
myself in one piece is
~~doubt~~ the ultimate victory.

no one else — wives
kids — etc. can say
the same —

So I guess in
the end I don't win.

Chapter 33

NO LONGER ALONE. WELL, THIS WAS going to be difficult because in my first two marriages I was alone in the sense that I was not a good partner. And even though Susan was kept from becoming close to me, we did have the children. That was reason enough to make it more special and demanding in the sense that my daughter and son, Dawn and Joel, were living proof that I must have been something more than just a partner. I had foolishly thrown away that responsibility to be a star and a man whom I would despise for the rest of my life.

But now I was becoming a (step) father, which thrilled me. It also came with a few surprises. This time, I told myself, I would make up for the lousy father I was to Dawn and Joel, and I would be a wonderful father to Tom and Ian. It was a nice thought, until I discovered what the role of a stepfather really was: all of the responsibility and none of the authority. Just because I was the co-guardian for Megan's boys didn't make me their father. That was something that only years of dedication, love, and friendship might bring as the boys grew into manhood, and finally understood the sacrifices I made for them.

Megan and I got married, but it got off to a rough start because I hadn't informed any of my previous female friends. One day—possibly two days—after we were married, Megan discovered I still had telephone numbers and photographs in my phone book of all the women I had been seeing up until the marriage. She called one of the women and was astonished to discover I had not made her aware of our marriage. From my point of view there was no harm in that. It was something I would communicate eventually, or I would simply not contact any of them in the future.

In Megan's price list of behaviors that I had to give up was one she absolutely believed was imperative for the success of our marriage. I was told to completely abandon any further communication with all of those women. That is what I did. After all, they were sexual relationships for the most part and Megan more than satisfied that need. Megan was a woman who could carry herself with dignity, respect, beauty, and a charming personality in public, but when it came to the bedroom she was very much . . . let's just say she was a master.

Since I was being truthful, I told her that one of the songs on *Rite of Passage* was written for another woman. The title was "By the Feel," a nice little jazz number I had written while driving down Hines Drive in preparation for the album's songs. Megan began packing her bags to go back to America. I begged her to stay and after some long conversation she complied, but it let me know just how deeply she held her beliefs. It didn't seem to matter that the song had been written before we were married.

This tough stance was applied to my replacement addictions as well. For example, if I gave up women I tried to take up drinking again. If I gave up drinking I tried to start gambling and on and on in the truest tradition of the addictive personality. That was the big picture and through our years together we fought each battle. I felt as if my freedom of choice was being totally taken away and that she was trying to control me. She felt that unless I was willing to give up those pursuits that were destructive to the relationship, we could not succeed. In the end she was right and now I see it. But there would be a few more betrayals on my part before I finally understood what it would take to stay in a relationship with her.

There were years and years of therapy—couples therapy, family therapy with Megan and me and the children, children's therapy, and individual therapy for the two of us. In addition, we were ardent practitioners of Al-anon, A.A. and N.A. meetings.

◆

The recording came to an end and I had, with the help of Engerling and Joe Gutc, continued my uphill pursuit of claiming my place in history as a true artist, and not a star manufactured by Bob Crewe. The album was wonderful. There was one song in particular that I thought Huey Lewis might be able to do a good cover on. I didn't believe I would ever get justice in America from the industry, but I thought an established artist and acquaintance such as Huey might be the way to get my music out. Huey declined, but gave me a rational explanation as to why he couldn't cover it. He also said he understood why I had chosen him to cover the song. That was good enough.

Uwe Tessnow again took control of the masters in return for the expensive production. I didn't mind, because I was slowly reaching my goal and although I consider

Rite of Passage to be one of my best five albums out of twenty-seven, it did not artistically meet the standard I was aiming for.

The band and I toured and Megan always accompanied me. At first there was some resentment because the boys could no longer have their drinking buddy along while they continued to drink, but over time they saw the professionalism and quality performances they could turn in without having to think like a bar band.

Back in America the same mentality existed with the band headed by Barry George. His brother, Bobby, was a great singer and performer and he sang very well, but he liked to drink before the show. The same was true of his other brother, David. Pat Harwood sometimes drank and sometimes not. This was the case with Robert Gillespie, as well. I tested these waters quite a few times with the German band and the American band until Megan threw down the gauntlet. Little by little I begrudgingly gave ground to her demands. Even when she wasn't on the road I abstained from drinking.

But then we began to do more casino gigs, and that was another challenge. And in the same way it was beaten back. I don't know why I can't just embrace her philosophy. I mean, we have four casinos in the Detroit area that I never frequent, but when I'm on the road and there is nothing else to do, so every once in awhile I believe I can win some money. God knows we can always use more of that. The costly divorce from Kimberly and having to support a growing family at the same time took its toll, given the reality that my income was so different from year to year.

Now, because *Rite of Passage* did not ignite the public's imagination (this had a lot to do with Uwe's power as a label) he abandoned any future plans to record. We did continue to tour Germany, but without the advantage of fresh product. We never had fresh product in America, but I had done a parody recording for Black Market Productions about Colonel Oliver North, "Good Gollie, it's Ollie," on which the Paul Schaeffer Orchestra played.

Mark Black and his partner Ed Bialak approached me about creating words and melody for sessions they had done with experimental music forms. When I received the music I was asked to integrate myself with, I thought it would be impossible. I simply couldn't listen to it. It was different from anything I had ever heard and not like anything I would ever create on my own. But, since he was a friend, I spent day after day with the tapes until I finally discovered a way to enter into the music without changing their intentions. It was one of the most demanding and exhausting creative efforts I have ever made, and in the end it was a work of genius totally rejected by the American public.

Phil Stemelo, an ex-Marine who helped me dress accurately for the Oliver North spoof became an investor and wrote the liner notes for the project that became *Monkey Island*. Phil was also a teacher in the Detroit public school system. *Monkey Island* was picked up by Uwe for Germany, but because there was no promotion, it disappeared. This project also signaled the end of my relationship with Uwe. Uwe, the man who gave me a start, had a few complaints about issues of trust and honesty with me, and I held an equal amount with him. Once distrust exists in a partnership, you can kiss it goodbye. And that is what we did. Line Records was no longer my recording company.

Eager, if not almost panicky, to continue a steady stream of new music and continue to improve as an artist, singer, and writer I approached Gert Leiser. Gert said he might be able to get me a deal with the label Engerling was on. It was an older established Eastern Bloc label run by Dr. Klaus Koch. We had a meeting and Dr. Klaus agreed to take me on for a project. We are growing together. He has managed to get my music in all the major retail outlets throughout all of Germany, East and West. He has discovered other delivery systems as well, and we are now at the point where I have given him four albums for the small but wonderful BuschFunk label.

The first was *The Old Man Springs a Boner*. It was a collection of recordings from four different live performances on one of our tours. We had begun doing incredible shows, shows that would go for two and a half hours without intermissions. My voice was becoming stronger, the confidence in the band was stronger, and our fans were growing more appreciative. Dr. Klaus was not shy about spending money. No, it was not the standard amount prevalent at the time, but it was way more than Tessnow ever invested and it allowed me the time and space to create to my fullest potential.

I also began a co-production with Manne Pokrant, who not only held great technical knowledge, but was a talented and creative personality in his own right. The next CD, *A Dark Caucasian Blue*, barely missed the mark but was a triumph for my writing ability as I closed in on my life-long pursuit. I was no longer thinking in terms of commercial recordings, but strangely, because Dr. Klaus insisted I be given free range to create anything I wanted, many of the songs did qualify as accessible or commercial.

Megan and I came over together for the next CD, and we brought our puppy Poindexter, a four and a half pound Yorkie. He was very calm and relaxed, and I found that to be extremely helpful for the mind-set I needed to create.

Another thing Megan and I marveled at was how the candy companies in Germany tried very hard to convince parents and children of modern day Germany that there was something missing from their lives that they absolutely must have. Halloween. I don't think it has really taken hold yet, but it is such fun to see the children trying to get the hang of this free candy concept from America. Some of their costumes are very entertaining—it's like Carnival for children, with candy instead of alcohol.

We next began work on *The Aquitted Idiot*. Right from the beginning the ideas flowed freely and effectively. All of the players had no trouble reaching the perfection I was asking. My voice was stronger than it had ever been, and the songs and musical arrangements were the best I had ever done. I had whatever I wanted: background singers of high quality, specialized musicians from all over Europe, and a happy spirit within the studio and the musicians. Even the saddest songs had a magical humanism and connection within each note.

This album, *The Acquitted Idiot*, was an exploration of my faith and belief in organized religion, God and Jesus Christ, and how that all impacted my life. The musical styles flew about freely from an Otis Redding style, to rolling in the aisles gospel, to soft moving ballads and high-energy testaments. There were compliments to my Motown heritage and, as I had done on *A Dark Caucasian Blue,* I wrote and sang one or two songs in the native tongue of my beloved host country.

In my mind I had finally, after many decades, reached my goal. I had, in arguable terms, created the best album of my career. I was relieved and proud and happy at last. No one in America would ever know about it. My time to share this great achievement with the American public had long ago passed. But what was important is the fact that I created it.

When I returned to America I listened for the first time in decades to the radio, and then I played my CD. I knew then, if history ever had the courage to honestly judge my career-long struggle, I would finally be given the recognition I felt I deserved. I had worked so hard through all the years of artistic growth, the struggles with substance abuse, and the painful but rewarding sacrifices, to find love and simply stay above the poverty line.

Very few historians took note of my achievement. Those who did were surprised to discover I was capable of resurrecting myself. Not in the sense that I was a commercial vehicle again, but that I had made a life-long commitment to an end and had succeeded. Those secret, below the radar reviews from men of honor and integrity in the music business, were all I needed to be happy. Fortunately, a few of my hard-core American fans were able to weigh in on the achievement and their consensus matched that of the critics.

My world was a perfect world on the music side.

On one short tour of Germany, Megan decided to stay home. One of the most precious gifts I was able to give her, and she freely admits this, was the ability to not work for most of the time, and to stay at home to be a live-in mother to her two sons. While I was away on the tour one drunken night in Cologne, Germany I took a woman, a stranger, to my room after the show and had sex.

When I returned, my guilt got the better of me and I did what I thought was the right thing. I tried to be honest with my wife at all times. But I also did what the centuries old rule of conduct as set forth by men dictated I should not. The rule was "never confess." After the confession (where I knew there would be problems), I fully expected she would be hurt, but I though because I confessed she would try to work it out. Instead, she filed for divorce.

It was very difficult, mostly because we had very little money and I was trying to stay in the home while we waited for the divorce to become final. Finally the day came when I could afford to move out, but it was only through the good luck of having an old acquaintance being the owner of some apartments.

My credit had gone from very good to high risk over the years. Not only had I neglected bills while paying alimony to Kim and trying to keep my family with Megan afloat, but Megan had serious health issues with her heart that only became worse with time. Doctor after doctor would perform serious malpractice, putting her condition in a steep decline.

When I first met Megan she was fine, but she suffered from STVs, a condition where her heart sped up to an unsustainable rate, especially in recent years. She opted to have an electronic oblation and was guaranteed by the premier school of medicine in Michigan that it was an outpatient situation and she would be home the same day. The professor physician, well qualified to perform the new medical procedure, allowed a visiting student doctor from France to take the reins and they ended up putting her into third degree heart blockage, requiring her to get a pacemaker implant while in her early thirties. In subsequent replacements and extractions more damage was done.

During the first extraction to replace the original pacemaker Megan died on the table twice and was beaten back to life twice. I visited her in the hospital and she complained about serious pain she had experienced through the night. It seems the doctor, in installing the new pacemaker, had punctured her left lung and caused it to collapse. They had given her a pump to keep the lung inflated, but it was still very painful. And Megan can take a lot of physical pain. She had to, because she now has been clean and sober over twenty-two years and has always rejected pain medication. We couldn't figure it out until I followed the pump's cord down to the electrical input in the wall, where it lay on the floor having been disconnected the entire evening. Megan was a mess from fighting with the pain and had gotten no sleep but refused to accept any meds. I took the doctor aside and told him to slip some painkiller into her IV and I would take full responsibility. Finally she slept.

That experience and subsequent mistakes with the next two implant replacements (a clotting disorder that she developed, two pulmonary embolisms she had blown in her lung, scar tissue from the lung collapse, a small clot that hit the back of one eye taking away some of the sight, injections of expensive blood thinner for the rest of her life, shots to diminish bone density loss, and many other offshoots of the "original sin"), plus the cost of our medical insurance, which is twice the national average for poverty for a family of two, and the cost of protecting the degenerative nature of her teeth due to the injections, have taken a heavy financial cost and thrown it directly upon my back. That and legal costs for a variety of issues we have faced together, now give me the credit rating of a rail car hopping hobo. By the way, the wonderful doctor who caused all this fled South after saying he was sorry.

Anyway, Megan and I divorced, but I was ordered to maintain her health insurance by the court. It was during this time that I started work on this book. Sure, I was lonely. I missed the boys and my dog, Sahne, but I wasn't sad. It seemed with Megan that I was always sad or mad about something.

As the years of alimony went by it became apparent to me that things were going to get extremely difficult for Megan because her health insurance was about to end. Because of previously existing conditions, she would never be able to regain private insurance. I cared so much for Megan I told her I would re-marry her so her insurance would not be interrupted. She understood, but she also believed she loved me and was willing to give me a second chance.

Today, even though I still think about the old behavior I hated giving up so much, I struggle to toe the line but occasionally find myself wanting a drink around the holidays. After a while the urges pass and I have pretty much adopted those rules of conduct I once so defiantly rejected as too invasive of my private rights. I understand the reasons for them being kept in place and I think Megan and I are going to make it.

Megan and I still have fights, but they are only about the way we communicate. They are no longer about the damaging actions that people foreign to love bring upon each other. And that is one of the major blessings I have been afforded by something more powerful than my faltering yet supreme ego. To be with a woman who has so many real problems to face every day, and to be around her as she awakens each day full of life and ready to face her destiny with confidence, gratefulness, and happiness is indeed a blessing.

Megan recently went with me again to Europe where I created (some say) my best CD yet, *You Deserve My Art*. And now that CD is finished, a book written by James Mitchell titled *It Was All Right: The Story of Mitch Ryder's Life in Music* has been released through Wayne State University Press, work on my first American CD in over twenty-five years will be finished this year, and this autobiography will be released soon as well.

But more important is finding out what love is truly about and sharing it with those close to me—especially my wife, who loves me but has stated there is a limit to her patience. I learn in spite of my protests, and my friends . . . that's the payoff.

But there is also an ugly downside. Once you have cheated on your wife you cannot expect forgetting or forgiving. Ever. It no longer is a part of your partner's vocabulary. It makes me wonder how former President Clinton and his wife have come to an understanding.

I, for some reason unknown to me at this time, believe in my deepest intuitions. These tell me that I not only suffer from low self-esteem, but I also believe women want to dominate me. That is why I show a great deal of disrespect to them. I also believe Megan could have chosen someone better than me, not because it is so hard to make the changes she requires me to make in my life choices, but because I am now in a place where I cannot financially give her the life she wishes to have. The same was true for my other two wives. I believe to the core of my soul I have indeed become the artist I so badly needed to become, but the truth with regard to my financial situation and abilities to provide is pathetic. Please, I beg you. Can you get a letter to the outside?

From Megan

11/16/07

Billy-

REMEMBER when I ASKED you IN Berlin why you ARE so MEAN to ME AND you SAID you ARE SEEING how much I will LIKE?? AND before when you told ME BARRY FAYNE told you to treat me BAD AND FORCE ME to file for A DIVORCE so you could MAKE out better FINANCIALLY???

WELL- At 49 YEARS old I think I DESERVE to be IN A RELATIONSHIP that IS loving AND not some stupid GAME of how much will she LIKE. I have REACHED that point that you have BEEN WORKING TOWARD.

I have never encountered such an emotionally egotistical and self loving person in my life. If anything that comes up is not <u>All About You</u> — then someone is going to catch hell. Every situation is —

(1.) How does this impact me?

(2.) How does this serve me?

(3.) How can I use this to my advantage?

(4.) ME — ME — ME — ME — ME — ME — ME ME.

I really at some point hoped
you would _Grow_ _up_ and
Allow that when in a Relationship
sometimes ~~####~~ one person is
slightly inconvenienced for the
sake of something important to
the other person.

But _Not_ _here_ !!!!

If it involves more than the
certain amount of money you
decide to throw at it.

And certainly anything deeper

than money — you can't
be expected to step up to
the plate. But everybody else
is supposed to accept whatever
you may dump in their life
just because it made you feel
Good for the moment no matter
how self destructive it may
be or how it may salvage
the relotionship —

You are cruel and
thoghtless and I have no
RESPECT for you as a person.

Let Alone a partner.

I want out—

I have reached the point
where I can see that
you will never love me
the way I deserve—

You can't be that
unfaithful to yourself.

My plane leaves at
10:43 tomorrow.

My lawyer will contact

you to discuss how
to divide our lives.
I dont even want
to speak to you.

Chapter 34

THE BIRTH OF THE PROBLEMS I have faced throughout my life, my reaction to the same in the form of my behavior, the continued presence of my low-self-esteem, the daily fears I battle or run from, and the difficulty I struggle with to find trust and love are all explained in the very first chapter of this book. I know this is a hard read for most people, because I am not a writer. I didn't even find out until a couple of months ago that, today, most celebrities who write books do so with the help of other writers. So I understand and appreciate your patience if you have managed to get this far.

Like every other person born into lower working class conditions, sometimes drifting between that category and poverty, we are fearful of so many things. We try to isolate ourselves from that fear by purchasing material things and end up hiding our fear in exchange for financial debt. The decisions we've made have never been made from a position of strength, a wonderful place reserved for the wealthy where, if you don't like your decisions you can simply throw them away and move on to the next. No. The decisions we make are trade-offs where if we have gained something temporarily we have also had to give up something else—hopefully not permanently. Many times we give up something we may have liked to have kept. Many times the exchange is a momentary pleasure that cannot be held onto and damage us. These trades we've come to accept are not only material. They are also trade-offs of our moral beliefs, our ethical standards, and assaults upon our character and standing in the community. The cost is an investment from which we may never realize a return. Our dignity. Our self-respect. Some of us then flee to the unknown for help. We go to church. We ask for direction and salvation. We become beggars of spiritual rescue.

Upon reflecting the scope of book, I understand completely that, in spite of what fame I have achieved, no matter how important that seems to be in our culture, it makes me no different from other people who are born from the same soil as myself. I was in some ways unfortunate to get a glimpse of the upper class.

Oh, I think it's marvelous that I belong to an elite club in the history of American musical culture and, as you noticed in previous chapters, there are rewards. But my truth as a fellow human to my peers of limitations is the fact that I am strapped in debt. I've been married four times because I traded love for my pursuit of a dream. I don't know my brothers and sisters beyond my teenage years, and my children have been handed the same dysfunctional characteristics with which they must now be burdened with for the rest of their lives. Every day of my life I must fight to not lose what little positive gains I have captured in regard to seeking a healthier way to live. This all comes to me so late in life, at a time when change is difficult, that it sometimes seems impossible.

But there is Megan. If I could give a Megan to every man who is lost and about to go under I would. She is my salvation. She's the one who said, "It doesn't have to be this way." I have two wonderful sons with Megan. Tommy and Ian, as they grew from little guys into men of the world they made a place for me in their lives that they didn't have to make.

When I hit the stage to perform I now do so with a confidence that comes from decades of knowing the territory. Even when the surprises come, and they do, I have bought and paid for enough real estate to know I would defend it to the death. I am happy to be making other people happy, because I understand how life tears most of us down and how important it is to find an hour or two of harmless pleasure in which we can all be entertained. You don't think I'm being entertained? When I'm on that stage, we are all being entertained. I'm entertaining you and you're entertaining me. If everything goes well, we all walk away a little bit better off than when we first came. But then, after the music is over, we go back to our private (not so private for me) lives and having had a short respite from the reality of life we somehow gather the resolve to go on.

I was speaking with a friend of mine in the business and we both agreed that most musicians and entertainers suffer from low-self esteem. That is why acceptance is so important, and that in turn drives you to have to be better than the competition. I have paid dearly for having low self-esteem. No matter what you do in life, whether you are a man or a woman, there are predators who can spot you like a hawk spots the field mouse. And they will take you down roads you would never take yourself, because you would be afraid. But they are not afraid. Why should they be? It's their road they are leading you down and you trust them. You are the prey.

I need to learn the territory that Megan allowed me to see, as I know the territory upon which my music exists. Here now in the eleventh hour of my days on this planet maybe I won't be able to get there, but the joy of chasing after that new dream will allow me to leave in peace.

We of the lower class don't need to be told to know our place. We need to enter the race. We need to stop hurting each other and come together in one voice and say to those who have deserted us that, "You cannot continue to abuse us. This democracy we are a part of did not give you license to treat us less than you, simply because you had the means to do so. We are all going to be buried in the same cold ground, and all of the people you have hurt, disregarded and stepped upon to raise yourself up will be there with you eventually. Your heaven on earth is temporary."

In the meantime, we can help each other. We can educate the uneducated. We can be kind to each other. We can stop victimizing each other. We can stop hating each other. And we can find a leader who believes we deserve to be a part of and share in the blessings and promises of this great country. Someone willing to hold the wealthy accountable for the pain, suffering and hate they have visited upon our class. Is there one person born of our social class that honestly believes the wealthy care about our fate? No. They do not. Not one little bit. What about all the good, charitable acts the wealthy constantly perform? You gotta know that they had a tax break or some other mechanism that worked for their financial gain. They wouldn't have given a shit if there was nothing material in it for themselves. It doesn't come from honest compassion.

I do charitable performances quite often and I receive nothing in return except the knowledge that I have helped my fellow human beings with no strings attached.

Volunteer work is admirable as well. There are a lot of good people in this country, but they are not from the upper class. They sincerely want to make a difference and, as small as it may seem to others, they understand that every little bit helps.

Steven Tyler and Mitch in 2009 at Book Expo America at the Javits Center in New York.

Hold on now and watch as your boss or the CEO of your company or whomever you work for doesn't blink an eye when your job and future are given away with no remorse. They don't have their lives shattered so completely, so very easily.

Some of you will laugh thinking to yourself, "What is he saying? The nerve of him! How ungrateful. He's one of the lucky ones. How did this hypocrite Mitch Ryder get a book deal if everybody wants to see him fail? What a crybaby. He makes me sick."

Good. It proves that the sick can be made sicker than they already are.

For one thing, I've spent a good deal of my life with my creative abilities pushed by sheer will beyond my inherent capabilities. "He's famous, or he used to be famous." No, there is no past tense for fame. Once you earn it fame is yours for life. But fame, at the end of the day, does not magically turn into food on the table. The benefits of fame for me are the blessings I have mentioned, and the fact that I love what I do when I can do it. In my mind I have proven what I set out to do. I am an artist of great achievement in spite of the music industry's best efforts to stop me. I possess one of the most unique voices in music and my lyrics are among the most truthful you will hear. Plus, I get better every day.

I also have my fans but they, like myself, are growing older and fewer. I remember telling a friend of mine a long time ago that, "my fans, the people I can most relate to, can't afford to buy my records and books." It turns out I might have been wrong. I think the people I can most relate to will find a way hear my records and read my books. It has nothing to do with afford.

Just as I stated in the beginning of this book, I look out upon the world of my misshapen time. The Midwestern staple of parochial intelligence, stripped naked by the cutting wind from the east, reveals itself embarrassingly thin and overmatched as it's streaming, tattered flag of pride is ripped from it's champion's broken, bloodied hands and thrown upon the dirt of it's own impotence. Democracy, taunting a person ho is afraid of water, invites him in for another swim through the cold raging waters of blessed freedom.

THE END

From Megan

Dear Billy—
When you met ME I was on
ADC because I was going to school
to earn a living for myself. Jim had
offered to put ME through school and
take care of ME and the boys but
I was determined never to rely on
any man again since I found out
that Edward was lying and using
drugs and I did not want ~~this~~
addiction to be part of my life Ever
Again. I would have been able
to support myself and my children
but you did not want me to continue
with an education ___ you wanted
me to stay at home and help you with
your ~~life~~ career and life. At the
time you were clean and I
thought a faithful, decent man

who wanted a better life than the one he was living.

What I got was a man who doesn't know the meaning of the word faithful — doesn't care enough about himself or me to choose the right thing in any situation. I have put ~~them~~ more than you into this relationship purportionally — 200% —

I have been faithful — worked hard inside and outside this house — given up my education — catered to your needs; eaten every shitty thing you dished out — made due with every

situation handed to me —
stayed clean — ~~XXXXXXXX~~
lived through countless heartbreaks.
And for what —
to be continually
berated — unloved —
and generally abused
on every level you could
sink to —
I have had enough —
You will never change.
And I am not
going to live in this

well ANY MORE —
I UNDERSTAND — AND you
HAVE STATED it OVER AND
OVER to ME AND
EVERYONE ~~ELSE~~ ELSE YOU
CHOSE to ~~that~~ you
ARE HERE BECAUSE you
FINANCIALLY NEED ~~to~~ be.
So — I will try to
buck up AND Allow you
the time to find
OTHER ARRANGEMENTS —

but do not think that
this is a free ride
as far as that you can
say whatever you want
to me and continue &
live here — you stay
in your room and be
cordial — I will be
in mine and do the
same ——————
you are right —
I have nothing &

GIVE you AYMORE —
I AM SpiRitwally —
AND EMotionAlly
bankrupt

GERE —

there is No Light
that you hove Not
HANDED ME — No
line you love Not CROSSED
No Abuse you hove Not
CAUSED ME ———
I AM through —

APPENDIX A

When I am onstage I sometimes tell my audiences that one of the great blessings I have enjoyed from my roughly fifty years of entertaining is the opportunity to come to know many of my heroes. I take every chance I can to meet, and maybe sit and talk, with voices and musicians I have come to love and appreciate though their music. Sometimes there is even the chance to perform on the same stage or show with them. In the book *The Rolling Stone Encyclopedia of Rock & Roll* are approximately twenty-six hundred groups and artists dating back to the late 1940s. That is over fifty years—half a century—with fifty-two names a year on average. I am grateful and proud to be listed among those artists, so I thought it would be helpful to go through the list and see just how many of them I knew or had met or had played on the same bill with.

It starts with Byron Adams whom I met when John Mellencamp took me to Philadelphia to hopefully perform with him at J.F.K. Stadium. Adams, when introduced, was kind enough but his face said something like "Where will I be in thirty years?"

The Allman Brothers: I met Frank Barcelona for the first time in over four decades with Mellencamp in Philadelphia. The band Detroit and I were on the same bill in Florida with the Allman Brothers and Tom Petty and the Heartbreakers. That was an energetic show.

Eric Burdon and the Animals: Eric and I go back a long way, from the time I sat in his trailer in Central Park and convinced him to perform a second show for the almost rioting fans, to several engagements over the years on shows all over the country. The last time I saw him he greeted me by saying, "Mitch, you son of a bitch," and I responded with "Eric, you fucking British twit." I'll never consider Eric anything less than competition.

Asleep at the Wheel: We did some gigs with these guys in Oklahoma and that part of the country, and also in Michigan while we were under direction of Barry Kramer with the band Detroit.

The Association: They are always on the higher priced oldies act circuit. You didn't know there were different levels of oldies acts did you? I've done a few performances with them over the years. What is interesting is that my former bass player, Mark Gougeon, had a brother who worked with them.

Chet Atkins: I had the pleasure of meeting Chet Atkins at a guitar clinic that I attended with Jimmy McCarty. Here was an opportunity to watch a mature artist work his craft for a bunch of uninformed young aspiring musicians. This did not happen too many-times in my life. Everyone there knew what Chet had done for the guitar. He was fast, innovative, and not being a guitar player per se, I sill had a huge appreciation for his skill. What was impressive about it was that he wasn't a peer. He was a level above me. He was one of the masters, and I am grateful for the opportunity to learn for him.

Bachman-Turner Overdrive and The Guess Who: I've met all of these guys and played on bills with them in all of their different incarnations. They are nice people, maybe because they started out in Canada.

Badfinger: The only one left is Joey Molland, and we've done countless shows together. I admire Joey's vision of his future in entertainment. He is humble when it is appropriate and arrogant when it is necessary.

Long John Baldry: I worked with him when I was in exile in Canada, and he is a marvelous student of R&B. Like many on this list he is no longer with us, but that never takes away from his contribution to music. Never.

Hank Ballard and the Midnighters: I saw Hank Ballard perform when I was first coming up at the Village. Talk about a man who got screwed over. Chubby Checker wouldn't exist if it wasn't for Hank Ballard.

The Band: I have worked with Levon Helms at his studio in Woodstock. More than anything else, I remember how their *Big Pink* sent the British running and hiding when it was released. This came as a great surprise to me because I always held Levon in great esteem. I remember feeling it was an honor beyond belief when I was invited into his home to work in his home studio.

The Barbarians: They make me wonder whether or not the band Detroit was the most uncontrollable band ever produced in America.

The Beach Boys: Brian Wilson once paid me a high compliment as he wondered aloud about the magical qualities of my voice. I've also performed with The Beach Boys minus Brian. I did that performance blind in one eye because the retina on my left eye became detached. As it was a Sunday gig, no doctor was available. My doctor told me that happens to some people and someday it might happen to the other eye. He "wallpapered" it and reattached it with a laser. He did such an excellent job that I can see out of that eye perfectly. I also find it disconcerting that a band of so many unique players such as The Beach Boys could remain broken and never come back together, but then again, that is the same thing that happened to my group and me.

The Beatles: I've already commented on John and Ringo and George. I don't know that much about Paul except that he loved Linda with all of his being and I will say nothing to make that any different. I wish I were capable of finding such a deep love.

Jeff Beck: I've also spoken of Jeff, except to comment on his passion for American muscle cars.

Archie Bell and the Drells: When I performed with him and his group I asked him if he really was from Houston. It was an oldies show but, when you take into account the age of most of the people on this list, any of them could be considered oldies shows.

Brook Benton: What a deep soothing voice. I was happy to hear it up close on the same bill.

Chuck Berry: He taught generations of American youth how to make rock 'n' roll and how to not get screwed. I've worked with him many times and understand how an ego such as Keith Richards might become upset with an ego as big as Chuck's. My fondest memory of Chuck was a date we did together in Louisiana. We were sitting backstage waiting for him. He was late and the house band was nervous because they had not rehearsed with him. This was because Chuck said anyone who doesn't know Chuck Berry songs doesn't deserve to play with him. Just before show time, down a dusty road came a long black Cadillac. Chuck stepped out and didn't say a word to anyone. Instead, he looked around, walked to young man, and asked for promoter. The young man said, "That's me." Chuck opened the trunk of car to get his guitar, then he turned without a word and put his hand out. The promoter understood then that he had to pay right then or there would be no performance. Chuck played exactly sixty minutes, as contracted. There was thunderous applause from the audience, and the promoter said, "Why don't you do another." Chuck again held hand out. The promoter rounded up a few thousand dollars and Chuck played two more.

Elvin Bishop: I first met and performed with Elvin when he was with the Paul Butterfield Blues Band. When I heard him play I had a deep sense of his ability to go well beyond where he was at that particular moment as far as his stature as a guitar player, and he did.

The Black Crowes: Obviously someone else loved Otis Redding besides me. I opened for them outside of Lansing Michigan at a show where both our bands totally thrilled the audience. I enjoy playing with Southern bands because they think the same way about African American music as I do. I believe it is a labor of love for them, as it is for me, and clearly it is an inspiration.

Bobby "Blue" Bland: The first recording I bought of Bobby's was "Two Steps From The Blues. His "Turn On Your Lovelights" became a staple in my early shows. I also learned to appreciate the use of string arrangements in blues thanks to Bobby.

Blondie: I was at a gig in Michigan standing on the side of the stage when "Blondie" became upset over something and was leaving in the middle of the performance. The band stayed on stage while I convinced her that the right thing to do was to go back out and let the audience enjoy the rest of her show. She did. It's not uncommon for something to occur on stage between musicians that cause one to want to leave, but you have to understand that the public isn't aware of it and shouldn't be denied a professional show for which they have paid money. How do I know? I'm the guy who did walk off stage, and it caused a riot where people were hurt.

Mike Bloomfield: Our paths crossed many times, as documented in this book. The last time I saw Mike he was headlining a show in Colorado and his opening act was Steve Martin. I borrowed forty-two dollars from him that night because I was broke. Then I heard he died from an overdose while sitting in his parked car in L.A.

The Blues Brothers: Barry Kramer took me to see them perform at Pine Knob in Michigan. Between sets we went back to meet John Belushi and Dan Aykroyd. This was the same John who had ridiculed me when I was under Bud Prager's punishment, but that was in the past. Now he was coming out of a shower with a towel around his still wet body trying to freshen up for the next show. He was very cordial and happy to see me. I believe he had come to a point where he understood what I had been through and was applauding me for coming back to entertainment. Then I went down a hallway while Barry and John spoke and came to Dan Aykroyd's dressing room. Dan showed the exact opposite of John's behavior. He sat alone in a darkened room with dozens of empty and half-filled bottles of alcohol. The room was filled with smoke and there were cigarette butts all over the place. He stayed in his soaking wet and wrinkled clothes and waited for the next set. Dan was also very cordial but I was struck by the difference. In the future, Dan would invite me up to his hometown in Kingston, Ontario to perform and would proclaim it one of the best concerts he had ever witnessed.

Gary U.S. Bonds: I hadn't made my first recording when I first heard Gary's music. I loved the energy and grooves he was working with. In the future I would do many shows, sometimes just he and I as the only two acts on the bill. Gary is a very nice man.

Booker T and the M.G's: Beyond what I've already stated, was the Southern hospitality that still existed when I did *The Detroit-Memphis Experiment* with them. I stayed at Duck Dunn's house and at Steve Cropper's house rather than being locked away in some cheap motel for the project. I've been on charity golf outings with Steve since then, but people change and life becomes something less than we hoped for.

James Brown: One of my early teachers. James once said on a national TV show that in his estimation Mitch Ryder was the most soulful white singer he could think of. I went to visit James at a show at Harpo's in Detroit quite a few years ago. I was let in the dressing room where James was drying his hair under one of those old space ship looking hair dryers that completely covered your head. I said hello, and James signaled me with his hand to come closer because he couldn't hear me. I spoke again, and again James summoned me closer. This went on a few more times until I was actually down on my knees at his feet and looking up. Nothing further was said. He just broke out in a huge grin having achieved his goal. But it was his influence on a fourteen-year-old Detroit boy that led me to the music I would chase after the rest of my life.

Brownsville Station: It was Cub Coda that I would come to do many shows with and befriend in the years shortly before his death. What a wonderful man he was. We were doing an oldies show in Cleveland I believe, and Cub didn't have anyone there to watch out for him. He had an attack and I took him to his room and got him what was necessary to normalize his situation. I didn't think of it as a big deal, but he did and so did his wife, Lady Jane. It was my honor to serve him.

The Buckinghams: I always think Chicago when I think of these guys. Mostly oldies shows, but a very competent group and their audiences loved them.

Tim Buckley: I was pissed off with him and Kimberly after she went to get his autograph at a Detroit performance. She was gone half an hour and came back with his autograph signed on the back of her prescription for birth control pills.

Buffalo Springfield: I knew Dewey Martin best and we did a few shows with them while I was still a big star, so to speak. The group was so enormously talented that the members went on to form several other successful groups.

Jerry Butler: I met Jerry while taping an oldies package for TV. He was one of the most pleasant men I've ever been introduced to.

Paul Butterfield Blues Band: Again a Chicago creation, but a group I thoroughly enjoyed. We did some TV shows with them while I was with the Wheels.

The Byrds: I performed on arena shows with them and was influenced most by the use of the twelve-string guitar sound. When thinking about the group I have to admit I felt they were almost as inventive as the English were during that period in the history of rock and roll.

Freddy Cannon: Another name from the Bob Crewe era and stable. We were on oldies shows on the mainland and Hawaii together. Freddy has a lot of energy for his age and he's one of those audience participation people, like so many from his era. I do it myself sometimes, but I wouldn't go to a show to participate. I'd want to sit there like a blind man and enjoy the sound from the stage.

The Cars: A couple of the members of the cars came to one of my shows in New York as the guest of John Badanjek. They liked his drumming. Who wouldn't?

Gene Chandler: Another oldies show. Gene Chandler was a showman in the old school tradition and he often entered the audience. I always wanted to steal his cape.

Cheap Trick: I performed with them in their home state of Illinois. They were good!

Chubby Checker: I wish I knew how to turn a penny into a dollar like he does. Every hit record he had came from somewhere else, but he managed to take million sellers and turn them into multi-million sellers. In a capitalist society, that is probably the greatest achievement of them all.

The Chiffons: Like a good portion of the groups or personalities I'm describing, the Chiffons are one of those groups I have appeared with on an oldies show. I can't really point to an individual because many of these groups have few, if any, of the original members left. But they wouldn't be working unless they had talent and were good at what they do. I apologize.

Lou Christie: If ever there was a self-promoter it is Lou Christie. If you enjoy intense monolog between artist and audience you'll love Lou. He comes from the Peter Noone school of "Let's Talk." Get to know me. When he does sing, he does it very well.

Eric Clapton: Beyond what I've described in the book is the fact that Eric is one of the few who either through luck or connections has attained superstar status. As a singer myself, I don't believe there are many guitar players as good as he is.

The Dave Clark Five: Uh . . . oh yeah, they finally got inducted into the Rock and Roll Hall of Fame. They had to be, given the fact they were robbed of the induction previously. The Rivieras and I took care of them before we ever had a hit.

George Clinton: Where would Stevie Wonder or Prince or Sly and the Family Stone be without George Clinton? Probably the same place I'd be without James Brown or Little Richard or Hank Williams. Everybody in this select group influences somebody else and on and on.

The Coasters: They influenced me before I knew I was being influenced. Today you have many choices of Coasters. Pick well. "Poison Ivy," and then "Searching," were the first songs of theirs I heard. The problem today is that many of the original members either sold or gave away rights to cousins, relatives, or strangers who paid them. All of them are good at what they do, but it's like looking at The Temptations, none of the original members are there anymore.

Albert Collins: Chicago. Blues club. Sweat and singing guitars.

The Comets: I was barely a teenager when "Rock Around the Clock" came out, but I did perform on a show with The Comets on an oldies package on the East Coast at a huge Indian Casino. They blew me away. Their eighty-three year old drummer did a ten-minute drum solo. And then I got to ride to the airport with them the next day. It was wild, hearing their conversations about health problems and social security.

Commander Cody and His Lost Planet Airmen: When Barry Kramer took over Mitch Ryder these guys were at their peak. Interesting approach to musical entertainment with very talented musicians.

The Contours: Pure Detroit Motown soul. I always loved "Shake Sherry Shake" but "Do You Love Me" is still my favorite. We did quite a few gigs with them over the years. Strictly professional.

Alice Cooper: I met Alice, or Vince, when he had his farm in Michigan. He wasn't from Michigan, but at this time in the history of music Detroit was a hot place to be. His manager thought it would be cool, so Alice moved there to be more visible. His farm was a very utilitarian place with no animals. It had running water and several vacant fields of weeds close to the expressway. He used the farm for rehearsing, and really, everything about him was about music. I actually played guitar for a rehearsal of "Under My Wheels." What a thrill.

Marshall Crenshaw: A hidden jewel.

The Crickets: Almost like The Comets with no Bill Haley, The Crickets were without Buddy Holly, but they were wonderful. It was a show in Deadwood, South Dakota, and also on the show was Bobby Vee. Bobby had hired me and I was mystified to find out that Bob Dylan had worked for him way back when.

Crosby, Stills and Nash: I did two different arena shows with them in the early days. What amazingly different harmonies. Not as compelling as The Beach Boys but none the less groundbreaking for white voices.

The Crystals: I love them. I mean, here we are some forty years later and they all look like they are in their twenties and thirties.

Ron Dante: What I find interesting about Ron Dante is his close ties to Bob Crewe in Los Angeles.

Bobby Darin: He was making records before I made my first recording at the age of sixteen. One day in Detroit he was the guest of some mutual friends and we had a chance to walk along the shores of Lake St. Clair in Grosse Pointe and chat about show business. What a career he had.

Spencer Davis: My favorite Englishman. A hard worker, biligual, a teacher, and a musician. Every time I play in Germany I bump into his posters. We've done many shows together and he always pleases the audience. I also thank him for Stevie Winwood.

Bobby Day: California. Nice make up. Better than Little Richard's.

Delaney and Bonnie: Kimberly and I had a chance to meet with them in their hotel room back in the day and they were great hosts. I wonder how Bonnie likes my recording of "Ain't Nobody White Can Sing the Blues"?

The Del-Vikings: Recently, I finally had the chance to perform on the same stage with some of the men who had created one of my all time favorite records.

Rick Derringer: What a talented guitar player. I've done many shows with Rick and he puts everything he has into his performance. I was very disappointed to discover that he had been sleeping with Sarah Smithers after we had broken up.

Willy DeVille: The classic "I will stay on the edge whether I like it or not" logic. So much talent, so little time.

Neil Diamond: I got to meet Neil in a California recording studio. My favorite story about him takes place in Germany. When my road manager, Neil Thompson, woke me up early on a Sunday to say we had reservations at a very private and exclusive golf course near Frankfurt, I bitched because I was still drunk from the night before. But, Neil assured me I would enjoy this. I asked how we could pay for such an expensive outing and he said, "Don't worry, just come down to the lobby." I arrived at the lobby and out front was a huge Mercedes limousine. I again asked what was going on and Neil again said, "Don't worry." When we arrived at the clubhouse the limo came to a stop and the driver rolled down the windows to the back. A man stuck his head in and said, "Welcome to our course. You will find everything you need in the clubhouse." He was the owner of the golf course, and, as promised, we found everything from clothes to clubs. We got a cart and proceeded to play golf. At every green a uniformed servant came out to supply us with drinks. After the first nine we were getting tanked and there were more divots than an army of gophers could have created. We were playing so slowly that a Japanese foursome played through. After eighteen we went back to the clubhouse, showered and dressed. I again asked, "What the fuck is going on?" Neil again said, "Don't worry about it." As we were leaving in the limo to go back to our cheap little hotel the driver again stopped and rolled down the windows. The same head popped in again and said, "Thank you for coming, Mr. Diamond."

The Diamonds: Another chance to be on a stage with one of my early memories. But much larger and more important was the fact that when I was in the fifth or sixth grade I was entranced with their recording of "Little Darling." One morning before leaving for school my mother took off her wedding ring and put it on the windowsill. I pocketed her ring, and hummed the words to the song all the way to school. I couldn't wait to give my girlfriend the ring. My girl was an army brat. I knew she and her family were moving away, and I wanted her know how devoted I would always remain to her. Two days later her family moved and we never got the ring back. Mom frantically searched all over the house for the ring. I could have redeemed myself and told Mom I took it, but I never did. I felt guilty, but I was in love. I still feel that guilt and shame now, even though Mom passed long ago.

Bo Diddley: Other than what I have previously written, was my amazement at his ability to walk after having been shot in the leg by one of his girlfriends while onstage.

Dino, Desi and Billy: It was one of the first Dick Clark appearances we did with the Wheels and I remember thinking how unfair it was for people to get breaks in showbiz because of who their parents were. I was still naïve, but not respectful enough to keep from blowing them off the stage.

Dr. John: After "Dr. John, The Night Tripper" I was a fan for life. I finally met him at a gig in Ann Arbor that I attended with John Sinclair. Dr. John gave a walking stick to John Sinclair, and it was a walking stick that, for many reasons John Sinclair cherished. One of the band members from the group Detroit stole it and Sinclair was understandably very angry.

The Doobie Brothers: Michael McDonald was the only Doobie Brother I got to meet. We met in North Carolina at a hotel where we were both staying. Michael McDonald, the late Robert Palmer, Stevie Winwood, Delbert McClinton, Elton John, The Righteous Brothers, Paul Rodgers, and a very few others fit into that category of white boys who actually comprehend R&B and blues and execute it with conviction and credibility. There may be more . . . I'm simply talking about the ones I am aware of.

The Doors: Even though I did attend a few of their concerts and made the pilgrimage to Jim Morrison's grave in Paris, I've only spoken to Ray Manzerak. It was around the time he finished his first book about The Doors, and I think I scared him off when I changed the subject of our conversation from music to personal relationships. More specifically, I wanted his advice about some marital problems I was having.

Bob Dylan: When I first played his acoustic stuff for the Wheels, the only one who ventured to listen was Jimmy McCarty. He held some reservations, but Jimmy was a true musician and would sample anything out there. As far as meeting Bob Dylan, sorry. The closest I got was the control room as he recorded. But, he set a standard in writing that no other American or British musician or songwriter has come close to. He remains my number one inspiration for writing. Maybe after I get a brain transplant I might try to equal his stuff.

Steve Earle: I met Steve Earle through my old friend George Konig. His talent is rewarding, but his demons won't leave him alone. He deserves more than he has, which he has proven on many occasions when his demons have left him be.

Dave Edmunds: Berlin and a sweet introduction to tasty music.

The Electric Flag: What I remember most is my blown opportunity to be their singer. We were doing a multi-act show in Wisconsin when the band's founder, Michael Bloomfield, came to my room and said he loved me as a singer. He said Columbia offered them a record deal and he wanted me to join them. I now regret not taking his offer as it would have put me on a major label, rather than the independent label I was on.

Elephant's Memory: For me this was all about Wayne Gabriel and how he complimented John Lennon's later creations. We had worked together twice before and I'm convinced he was happiest in a studio as opposed to live gigs.

Fabian: He hosted a made for television concert on which I appeared with the Thrashing Brothers, Mary Wells (God rest her soul), and Del Shannon, another talent no longer with us. Fabian was the first national white singer I went to see when I was young. He was at the state fair. Unfortunately, that was also the year I saw James Brown. Making the comparison between the two of them changed my life.

Marianne Faithful: The book tells the story, except it doesn't say how she has completely turned her life around for the better. I hope she keeps going. I love her voice.

The Flamingos: What heavenly harmonies. Amazing.

Fleetwood Mac: We opened for them in Germany at a huge outdoor concert. I remember buying one of their albums and loving every single song on it.

Foghat: My group that worked with my man Danny McAleer has to be special.

The Four Seasons: Because of their involvement with Bob Crewe, I got to see the creative side to their hits. One of the funny things was that when I was still at the Village, my brothers in the Peps loved the song "Sherry." They thought Frankie Valli's high falsetto was perfect.

The Four Tops: My favorite male Motown group. "Bernadette" and "Standing in the Shadows of Love" were two of the best productions ever created by Holland, Dozier and Holland.

The Gap Band: Perfection through simplicity. That was the lesson I learned from them. I even used a modified version of a keyboard line of theirs that I loved on my *Acquitted Idiot* CD.

The J. Geils Band: We were fans of each other and it was sad to see them pull themselves apart. It was like watching a replay of the Mitch Ryder and the Detroit Wheels break up.

The Go-Gos: Working with Gina Schock was great. Gina came into drum on one track on the John Mellancamp produced *Never Kick a Sleeping Dog* album for me. I appreciate the group itself, and her skills as a drummer even more.

Barry Goldberg: Barry played piano on some of my tracks in New York and was most concerned with perfection. He is way under-rated for his abilities.

Lesley Gore: We did many shows together and we almost did some summer stock in the early days. She has a good sense of her place in the history of music.

Grand Funk Railroad: A Michigan group I've done a few shows with. Their story will make for interesting reading when it becomes available. Mark Farner is the one member I am most familiar with.

The Grass Roots: Another of those oldies hit makers who command a higher price than most. And why not? They do a great show and they've got the hits.

Buddy Guy: I was one of the many happy people fortunate to have gotten a ticket for one of those nights he decided to let it all out.

Nina Hagen: Nina is from East Germany and I am talking to her about doing a duet on one of our next recordings. I don't know if we will sing in German or English, and it doesn't matter. Her voice is one for the ages.

Screamin' Jay Hawkins: California. He came out of his coffin to practice some kind of voodoo. He put a spell on everybody.

Isaac Hayes: I met him while working down in Memphis with Booker T and the M.G's. He was very distant and not as pleasant as was Don Davidson.

Jimi Hendrix: Music for the ages. I knew him better than most and, of course, I've told my story about him. But, after I turned down his offer to be his singer, around two years later a friend introduced me to Noel Redding, Jimi's bass player, in Detroit. Noel, I was told, was thinking about jamming together to see if we could make something happen. I had also gone out to Coney Island with Sarah, and Mitch Mitchell, Jimi's drummer, was a guest in our limo.

John Hiatt: John was doing an acoustic set at the Bus Stop in Minneapolis. I happened to be in town and went to see him, and there weren't more than twenty people there. After the show we spent some time together talking about sobriety and alcohol. A little A.A. meeting if you will. I last saw him when I introduced him to Megan as he came through and played at Chene Park on the river.

John Lee Hooker: There is a *Rolling Stone* article that says John Lee Hooker and four other male voices, one being mine, were the most influential to ever come out of Detroit. I saw John Lee Hooker last at the Navy Pier in Chicago. He came out of his trailer, sat down on a chair and began patting his foot on the cement. Then he began to play guitar and sing. It doesn't get much better than that. It reminded me a bit of the time I saw Jimmy Reed, who was playing at the Village in Detroit long after I had left. He was pretty messed up that night but it was still okay. I've certainly done my share of shows not entirely sober.

Brian Hyland: A very nice man and a nice family. Like some of us, he continues to create and improve his art form in spite of the odds.

Iron Butterfly: I've worked shows with them here in America and in Germany. Very few people know that the catch line is a drunken slur of "In the Garden of Eden."

The Isley Brothers: One of the first gigs I did with the Wheels in Virginia was with the Isley Brothers. Pure funk.

Etta James: I was transfixed as she performed during a show in Mississippi. What a voice. It was one of those lasting heaven-sent voices like Aretha Franklin's. I thought hearing her voice move me like that would only be an experience I could enjoy from a live performance, so I was stunned some months later when the same goose bumps appeared on my skin when she sang on television. People don't know how difficult her career and her relationships with men were.

Tommy James: Another Michigan guy who had the great misfortune of working with Morris Levy. I've done several shows with him but could never appreciate it. More my problem than his.

Jan and Dean: California. That whole California surf thing confuses me, but as I watched them I kept thinking about Brian Wilson and how he was able to make that a small and temporary part of what he was doing.

Jay and the Americans: I was on a show with them in New York City when Jay popped a vein in his throat and had to leave the stage in panic because of the blood in his throat.

Jefferson Airplane: San Francisco. Marty Balin. Jefferson Starship. White Rabbit. Oh man, that was what was driving me crazy as the West Coast sound blew the Midwest sound off the map and went toe to toe with the Brits.

Billy Joel: I met him once in a restaurant and again near an aircraft carrier in the Hudson River. He took my drummer, Liberty Devito, and made him famous, but I can't hold that against him. Billy genuinely seemed to like me and what I had to contribute to music, but once we both broke from Paramount our communication ended.

Elton John: I allude to Elton in this book, but I can't bring myself to call him Sir Elton John. I just have weird visions of Sir Elton, Defender of the Realm, wildly swirling a lethal sword around and causing much havoc and injury. He has one of the most beautiful voices I've ever heard and thank you for "Yellow Brick Road." It pissed off Bud Prager when I sent him a copy.

Janis Joplin: Last time I saw Janis we spoke for a few minutes in the Memphis airport between planes. She looked done in by the guilt of innocence as we talked about how tired we both were, where we were going, and how much we loved each other. The one thing people walking by the two of us would have seen was that we looked like two penniless vagrants, and here we were both stars. It was a surreal scene. We both loved R&B so much. My passion and goal as a singer was to be the best white male R&B singer, and she confessed to me that her goal was to be the best white female.

Journey: The white singer who sounds like Sam Cooke. Splendid. My daughter begged me to take her to see Journey when she was a young lady, and the group allowed us to stand backstage for the show. Thanks, guys, for making my daughter happy.

The Knack: Doug Fieger is the brother of one of my best friends Geoffrey Fieger. We are both proud of you Doug.

Billy J. Kramer: I got to know Billy very well on the oldies packages put together by the agent Wendy Kay. His is an interesting story. In fact, I'm sure that anybody I've mentioned has an interesting story, because fame is so hard to reason out.

Patti LaBelle: Alan Stroh first took me to see Patti because he wanted me to see what the competition and expectations would be like in my own career. What I learned from Patti was that when you are on stage you give 100 percent. All of the time.

Brenda Lee: Before I was old enough to drive I hitch-hiked twenty-seven miles to see her appearance where she lip-synched "I'm Sorry." I was in love with her voice. When she finally left through the rear door where I had been waiting, I lost my courage and watched her drive out of my life.

The Left Banke: I befriended the player whose father worked with the symphony and helped them make their string arrangements. They were better than they got credit for. Jesus, The Four Tops covered one of their songs.

Gary Lewis and the Playboys: We did mostly Wendy Kay oldies shows together. Over the years, I got to know the band very well. They always made me sound good when they backed me up. Gary was different. He was, and is, a "keep to himself" person and in spite of my constant reaching out to know him, he prefers his privacy. I don't know if it's the famous father syndrome or what, but Gary is one of the ones who decided it was not worth continuing to chase his dreams and settled for living out his career based upon his past accomplishments.

Huey Lewis and the News: Besides what I have documented already, Huey also has the ability to act. Last time I saw one of their shows was at Lake Tahoe at a casino.

Jerry Lee Lewis: The Killer. I saw Jerry at a small performance in a small club on the East side of Detroit where he stopped his drummer from jumping off the stage to kick my ass. I also saw him go head to head with Little Richard in an arena and got pissed off, because that's what Little Richard would do to him. And, I opened for him the night we all glanced up to watch the beginning of the first war in Iraq on TV. One of the first records I ever owned was given to me as a Christmas gift. It was "Whole Lotta Shakin' Goin' On."

Little Anthony and the Imperials: I was on the same show with him on three different occasions. He still has his chops.

Little Richard: I've met him, made a lot of money for him, played on the same bill with him, and know more about him than he probably knows about himself. It was his voice that taught me about energy. He definitely doesn't suffer from a lack of ego.

Nils Lofgren: The Rock Palast Show in Germany.

Los Lobos: A fine, fine group. I like their cover of "Devil With a Blue Dress On" in Spanish, and "Jenny had a Pony." I met two of the guys in Arizona at the hotel we were staying at.

Trini Lopez: One of the first singers Alan Stroh took me to see. Not because he was special, but because my manager wanted me to experience standing ovations at Basin Street East in Manhattan.

The Lovin' Spoonful: We did a show in Florida together. I thought they were one of the best American groups I had ever seen. I remember our engineer at Bell Sound in New York brought us into the control room to hear an early preview of "Summer in the City," and we flipped out. It was such a radical change from "Do You Believe in Magic," which was out just before that.

Lulu: Thanks for being a good friend to my wife Susan during our night of terror with three of The Beatles—minus the good one, John Lennon.

The Mamas and the Papas: Cass Elliot was the member I befriended. She loved life and it was hard to understand how she lost it. What a powerful voice.

Martha and the Vandellas: Interestingly enough, Martha for a while sat on the city council for the city of Detroit. But, I've shared stages with her my entire career.

The Marvellettes: It depends on which of the two available Marvellettes you are talking about.

The MC5: Wayne Kramer is my connection to that group. Wayne and I have worked together quite a few times in different forms over the years. *Ramblin' Rose.* If anybody wants to question the authenticity of this book, Wayne would be the guy to talk to.

Cash McCall: Straight from the Dick Clark Caravan of Stars.

Melanie: I didn't even know she existed until I did a two-year run with a package show called HippieFest. Her son is one of the best guitar players alive. He's absolutely brilliant to the point that he stole the show from his mother.

John Mellencamp: John and I will be forever linked with the album *Never Kick a Sleeping Dog.* We are too much alike to ever be friends, but I thank him for his belief in me.

Buddy Miles: Too bad I can't play drums like that.

The Monkees: I was still a "star" when they burst onto the scene. I spent time with Peter Tork as a house guest, and did a show or two with Mickey Dolenz. My wife and her sisters each had their favorite Monkee to pine over.

The Moody Blues: I've only performed with the man whose voice cut through the race barrier in Detroit when he sang "Go Now."

Mountain: It's already been stated earlier: Leslie is very much under-rated for his ability as a singer and guitar player, and Corky will always be an excellent drummer.

Nazareth: They once kicked me out of their dressing room after I had been invited in. The guy who invited me disappeared and they didn't know who I was. Or was it they knew who I was and were just being British?

Willie Nelson: I saw him perform at the Macomb Center for the Performing Arts. Another good book to read.

Randy Newman: I saw him at the Royal Oak Music Theater. I wasn't expecting to see just him and a piano. Neither were the other hundred or so customers. He signed an autograph for me, and when I introduced myself as Mitch Ryder, his mind began racing. Had I waited, there might have been a song.

Ted Nugent: I've only played on a few shows with Ted. The one I like to recall is when he hid in the rafters of the arena. Then, when he was introduced he came swinging down to the stage from the ceiling on a rope and began playing immediately. He has professed to be a life-long fan.

Tony Orlando: I met him at a party at his home in Branson, Missouri where he was booked for something like five hundred years. He was kind enough to talk to me, but like every artist who works Branson regularly, he had the look of a prisoner in a work camp. You are booked there for months, and except for the water ride, the only other thing to do there is sit in traffic. He never introduced me to Dawn.

Les Paul: Another guitar clinic promotion appearance, but that couldn't replace the memory of him playing on TV with his wife as guitar strings went popping.

Wilson Pickett: Wilson and I made history when we did a series of mixed race shows during the height of the Civil Rights movement. He was also my intro to the Apollo Theater, as he was the first black artist to bring me onstage and sponsor me.

The Platters: I worked with them at the Grand Hotel in Upper Michigan. It was like going back to a time when my parents might have bought one of their recordings, even though I knew all the words and melodies.

The Police: It was an Easter show in Berlin way before the wall came down and we opened for them. I have that performance on tape and it is hot. Thrashing Brothers and I rarely did a better show.

Billy Preston: I attended a party at his sister's house in Palmer Park in Detroit, and finally met Billy on the same show as The Comets played.

Prince: There's nothing to say except he is an eccentric.

Procol Harum: Gary Brooker and I were both signed to Line Records when he tried to establish himself in Germany.

Gary Puckett: What a wonderful voice. I don't care all that much for his style, but he has a beautiful voice. We worked together on a couple of shows.

Suzi Quatro: A Detroit girl. Last time I saw Suzi was at one of my shows in Hamburg, Germany.

Queen: Just a meeting in Germany at an empty bar. I later heard their music with a few of the original members when Paul Rodgers invited me to a Queen reunion several years ago.

Question Mark and the Mysterians: I did a couple of shows with Question Mark. I most liked his tailored pants that would split in the back every time he turned his back to the audience and bent over.

Bonnie Raitt: I first saw Bonnie at the Ann Arbor Blues and Jazz Festival in the early seventies. She couldn't have been more than fourteen. She also was gracious enough to appear on my radio show.

Rare Earth: I've done tours with these guys as my back-up band. At one time they wanted me to be their singer when I was living in Colorado. Great guys, great music.

Otis Redding: The first song I heard from Otis Redding was the ballad "Try a Little Tenderness." There will never be a more moving voice such as his in music. Ever. "Mr. Pitiful" was a hit for him when I first arrived at Trude Heller's. But being on stage and having him wrap his arm on my shoulder, rocking back and forth together as we sang a duet was one of the highlights of my musical life.

Lou Reed: I appeared on stage with Lou at the Masonic Temple in Detroit.

Paul Revere and the Raiders: I did many Dick Clark shows with them and live performances, too. I continued working shows with Mark Lindsay after he left. Many of these groups that changed people or broke up have legal stories that could fill a book.

The Righteous Brothers: "You've Lost That Loving Feeling" was the song I listened to on the radio as I drove up and back to Michigan State to visit Susan. Later on in my career, I was told by Mr. "Unchained Melody" that I was one of the best white R&B singers he had ever known.

Johnny Rivers: The rumor was that Johnny was very difficult to work with. Piss on that. Everyone on this list had to be difficult to work with at one time or another. We're all only human and the lifestyle we've chosen leaves us vulnerable to intrusions from all sorts of disagreeable persons. He does a very professional show.

Smokey Robinson and The Miracles: My first recording by this group was a song called "Way Over There." I don't think it ever was a hit outside Detroit, but that was the beauty of Motown. By living in Detroit we got to hear the test models before they went national. I saw Smokey perform in the early days in Detroit. What a marvelous voice. Smokey was also a very good businessman, and beyond Jackie Wilson, got Motown off to its start. Marv Johnson could be included in that bunch as well.

Tommy Roe: We did a date in the Midwest together, and I was a fan of "Sweet Pea."

The Rolling Stones: For me . . . silence is a virtue.

The Romantics: Again, a Michigan group. I played with them on a number of occasions, the most memorable was singing in front of them with guitarist/songwriter Robert Gillespie at the baseball All Star Game in Detroit.

The Ronnettes with Ronnie Spector: An oldies show with higher priced talent on the bill. Some of these groups I mention had hits, but some had hits with very special voices. Here is a very special voice.

Diana Ross: I ran into her before Berry Gordy had finished his grooming process. It altered my take on the group as a whole, but we are talking about numbers. They had a lot of them. Somehow I don't think Diana is going to die on welfare.

Leon Russell: From the time I met him and Denny Cordell in Washington State, until the time I saw him perform at a club that held two hundred people, I've wanted to understand his story.

Sam and Dave: When I first broke into the top ten, Sam and Dave were there to greet me. I've always thought that "Hold On, I'm Coming" was Stax and Booker T. and the M.G's at their finest.

Bob Seger: One time I went out to Bob's house on a lake to write, or try to write, songs. My little son Joel had fallen asleep on Bob's bed, and had wet the bed. It was the last time I was invited. Over the years Bob, in spite of Punch's protests, has been very respectful of me. I return the respect. "Turn the Page."

Sha Na Na: The best part of this story is how the powers that be tried to eliminate their appearance at Woodstock. Revisionist history never works guys. Give them their due. Call Woodstock what it was, not what you want it to be. This is as sick as the Rock and Roll Hall of Fame. I worked with Bowser (Jon Bauman) on a few gigs.

The Shangri-Las: Quite a few appearances on oldies shows. Fun to be around.

Del Shannon: He was on a TV show I did with Mary Wells. Del had some demons he couldn't get rid of.

The Shirelles: They were my early soundtrack before I went to New York. The one song I especially like was "Will You Still Love Me Tomorrow." That was hot when I was in love for first time as a teen. What great memories! I didn't know for a long time that the song was written by Carol King. I loved the group arrangement on it.

Paul Simon: I've always wanted to work and record with Paul Simon because of his ability to create exciting music. I often thought that my voice on his music would be something special.

Percy Sledge: I saw him from the side of the stage as the cue to take the knee-drop was given. This was in the 1960s, maybe about 1967. My manager said, "I want you to watch this. Watch Percy." There he was, singing his heart out on stage. But, he never knew when to do the knee drop except to watch his manager. After the drop, his manager brought his hand back up and he got up and finished the song. Amazing.

Sly and the Family Stone: I've already stated what my relationship to the group was. I think a lot of Sly's bad reputation is the product of a vengeful enemy that occupied his camp at one time.

Southside Johnny: These New Jersey guys are relentless in their plan to rule the world. They just keep coming. Johnny was just one of the first. I played with him on the infamous Rock Palast Show in Germany.

Rick Springfield: I met him when my ex-drummer Jack White was working with him. He was a nice guy. I like his acting.

Bruce Springsteen: In my office hangs a picture of Bruce and me performing together on stage. Bruce is one of many performers on this list who asserts I was an influence on his career. This is much the same way I give credit to Little Richard, James Brown and Hank Williams. We all have influenced each other, and when a new artist comes out he or she is the distillation of a lifetime of previous artists having impact on each new generation. It is a gift we give to each other, kind of like passing the torch. The best part is that the public is the beneficiary of these transitions.

Steppenwolf: I've performed many times with them over the years. John Kay caused me to go out and purchase one of his albums at a time when I could have had it for free from my promo man, but I didn't want to wait two hours.

Rod Stewart: Ohhh . . . let's move on.

Barrett Strong: The original moneyman from Motown. The Beatles thought enough of Barrett to cover one of his songs.

The Temptations: I've known them from the beginning through the present and like many of the groups have watched the older members disappear. I use to sing down at the Village with one of their first replacements, Richard Street. Richard Street now bills himself as the Richard Street Temptations. All these evolving older groups are passing the money making name on to relatives or friends. It makes me grateful that there is only one Mitch Ryder in music. There is, however, a Mitch Ryder porno star, and a Mitch Ryder wrestler from Indiana, and of course, Winnona Ryder, the actress whose parents were fans and gave her my last name. Maybe. I wonder if I ever knew her mother?

George Thorogood: I worked with him in Washington, his home state. Good show.

Three Dog Night: I've only had the pleasure of working with Two Dog Night, or Chuck Negron, by himself. Even today, Chuck has a remarkably beautiful voice.

Tiny Tim: I worked with Mr. Tim in Nevada and later he sent me a talking Christmas card with Christmas greetings in his own voice. I will cherish it forever. He is definitely the person, of all the people I've known, that I was the most intrigued by. For starters, he had no sense of oral hygiene. And, he always addressed gentlemen and ladies as sir and ma'am, like we did down south. He was very formal and also, at the same time, very eccentric.

The Tokens: Many oldies shows in America and a universal hit record to last forever. When I look at this list, more than half of the artists have appeared on oldies shows with me. That causes two reactions from me. First, I am grateful to be able to perform for my American fans as long as I can. Secondly, I am grateful to have a second career in Europe with fresh product nearly every year.

Ike and Tina Turner: "Fool in Love." That was my first experience with their music. I remember how funny Ike was, though. One night in L.A., I went to a club called the Maverick and went backstage to say hi. Ike answered the door. I told him who I was, and three seconds later the door flew open with Tina standing there naked. She was smiling wildly, and as she approached to give me a big hug she stopped short, looked at me, turned to Ike and said, "You asshole Ike, that's not Mick Jagger," then slammed the door in my face.

The Turtles: Another exceptionally gifted self-promoting entity. Their show is what I call Mickey Mouse safe, and I say this after having worked with them at Disney World. They were re-booked, I wasn't.

Stevie Ray Vaughan: We briefly shared the same management, and one night I opened for Stevie in Miami. Basically, we sat in the hallway unable to move, waiting for some passerby to give us more drugs.

Bobby Vee: Bobby has hired me for a few of his promotions. A genuine guy without pretense and a veteran performer.

Jr. Walker: One of the biggest mistakes I ever made. I was opening for Jr., and being that I had too much to drink I said to him as I walked on to perform, "Pay attention, Jr. You might learn something." He just smiled. When he came on for his show, that seventy-year-old man proceeded to kick my ass out of the state. I've never seen such energy from an old guy. Now I always keep my mouth shut.

Joe Walsh: I spent time in his trailer before he went on, talking about other artists, which is typical. He is special in his approach to guitar. Ry Cooder, Stevie Ray Vaughan, Eric Clapton, Jimmy McCarty, Jimi Hendrix, Jimmy Page, Jeff Beck. Those are his equals. It's the same way with harmonica players. You can create a list filled with accomplished harp players, but at the end of the day you begin your list with the best. In harmonica I always start with Sonny Boy Williamson and go from there.

Was (Not Was): Having been produced on a couple of different occasions by Don Was, it has become a much closer relationship. In fact, I performed with Was (Not Was) when they appeared in Detroit at the Majestic Theater, and it went very well. If you search, you can probably find it on YouTube. Over the years, Don has become a confidant to whom I often send my work to for criticism.

Mary Wells: I did an oldies TV special with her. She had so many hits for Motown, but I prefer the early Mary Wells to the later Mary Wells. The "Bye Bye Baby" to the "My Guy" Mary is gone now. Dead from throat cancer.

The Who: It is well documented that they got their first break in America by opening for me. Peter and I knew each other briefly, and it was fun being on the same bill.

Jackie Wilson: One day my body guard, Romeo, asked if I wanted to meet Jackie Wilson. I naturally said yes. He was staying in the same hotel. We approached his door, which was partially open, and knocked. We were told to enter, and when we walked in there was Jackie in the nude on a bed with a nude woman and we conversed for maybe fifteen minutes.

Edgar and Johnny Winter: I was introduced to these brothers on separate occasions while working with Barry Kramer.

Stevie Wonder: I met Stevie when he was called Little Stevie Wonder and we did a television show together. He's one of greatest chromatic harmonica players that the world will ever know. I only wish he had written all of his hits because I prefer his writing to the songs that were written for him in early days of Motown. When I was introduced to him for very first time he accidentally spit on me, but I didn't take it personally because he was blind. His contribution to music is sizable, no doubt about it.

The Yardbirds: This was the early days of success with Mitch Ryder and the Detroit Wheels. We approached our show with them the same way we did with all of the early English acts. We saw them as someone to blow off the stage. We succeeded.

Neil Young: I met Neil in California while he was waiting in the lobby of an agent. He sat there playing his guitar and trying out new lyrics, which I'm sure he had created to perform for the agent. We spoke briefly about nothing too important and I went in for my appointment.

The Young Rascals: I came to know them all very well. I used to drive or fly from Detroit to Syracuse, New York just to have some of their mother's lasagna.

The Zombies: I played on the HippieFest tour one summer with the Zombies. It was a good show.

That completes the national stars, for the most part but it doesn't say anything about the thousands and thousands of other musicians I've performed with who never made the cut, so to speak. These are men and women who, for one reason or another, couldn't survive the demands needed to sacrifice everything for a shot at stardom: financial responsibilities, families, health concerns. There is an endless list of demands that must be met for a shot at the big time.

Fame in America is so perverse that you find people willing to appear for fifteen minutes on national television. They go through every sordid detail, every humiliating experience, and every dark truth they have held onto just to be able to say, "Did you see me on TV?"

All my sordid details, humiliating experiences and dark truths are now documented for all to see in this book, but it took me much monger than fifteen minutes to survive them. It took me a lifetime. It was a lifetime of blessings from lessons learned and survived, and I am a better person for each of those experiences.

APPENDIX B

The rewards of a lifetime of entertaining can be measured in so many different ways, probably as many as when one would care to list the sacrifices they have had to endure, but I am going to stick to what I feel the positive rewards have been. I have, with and without Megan, been able to see and travel a lot of the world and discover the sameness in humans while overlooking cultural differences and any observations on personal relationships. I mean, why ruin everything by having to work hard on a vacation? This career of mine has taken me to many places on this planet that most people, other than the wealthy, will probably never see and I'd like to share my thought on some of those places with you.

Canada
In case no one has ever told you, the Rocky Mountains of Canada are far superior to the Rockies in the United States.

Germany
I have, over the years, covered every inch of Germany, probably more than the average German. My favorite places to go are the little, off the beaten path villages that survived destruction in the Second World War. It is fairy tale stuff. The rolling hills, the deep forests and the foothills to the Alps are all in my memory. Then you have the excitement of Berlin. So many artists of every stripe are trying to make Berlin worthy of its former great reputation prior to Nazi domination and persecution.

Austria
The Austrain Alps, the Sound of Music, Salzburg, Vienna, and the long history of classical music from Germany and Austria. I am a big fan of classical music and have visited the birthplaces of all of the great composers from Germany and Austria. One time we performed in a little town, and right below our hotel was a little stream that was the beginning of the wonderful River Danube, as we spell it. History is another magical thing for me in Europe.

Switzerland
The land of Heidi. It's not as beautiful as one might imagine unless you are willing to head into the mountains. Bern is wonderful, even more so than Zurich, which surprised me the first time I compared them. There is so little available flat land that the industrial complexes are almost always visible from the autobahn. It's better to get off the beaten path and discover the pleasant panorama of the mountains.

France

I have a few very good friends in France, some in the South on the Mediterranean and some around Paris. Everything you have heard about the romantic qualities of Paris must indeed be true. Megan and I spent our honeymoon there. The scenery is breathtaking, but after you become something more than a tourist you begin to understand the meaning of democracy, French style, and you don't have to stray off the beaten path too far to catch a glimpse of the Paris of the people.

Belgium

Sitting in Brussels and wondering how the country was able to maintain a sovereign status is always the question.

Luxemburg

Luxemburg is probably the only country where you will want to make a walking tour. One thing I was unable to avoid as my trips to Europe grew in frequency was the need to study the history, the wars, and the nobility concepts connected to the ever-changing borders of the many nations that now make up what the Europeans have accepted as inevitable: a United Europe. Just as we have a United States, the Europeans have essentially decided to become one big country. Gone is the charm of the different currencies, which are now reduced to the common Euro.

Holland

Amsterdam. The Paradiso. Dutch history. Tulips, wooden shoes, fine art, canals, brothels. It's all still there, but Holland is a very progressive state. Previously a nation like all of the others, I recall sitting at a party with the leader of the Hells Angels of Amsterdam. He was assassinated, according to his wife, by the CIA. But when you walk through the towns, many in which I have performed, you never lose sight of the romantic tourist view of such places. I've seen that. But I've also seen the darker side that gives all these countries powerful feelings a much different feel than when you walk outside the gates at Disney World in Orlando.

Spain

So rich and steeped in history, having spread a language and religion more aggressively than any other European nation. Bal-Boa, Madrid, and my favorite, Barcelona. There are few things I cherish more than sitting in a café in the afternoon and looking out over the Mediterranean Sea. Dreaming, always dreaming about living such a life every day. But for someone who is barely surviving, in fact collapsing, under the weight of my financial burdens, it remains just a dream.

Portugal

Like the Spanish, the Portugese were extremely aggressive in their approach to dominate unexplored new worlds as they reached the height of their power. Despite their geographic proximity to each other, Portugal was more than eager to conquer the new world. But when you walk through the villages and towns, it is very much like Northern Spain, and it is beautiful along the shorelines.

Denmark

Supposedly the land of the Vikings. I've never performed in Denmark, but because of its closeness to Germany, I've made a few holidays there.

Sweden

Sweden is very much like Denmark in that I have yet to perform there, but it is an exceptional country when you come to understand the rich history connected to it.

England

I've been there many times and a lot of memories have been tucked away. I've been quoted over the years declaring my hatred for the British, but I'm not talking about the general public. I'm talking about the music industry. I have a lot of fans in Northern England and have performed in England several times. I do, however, hold the same contempt for the music industry in England as I do for the music industry in America. I'm certain none of this will help me in the future. I don't know, how would you feel about an industry that tried to diminish and destroy you? Megan and I have been to England to visit the birthplace of her ancestors and their gravesites in Clovelly. We have thoroughly enjoyed it, and on our wall hangs a portrait of Megan that was done on our first visit.

Japan

The Japanese understand beauty to a degree that is unimaginable to the Western mind. Hard to believe, coming from a country of fierce warriors. Tokyo, Nagasaki and all the rest of the major cities were a part of my tour of Japan, but what most impressed me were the temples, and the attention given to landscape. I was told that 97 percent of the population is native born Japanese. That tells a lot about how they feel about foreigners.

Jamaica, The Bahamas, Puerto Rico, Bermuda, Majorca, Hawaii and Barbados

These complete the island visits.

APPENDIX C

The case I wanted to present in this book, beyond the obvious details of my personal life, deals with my acceptance and accomplishments as an artist. Before that argument can be presented it would help the public to be aware of my recorded history because that is where the issue of "relative success" can be best answered. So I have prepared, in chronological order, my discography. I begin with the single releases. These include my personas as Billy Lee, Billy Lee and the Rivieras, Mitch Ryder and The Detroit Wheels, Detroit featuring Mitch Ryder, Mitch Ryder, and Mitch Ryder featuring Engerling.

Singles

Label	Single Title	Date
Carrie	That's the Way it's Gonna Be / Fool For You	1962
Hyland Sundazed	Won't You Dance With Me? / You Know	1964
New Voice	I Need Help / I Hope	1965
New Voice	Jenny Take a Ride / Baby Jane	1965
New Voice	Breakout / I Need Help	1966
New Voice	Takin' All I Can Get / You Get Your Kicks	1966
New Voice	Devil With a Blue Dress On / I Had it Made	1966
New Voice	Sock it to Me, Baby / I Never Had it Better	1967
New Voice	Too Many Fish in the Sea / One Grain of Sand	1967
New Voice	Joy / I'd Rather Go to Jail	1967
New Voice	You Are My Sunshine / Wild Child	1967
New Voice	Come See About Me / Take the Time	1967
New Voice	You Get Your Kicks / Ruby Baby	1967
Dynovoice	What Now My Love? / Blessings in Disguise	1967
Dynovoice	Personality-Chantilly Lace / I Make a Fool of Myself	1967
Dynovoice	Baby, I Need Your Lovin' / Ring Your Bell	1968
Dot	Sugar Bee(We Three) / I Believe	1969
Dot	It's Been a Long Time / Direct Me	1969
Avco Embassy	Jenny Take a Ride / I Never Had it Better	1969
Paramount	I Can't See Nobody / Girl From the North Country	1971
Paramount	Sing a Simple Song / Ring Your Bell	1971
Paramount	It Ain't Easy / Long Neck Goose	1971
Paramount	Rock 'n' roll / Box of Old Roses	1972
Line	Nice N' Easy / Passion's Wheel	1979
Line	Freezin' in Hell / Long Hard Road	1979

Line	Rock 'n' roll / Soul Kitchen	1979
Line	We're Gonna Win / Beyond the Wall-Bare Your Soul	1980
Line	Ain't Nobody White / It's My Life	1980
Line	War / Don't Wanna Hear It	1981
Line	Red Scar Eyes / We're Gonna Win	1981
Line	Er Ist Nicht Mein Prasident / Berlin	1983
Riva	When You Were Mine / Stand	1983

Twelve Inch Singles

Label	Title	Year
Seeds and Stems	Rock 'n' roll / Soul Kitchen	1979
Personal	Like a Rolling Stone / Can Do	1985
S.O.S.	Good Golly Ask Ollie (plus dance mix)	1987

Albums

Label	Title	Year
New Voice	Take a Ride	1966
New Voice	Breakout	1966
New Voice	Sock it to Me	1967
New Voice	All Mitch Ryder Hits	1967
Crewe	All The Heavy Hits	1967
Dynovoice	What Now My Love?	1967
(Recorded, not released)	Spirit Feel	1967
New Voice	Mitch Ryder Sings the Hits	1968
Dot	The Detroit-Memphis Experiment	1969
Paramount	Detroit featuring Mitch Ryder	1971
Seeds and Stems	How I Spent My Vacation	1977
Seeds and Stems	Naked But Not Dead	1978
Line	How I Spent My Vacation	1979
Line	Naked But Not Dead	1980
Quality	Look Ma, No Wheels	1980
Line	Live Talkies	1981
Line	Got Change For a Million?	1981
Line	Smarts Ass	1982
Line	Never Kick a Sleeping Dog	1983
Riva	Never Kick a Sleeping Dog	1983
Line	The Legendary Full Moon Concert	1985
Line	In the China Shop	1986

Line	Red Blood, White Mink	1988
Line	The Beautiful Toulang Sunset	1990
Line	La Gash	1992
Line	Live a The Logo Hamburg	1992
Line	Rite Of Passage	1994
Line	Monkey Island	1999
BuschFunk	The Old Man Springs a Boner	2003
BuschFunk	A Dark Caucasian Blue	2004
BuschFunk	The Acquitted Idiot	2005
BuschFunk	Red Scar Eyes (double set)	2006
BuschFunk	You Deserve My Art	2007
Free World Records	Detroit Ain't Dead Yet	2010

APPENDIX D
AN ESSAY FROM MITCH

Attaching itself to the vulgar dust in the empty back room of my low rent home, the rank smell of love enters my nose. The stench resurrects my dormant self-destruction. Bitter cold rushes through my broken window, filling my aching cigarette-scorched lungs. Alone, the night-light defiantly challenges the evil that waits, hopefully out of reach, just on the edge of the dark. Another winter has arrived and I sink into another uncontrollable spasm of coughs. When it ends, I pull a handkerchief from my coat pocket and dry my eyes, for my view of the world is sad.

Outside, beautiful crystal ice has bonded itself to the blackened, frozen lives that slide down the sullen streets. Most people no longer have the will to conjure up hot blood and save themselves from the freeze. Democracy, taunting the errant revolutionary, invites him in for another swim through the cold, raging waters of freedom. The unforgiven liberal jade is no longer for trade. Criminally bent Einsteins, with conservative spines, feverishly work their long awaited revenge. Money, money, money. It is a loveless but powerful place. Only the rich and the pretty, or their brutish progenitor, are secure from the chill.

It's a fact that famous people are pitifully and faithfully connected to a marketplace that will eventually betray and destroy them. The less shiny and faded shell-shocked "somebodies" like myself walk on gilded splinters with our one-time servile followers, the nervous bullshit betraying the necessary alliance. It is a downturn. It is a correction. We have finally come home. Values have shifted. Stock has fallen. Morals have cleanly split in two. Things are being shattered everywhere you look. These aren't very nice times, as they are a submission to what truths remain for any human who has struggled for love in vain. All lies now are suddenly accountable. The apocalypse says we are damned. We only know we are cold and older.

What began with a visionary's hope for a life of happiness has become a life hardly worth living. The drug dealing medics, uninvited, are everywhere, clumsily plying their sweet, putrid relief at the sides of the inevitable fallen. It is a pain-free resignation to the defeat of the human spirit.

It was, in the end, too damned easy to get here. In this space, with myself and other veteran victims of this dishonorable disease, rest the bodies of my abandoned children, those worn-out, beat-down progenies of a faithless broken family. A generation of innocents have been lost to the ages.; children left to raise themselves by whatever means supplied.

The sadness is the fact that I never seemed to care. There was never enough pain, it never hurt quite enough. It was a hairline call that was most often about me, or fame, or my career. In this gallery of human sacrifice is the final testament to how terrible I am. How indifferent to my own I was, while caught up in myself. The endless excuses for cutting my children adrift and leaving them alone in a lethal sea of adult intentions replay themselves until I am sickened by my own presence. I had first been here when I was a young man. I thought I had, in the wreckage of my selfish pursuits, left it behind. But its spirit still exists. It stares into my twitching eyes and I am helpless to stop it. My selective memory has failed. I am vulnerable. The images play out, and I walk to the door. I look back, the way you might look at a scar on your body, with regret and sick infatuation at the loss of purity.

Beyond the filthy needles of inhumanity and its running dogs is the world I, at all costs, aspire to. After all, it must be better than yesterday. It is the only promise I made to myself: that world overdosing on the magnificent passion of sad and common characters, with broken and stolen dreams sent aloft on the smoke and haze of their exhausted, consumed brilliance. Such a dark vapor that, when lovingly inhaled, carries the communication of the arts through rebellious evolution and satisfaction of the retired senses, exhuming cerebral burial grounds.

There is the beauty of the ugly who think they're beautiful, and the holiness of undaunted, crippled believers with newborn, bird-like mouths open and crying for regurgitated life. A transsexual masseuse asks where it hurts the most. Eyes reflect the truth of their hearts. The world of consecrated refuge versus the unbearable reality of a society addicted to addiction.

There is betrayal on every front at the hands of invisible friends. It's still playtime, time so unwittingly given up in our youth to enter the cage of adult promise. It is, finally, a place where life becomes art and the only real harm that can come to you comes by your own hand. But now I'm left to wonder at the odds of keeping that while haunted by the cry of innocent, trusting children. I slap my face hoping to wake before I sink any further, and like a parent after an abortion, I turn to face the fire.

For my very life and damaged sensibilities comes the age-old question: what is love? Not closing the door completely, lest someone insanely love in a non-punitive way, I give the age-old answer. I don't know. Is it humanism in broad terms? I don't think so. I would give the same care to a hurting animal as I would to a human. Probably more. For my understanding, love must be about what did and did not occur in my family and career at the very precise and critical moment when my commercial Pop artist's flame was white hot. After that it would run a parallel descent alongside anything else of lesser value until the bottom, some short twenty-five years later, shook me hard enough to make me breathe again.

In a different climate or a different age, where my artistic credibility and history might have grown legendary with less opposition, such a confession of ignorance and supplication to the truth would sadly be enough. Here and now, however, at the callous feet of my critics and time, it is not. It is no good as an answer, and it's even worse as an excuse. "Wasn't it enough to simply care?" infuriates them. Furthermore, nothing I could say would please them. It becomes impossible to safely reach for the truth when surrounded and attacked by a pack of vengeful hyenas. These critics who would judge me are irrationally incensed. They are weary at my insistence of raising my head. They choke and become ill on air that I breathe and I wonder if their anger and frustration is with their inability to finish me off. After all, they thought I was washed-up. For them, my life as an artist was never considered an ongoing work upon which they should honestly weigh the merits of my talent and it's painstaking accomplishments. It was much more personal than that. What angers my enemies and critics is my presumption of heightened stature and my tarnished claim to artistry itself.

It seems to me that I have paid too many times for the privileges of birthright through imperfection and native intelligence. I am a common man indifferently caressed by uncommon graces. There was never a question of my capability to love, only my desire. Never a question of my justifiable need for revenge, only my courage. Never a question of my talent, only my commitment. Never a question of my fame, only my humanity. Where and how those truths can be presented lays a pall upon my spirit. This contest of my making, between children and self-indulging social art, even though settled by many accounts, continues to engage me.

To enter into an additional struggle with my elitist critics at precisely this moment should be more than interesting.

Index

The Promise is Mitch Ryder's newest CD and all twelve songs are available to you as a digital download free of charge with the purchase of this book.

To access the download go to: http://www.CoolTitles.com
Click on the Mitch Ryder / The Promise button
Type in the unique code shown below.

2b473d7

The Promise

1. Thank You Mama
2. The Promise
3. One Hair
4. Everybody Loses
5. My Heart Belongs to Me
6. Crazy Beautiful
7. Let's Keep Dancing
8. If My Baby Don't Stop Cryin'
9. Get Real
10. What Becomes of the Broken Hearted
11. Junkie Love
12. The Way We Were

Credits: Jamie Muhoberac, keyboard / Reggie McBride, bass / Randy Jacobs, guitar / James Gadsen, drums / produced by Don Was

"It has been a wonderful experience for me to work on *The Promise* with talented musicians who have worked with so many legends. Drummer James Gadsen, for example, has worked with such notable talent as Ray Charles, Marvin Gaye, The Isley Brothers, Frank Sinatra, Herbie Hancock, Joe Cocker, Beck, Justin Timberlake and Paul McCartney. Randy Jacob's credits include Steve Cropper, Stevie Wonder, Herbie Hancock, B.B. King, Bonnie Raitt, Ringo Starr, Kris Kristofferson, Michael McDonald, Paula Abdul, Jewel, Ringo Starr, Seal, Willie Nelson, and many others. Jamie Muhoberac's father, session musician Larry Muhoberac, worked with Barbra Streisand, Elvis Presley, Neil Diamond, Dean Martin and others, while Jamie's credits include Fleetwood Mac, The Rolling Stones, The Backstreet Boys, Bob Dylan, and the Goo Goo Dolls. Reggie McBride has performed with James Brown, Aretha Franklin, and Stevie Wonder, and many more.

"I am so proud to have worked with each of these musicians, as each has music in his blood. It is an honor to work with people who make great music their life. And, it is a special privilege that Don Was chose to produce me, as he has produced such notable artists as Willie Nelson, the Rolling Stones, Bonnie Raitt, Bob Dylan, Ziggy Marley, Bob Seger, Garth Brooks, Ringo Starr, Iggy Pop, Joe Cocker, Hootie and The Blowfish, Elton John, Stevie Nicks, Carly Simon, Brian Wilson, B.B. King, and numerous others. I tip my hat to Don, and to everyone who worked on this record with me. It was a joy and I thank you."

Mitch Ryder
November, 2011